RESEARCH AND PRACTICE IN SOCIAL STUDIES SERIES

Wayne Journell, *Series Editor*

Civic Engagement in Communities of Color:
Pedagogy for Learning and Life in a More Expansive Democracy
KRISTEN E. DUNCAN, ED.

Developing Historical Thinkers: Supporting Historical Inquiry for All Students
BRUCE A. LESH

Toward a Stranger and More Posthuman Social Studies
BRETTON A. VARGA, TIMOTHY MONREAL, & REBECCA C. CHRIST, EDS.

Critical Race Theory and Social Studies Futures:
From the Nightmare of Racial Realism to Dreaming Out Loud
AMANDA E. VICKERY & NOREEN NASEEM RODRÍGUEZ, EDS.

How to Confront Climate Denial: Literacy, Social Studies, and Climate Change
JAMES S. DAMICO & MARK C. BAILDON

Racial Literacies and Social Studies: Curriculum, Instruction, and Learning
LAGARRETT J. KING, ED.

Making Classroom Discussions Work:
Methods for Quality Dialogue in the Social Studies
JANE C. LO, ED.

Teaching Difficult Histories in Difficult Times: Stories of Practice
LAUREN MCARTHUR HARRIS, MAIA SHEPPARD, & SARA A. LEVY, EDS.

Post-Pandemic Social Studies:
How COVID-19 Has Changed the World and How We Teach
WAYNE JOURNELL, ED.

Teaching History for Justice: Centering Activism in Students' Study of the Past
CHRISTOPHER C. MARTELL & KAYLENE M. STEVENS

Civic Engagement in Communities of Color

Pedagogy for Learning and Life in a More Expansive Democracy

Edited by Kristen E. Duncan

Foreword by Ashley N. Woodson

TEACHERS COLLEGE PRESS
TEACHERS COLLEGE | COLUMBIA UNIVERSITY
NEW YORK AND LONDON

Published by Teachers College Press,® 1234 Amsterdam Avenue, New York, NY 10027

Copyright © 2023 by Teachers College, Columbia University

Front cover by Peter Donahue. Illustration by smartboy10 / iStock by Getty Images.

All rights reserved. No part of this publication may be reproduced or transmitted in any form or by any means, electronic or mechanical, including photocopy, or any information storage and retrieval system, without permission from the publisher. For reprint permission and other subsidiary rights requests, please contact Teachers College Press, Rights Dept.: tcpressrights@tc.columbia.edu

Library of Congress Cataloging-in-Publication Data
Names: Duncan, Kristen E., editor.
Title: Civic engagement in communities of color : pedagogy for learning and life in a more expansive democracy / Edited by Kristen E. Duncan.
Description: New York, NY : Teachers College Press, [2023] | Series: Research and practice in social studies series | Includes bibliographical references and index. | Summary: "This volume will assist classroom teachers, teacher candidates, and teacher educators identify where whitewashed civics curricula fail students of color. Topics range from issues facing Asian immigrant communities to the Black Lives Matter at School curriculum"—Provided by publisher.
Identifiers: LCCN 2023021158 (print) | LCCN 2023021159 (ebook) | ISBN 9780807768570 (hardcover) | ISBN 9780807768563 (paperback) | ISBN 9780807781838 (ebook)
Subjects: LCSH: Service learning. | Civics—Study and teaching. | Minorities—Education. | Curriculum evaluation. | Community and school.
Classification: LCC LC220.5 .C573 2023 (print) | LCC LC220.5 (ebook) | DDC 372.83—dc23/eng/20230526
LC record available at https://lccn.loc.gov/2023021158
LC ebook record available at https://lccn.loc.gov/2023021159

ISBN 978-0-8077-6856-3 (paper)
ISBN 978-0-8077-6857-0 (hardcover)
ISBN 978-0-8077-8183-8 (ebook)

Printed on acid-free paper
Manufactured in the United States of America

Contents

Foreword by Ashley N. Woodson   vii

Introduction   xi

PART I: CURRENT REALITIES OF CIVIC EDUCATION: PERSPECTIVES FROM THE MARGINS

1. Emancipatory Civic Education for Black Students: An Action-Oriented Literature Review   3
   Erica Kelley

2. "Have We Been Civically Educated to Seize the Present Moment?": Two Black Social Educators' Sense-Making of Civic Education   17
   Carla-Ann Brown, Rasheeda West, and Elizabeth Yeager Washington

3. Civics and Latinidad: Letters to the Past With Hopes for the Future   31
   Jesús Tirado, Gabriel Rodriguez, Timothy Monreal, and Tommy Ender

4. "I Understand Both of Them. But Nobody Understands Me!": Civic Dissonances Among Arab-Palestinian Students in Israel   41
   Aline Muff and Aviv Cohen

PART II: CIVICS EMBODIED IN COMMUNITIES OF COLOR

5. It's Been Here All Along: Integrating Local Stories of Struggle Into Civics Discourses   57
   Asif Wilson, ArCasia D. James-Gallaway, and Sabryna Groves

6. #FreeThemAll: Civic Action Through Southeast Asian Community Defense Digital Toolkits — 71
Van Anh Tran

7. More Than Talk: Youth Poets' Civic Action and How Youth Spoken Word Prepares Minoritized Youths as Civic Actors — 93
Camea Davis

PART III: POSSIBILITIES FOR CIVIC EDUCATION

8. Black Feminist Pedagogy for Anti-Racist Civics — 109
Tiffany Mitchell Patterson, Natasha C. Murray-Everett, and Crystal Simmons

9. "Responsible, Capable, and Whole Human Beings": The Value and Necessity of Indigenous Civics — 125
Leilani Sabzalian and Michelle M. Jacob

10. "It Didn't Mean 'Me' When It Said 'We'": Counterstories as Pedagogy When Citizenship Is Not Guaranteed — 141
Brittany Jones

11. The Black Lives Matter at School Guiding Principles: Fostering Black Cultural Citizenship Through Critical Civic Empathy — 153
Denisha Jones and Sarah A. Mathews

Endnotes — 169

Index — 171

About the Editor and Authors — 181

Foreword

What's your favorite scary movie?

It depends on how you define *scary*. If scary movies follow protagonists' attempts to escape or survive an ominous threat, then my favorite scary movie is *Roots*. If scary movies intend to elicit terror or fear, then my favorite scary movie is *Roots*. If scary movies are supposed to trigger shock and disgust, then my favorite scary movie is *Roots*. And if scary movies portray violent moral reckoning for those with poor character or past atrocities, then my favorite scary movie is either *Tales from the Hood* or the first *Candyman*. Maybe these are the same movies that give you nightmares, maybe not. Scary is in the eye of the beholder.

The dangers in some scary movies are context bound. If you avoid certain cabins, streets, forests, videos, or neighborhoods, you'll probably be okay. But some dangers, like those that our children face in the name of schooling, are more omnipresent. Every school, according to Brother Michael Dumas, is a site of social suffering. The story of schools, social studies, and civic education is scary because we are dreadfully aware that every child we love is vulnerable. Our failure to model a more expansive democracy places every child's future at risk.

If I had to assemble a team to combat this risk (think *Lovecraft Country* or *Vampires vs. the Bronx*), Dr. Kristen Duncan would be a first-round draft pick. After she and I realized we shared a love for brunch and justice, our sisterhood developed as many Black academic kinships do. We joked about how 3.4 ounces of twist cream was simply not enough to get through a four-day conference. We drafted theoretical frameworks on the long Uber rides to the Black-owned soul food restaurant closest to the conference hotel. Kristen had been in the game longer than I had, and did not hesitate to offer the kind of insights that made my survival in our niche field possible. She taught me how to speak social studies, which journals would reach my desired audience, and which service opportunities made sense to pursue. Beyond providing constant mentorship to me, Kristen broadly models politics of language, methodology, and citation that are both deliberate and emancipatory. She is one of the most intentional scholars I know.

That being said, when Kristen asked me to write the foreword for this volume, I don't think even she realized she'd curated what would amount to a horror anthology. Across the chapters, you will encounter a monster of an antagonist. We're up against a force that preys on the civic possibilities of children, shape-shifts to meet the imperial demands of global contexts, and simulates the immortal by reemerging (seemingly unphased) after each presumed defeat. Fear poses the question of our survival; this book is a collection of possible answers.

Whether critical race theory is explicitly invoked or not, all of the answers suggested across these pages show indebtedness to its principles. Aline and Aviv's chapter artfully examines related concepts of intersectionality and whiteness as property in the strivings of Arab-Palestinian students in Israel, while Leilani and Michelle take up Indigenous counterstorytelling as a tool to cultivate more just notions of civic belonging. The implied consensus on the validity of critical race theory is encouraging, especially across the diversity of subjects taken up in this text.

It's encouraging, but it's also a bit horrifying. As I read the chapters, many of which are written by brilliant early-career scholars, I can't shake the feeling that our field is credentialing new casts of academics into the same dark scripts, tropes, and settings. Consider it's been damn near 30 years since Gloria Ladson-Billings and William Tate published "Toward a Critical Race Theory of Education" and 20 years since the former edited *Critical Race Theory Perspectives on the Social Studies: The Profession, Policies, and Curriculum.*

I remember reading both of these for the first time and thinking that I'd found a conceptual home in teacher education. I remember hoping with Kristen, as we started writing articles and book chapters of our own. Once we joined the ranks of the cited, we wanted to believe that supremacy was maybe mortally wounded, at least in the academic spaces, classrooms, and street corners within our sphere of influence. We wanted to believe that the worst of Black children's erasure and disenfranchisement in schools was over. It absolutely isn't. And we should all be afraid.

You don't have to take my word for it. The authors in this volume do an outstanding job articulating why fear is really the only rational response to the current condition of our field. In Part I, authors demand that we acknowledge the ways we've failed to secure a safe, inviting, and expansive democracy for Black, Brown, and Beige children. Part II describes what we can learn from our children, and how we might engage their meaning-making practices to inspire new pedagogies. The authors in the third and final part anticipate sequels to what we are currently living through and how forthcoming research and activism will continue to defend against fascism. Kristen has engineered a choose-your-own adventure cliffhanger with the sequence of chapters, asking us what we will do with our fear.

One of Kristen's strengths, and a strength of this collection, is the interpretive primacy of Black women's scholarship. Tiffany, Natasha, and Crystal remind us that

Black women have always been at the forefront of nearly every progressive social movement in the United States. These are not falsehoods by any means. Although we are the first to show up, we are the last to be saved.

The wisdom and capacity of our children is also reiterated across the pages that follow. We don't have to be the adults in the Freddy Krueger movies or the *It* franchise, who are conveniently absent from or struggle to believe our children's accounts of horrific experiences. In the context of our scary movie, it is the expressive, resistant survival strategies of those we expect to die first that might save us all.

If you believe a more expansive democracy is necessary and possible through informed, empowering civic engagement of young people, this book should keep you up at night. Stay woke.

And don't read alone.

—Ashley N. Woodson

Introduction

Civic education scholars and researchers largely understand the goal of civic education to be to foster the development of citizens who will live in and maintain a pluralistic democracy. The realities of civic education classrooms, however, do not exactly align with this goal. Instead of learning how to uphold a democracy with a diverse citizenry, students often find themselves subjected to a civics curriculum that privileges white, middle-class cultural knowledge. Here, students learn to value particular ways of knowing and being, while other possibilities for civic life are discarded in the name of unity.

Traditional civic education emphasizes a mainstream, supposedly unifying narrative in which all students learn what it means to be an American, despite civic education scholars advocating against this (Banks, 2001; Journell, 2011; Parker, 2003). This form of civic education focuses on the development of the "personally responsible citizen" (Westheimer & Kahne, 2004, p. 241), as students learn that their role within a democracy is to vote, pay taxes, and donate to charity in addition to learning to be loyal to the nation-state in the name of patriotism. As this race-evasive form of civic education ignores oppression at the institutional and systemic levels, it reminds students of Color that whiteness remains a criterion for full citizenship in the United States (Ladson-Billings, 2004), often leaving them to understand the citizenship status of their racial and cultural groups as tenuous. Traditional civic education serves as a tool of imperialism (Sabzalian et al., 2021) and the centrality of whiteness can leave students of Color resigned to seeing themselves as "maybe citizens" (Johnson, 2019), anti-citizens (Busey & Dowie-Chin, 2021), or in possession of failed citizenship (Banks, 2017).

FRAMEWORKS FOR CENTERING THE MARGINS IN CIVIC EDUCATION

Scholars of Color have long understood that whitewashed conceptions of citizenship and citizenship education do not serve students of Color or their communities. For this reason, scholars have conceptualized various forms of citizenship and civic education that not only include, but honor the marginalized identities that students bring into classrooms with them. One such conception is cultural citizenship (Rosaldo, 1994), which focuses on a plurality where "one group must not dictate another group's notion of dignity, thriving, and well-being" (p. 410).

Scholars have also centered race and other marginalized identities through various conceptions of multicultural citizenship education, which would "enable students to acquire a delicate balance of cultural, national, and global identifications and to understand the ways in which knowledge is constructed; to become knowledge producers; and to participate in civic action to create a more humane nation and world" (Banks, 2001, p. 5). While scholars have theorized various forms of multicultural citizenship education (Ladson-Billings, 2004; Miller-Lane et al., 2007), Dilworth (2004) explains that there are several components that scholars agree are critical to this concept: (1) critical cultural consciousness, (2) ethnic identities, (3) cultural pluralism, (4) uneven distribution of resources and opportunities, and (5) sociopolitical issues rooted in long histories of oppression. Dilworth then defines multicultural citizenship education as "going beyond diversity and as a reciprocal undertaking in which students and teachers are challenged to critically examine curriculum content, themselves, and others through different and multiple lenses" (pp. 156–157).

One major critique of these conceptions of multicultural citizenship, however, is that they conflate race and Indigeneity, categorizing Indigenous nations as racially marginalized by the U.S. government and society while erasing notions of tribal sovereignty. Sabzalian (2019) notes that such frameworks for multicultural citizenship education are rooted in colonialism and proposed a framework for anticolonial civic education that explicitly supports Indigenous sovereignty. Additionally, after seeing how traditional civic education failed to help Black and Latinx students analyze their civic realities, Clay and Rubin (2020) offered critically relevant civics, which embraces tenets of culturally relevant pedagogy and critical race theory. With critically relevant civics, teachers bring resources that youth of Color use to navigate their civic worlds outside of school into the K–12 classroom.

CIVIC EDUCATION AT THE BOTTOM OF THE WELL

In recent years, researchers have begun to pay more attention to the ways Black, Indigenous, and other students and teachers of Color conceptualize, teach, learn, and enact civics. Communities of Color have reconceptualized civics in ways that fit their lived experiences and cultural values as a means of surviving the colonial project. As some Black teachers use their civics classrooms as spaces to help Black students navigate systems of white supremacy (Duncan, 2020; 2022), others reconceptualize the notion of citizenship, turning toward notions of citizenship that focus on community instead of loyalty to the nation-state (Vickery, 2017). Additionally, many

Black teachers find themselves engaging in the work of civic education in school spaces beyond the classroom (Thomas, 2022).

Black teachers are not alone in turning to spaces beyond the classroom to foster civic understandings, as Black and Latinx students turn to family members, community members, and social media to gain a greater understanding of their racialized citizenship (Clay & Rubin, 2020). These students are keenly aware of the chasm between the race-evasive civic education they experience in their classrooms and their lived realities as youth of Color in the United States (Rubin, 2007). Other research on students of Color has found that Muslim and Mexican American students use history to contextualize contemporary discrimination and sustain their civic identities (Yoder, 2020), and that the messianic master narratives used to present Black historical figures in school often stifle the development of Black students' civic agency (Woodson, 2016).

Additionally, civics teachers whose students are undocumented prioritize safety and provide their students with symbolic resources that allow undocumented students to see themselves as legitimate civic actors (Dabach et al., 2018). Meanwhile, teachers of Color understand the civics curricula provided to them often fail to consider the racial and cultural realities of their students and therefore, these teachers draw on their own lived experience to inform the frameworks of citizenship they embrace in their classrooms (Rodriguez, 2018; Salinas & Castro, 2010; Vickery, 2016).

STRUCTURE OF THE BOOK

The authors in this edited volume take up Banks's (2001) call to reconceptualize civic education and Vickery's (2017) call to "understand how individuals who are positioned as outsiders to the traditional meaning of citizenship create their own sense of belonging as a 'citizen/non-citizen'" (p. 320). If civic education is truly about helping students understand the concept of citizenship and belonging, it is imperative that social studies educators, teacher educators, and researchers gain a greater understanding of how people who exist beyond the bounds of whiteness, and therefore full, traditional citizenship, conceptualize and embody this concept. Traditional civic education relegates Black, Indigenous, and other students and teachers of Color to the margins. In communities of Color and Indigenous nations, however, where Indigenous and racially marginalized groups' cultural knowledges are centered, civic education, knowledge, and action can be affirming and center students' "enoughness" (Woodson & Love, 2019). The authors of this edited volume illuminate the ways that racially marginalized communities approach the notion of civics, both historically and contemporarily, disrupting the idea that civics is a singular notion that should be viewed solely through a Eurocentric lens. In tackling the intersection of race and civics, chapter authors move beyond the myopic, white-centered interpretations of civics that have dominated the field.

This book is organized into three parts, the first of which is "Current Realities of Civic Education: Perspectives From the Margins." In this part, authors discuss civic education in its current state and how it continuously fails to prepare students of Color for the challenges they face attempting to engage as full citizens in a democracy. Just how does traditional civic education impact Black students? In Chapter 1, Erica Kelley helps us answer this question, providing a critical race theory analysis of the research on traditional civic education and its impact on Black students. Kelley discusses issues with traditional civic education curriculum, the ways traditional civic education contributes to Black students' civic estrangement (Tillet, 2012), and the chasm between traditional civic education and Black students' civic realities. All hope is not lost, however, as Kelley also uses research to imagine a pathway toward an emancipatory civic education that acknowledges the realities of Black students and empowers them to develop their own civic identities.

In Chapter 2, authored by Carla-Ann Brown, Rasheeda West, and Elizabeth Yeager Washington, the authors work to make sense of the civic education they received as students and reimagine civic education for the Black students they teach each day. As they reflect on the civic education they received as students, they begin to understand how the race-evasiveness of the civic education they received impacted them. They close out the chapter discussing the civic education they wish they had received, along with the civic education they hope to provide for their students. This kind of civic education centers race and helps students understand the connection between race and citizenship.

Chapter 3 finds Jesús Tirado, Gabriel Rodriguez, Timothy Monreal, and Tommy Ender crafting letters to their former K–12 teachers. In these letters, they discuss feeling othered as Latinx students, as issues specific to Latinx communities went ignored in their classrooms. They conclude this chapter by suggesting ways to push the field of civic education forward to better serve Latinx students and all students of Color.

What is civic education like for marginalized groups in international contexts? In Chapter 4, Aline Muff and Aviv Cohen provide an answer to this question with their study on Arab-Palestinian students. Their study illuminates these students' understandings of citizenship, civic identity, conflictual reality, and their educational experiences, leaving readers with questions about what it means to belong and how we construct notions of citizenship.

The second part of this book is "Civics Embodied in Communities of Color." Chapters in this section focus on the ways communities of Color engage in civic action beyond the typically accepted personally responsible (Westheimer & Kahne, 2004) civic tasks of voting and paying taxes. In Chapter 5, Asif Wilson, ArCasia D. James-Gallaway, and Sabryna Groves provide us with both historical and contemporary examples of enacted civics in communities of Color. They use community cultural wealth and justice-centered educational praxis to analyze instances of civic action that include Black students' resistance to discriminatory desegregation tactics and programs that help youth see how their community historically engaged in civic action.

In Chapter 6, Van Anh Tran analyzes the digital curricular toolkits that local and national Southeast Asian organizations use to resist unethical deportation policies. Given that immigration has been painted by both politicians and mainstream media as a Latinx issue, these toolkits remind us that problematic immigration policies affect numerous communities of Color. Tran's analysis of the toolkits provides tremendous insight into how Southeast Asian communities engage in civic resistance, as well as how community members are invited to engage in that resistance.

This section closes with Camea Davis's discussion of youth poets as civic actors. In Chapter 7, Davis discusses the ways youth poet laureates engage in civic action both with and beyond their poetry. Her chapter expands our understandings of how youth of Color comprehend the necessity of civic action and participate as citizens in their communities.

The third and final section of the book is "Possibilities for Civic Education," and the authors of these chapters provide us with a glimpse of what is possible in and for civic education when communities of Color are centered. This section begins with the work of Tiffany Mitchell Patterson, Natasha C. Murray-Everett, and Crystal Simmons in Chapter 8, as they utilize Black feminist pedagogy to construct a framework for anti-racist civics. Their RESPECT framework centers Black women's civic knowledge, scholarship, and activism, and provides teachers and students with the opportunity to work toward justice from a perspective that refuses Eurocentric notions of civics and focuses on principles such as collectivism and truth telling.

In Chapter 9, Leilani Sabzalian and Michelle M. Jacob show us what is possible when we move Indigenous civics from the margins to the center, illustrating how core questions and practices in Indigenous civics can lead us to have more humanizing and ethical relationships with each other and with the land. Sabzalian and Jacob also note that an Indigenous civic education not only benefits Indigenous children, but it works to benefit *all* children.

One of, if not *the*, primary issue with the whitewashed ways in which civics is typically taught is that teachers and students of Color often know that they are not included in the "we" that constitutes "we the people." In Chapter 10, Brittany Jones explores how Black teachers navigate the tensions in teaching about citizenship using counterstories. Her chapter helps us understand how Black teachers use counterstories to help their students see the contradictions between the grand narrative of full citizenship and their own lived experiences.

Finally, as the Black Lives Matter movement gained momentum in recent years, principles of the movement made their way into classrooms and curricula. In Chapter 11, Denisha Jones and Sarah A. Matthews help us understand how teachers' use of the 13 guiding principles of Black Lives Matter at School supports the tradition of Black citizenship education and cultivates cultural citizenship for Black lives. These authors help us understand how teachers should use the guiding principles to reinforce and expand notions of citizenship.

The goal of this volume is not to compare communities of Color to dominant white society but to explain how communities of Color have taken up our own definitions of civics and enacted it in our own ways. The chapters in this volume go about this by helping us understand how traditional civic education fails to serve students of Color, some of the ways that communities of Color engage in civic action, and what is possible when racially marginalized groups and Indigenous nations are placed at the center of civic education. Ultimately, through this volume we aim to center our "enoughness," as we work to design and enact civic education that does the same.

REFERENCES

Banks, J. (2001). Citizenship education and diversity: Implications for teacher education. *Journal of Teacher Education, 52*(1), 5–16. https://doi.org/10.1177/0022487101052001002

Banks, J. (2017). Failed citizenship and transformative civic education. *Educational Researcher, 46*(7), 366–377. https://doi.org/10.3102/0013189X17726741

Busey, C., & Dowie-Chin, T. (2021). The making of global Black anti-citizen/citizenship: Situating BlackCrit in global citizenship research and theory. *Theory & Research in Social Education, 49*(2), 153–175. https://doi.org/10.1080/00933104.2020.1869632

Clay, K., & Rubin, B. (2020). "I look deep into this stuff because it's a part of me": Toward a critically relevant civics education. *Theory & Research in Social Education, 48*(2), 161–181. https://doi.org/10.1080/00933104.2019.1680466

Dabach, D., Fones, A., Merchant, N., & Adekile, A. (2018). Teachers navigating civic education when students are undocumented: Building case knowledge. *Theory & Research in Social Education, 46*(3), 331–373. https://doi.org/10.1080/00933104.2017.1413470

Dilworth, P. (2004). Multicultural citizenship education: Case studies from social studies classrooms. *Theory & Research in Social Studies Education, 32*(2), 153–186. https://doi.org/10.1080/00933104.2004.10473251

Duncan, K. (2020). "What better tool do I have?": A critical race approach to teaching civics. *The High School Journal, 103*(3), 176–189. https://doi.org/10.1353/hsj.2020.0011

Duncan, K. (2022). 'That's my job': Black teachers' perspectives on helping Black students navigate white supremacy. *Race, Ethnicity and Education, 25*(7), 978–996. https://doi.org/10.1080/13613324.2020.1798377

Johnson, M. (2019). Trump, Kaepernick, and MLK as "maybe citizens": Early elementary African American males' analysis of citizenship. *Theory & Research in Social Education, 47*(3), 374–395. https://doi.org/10.1080/00933104.2019.1582381

Journell, W. (2011). Social Studies, citizenship education, and the search for an American identity: An argument against a unifying narrative. *Journal of Thought, 46*(3–4), 5–24. https://doi.org/10.2307/jthought.46.3-4.5

Ladson-Billings, G. (2004). Culture versus citizenship: The challenge of racialized citizenship in the United States. In J. A. Banks (Ed.), *Diversity and citizenship education: Global perspectives* (pp. 99–126). Josey-Bass.

Miller-Lane, J., Howard, T. C., & Halagao, P. E. (2007). Civic multicultural competence: Searching for common ground in democratic education. *Theory & Research in Social Education, 35*(4), 551–573. https://doi.org/10.1080/00933104.2007.10473350

Parker, W. (2003). *Teaching democracy: Unity and diversity in public life*. Teachers College Press.

Rodríguez, N. (2018). From margins to center: Developing cultural citizenship education through the teaching of Asian American history. *Theory & Research in Social Education, 46*(4), 528–573. https://doi.org/10.1080/00933104.2018.1432432

Rosaldo, R. (1994). Cultural citizenship and democratic education. *Cultural Anthropology, 9*(3), 402–411. https://www.jstor.org/stable/656372

Rubin, B. (2007). "There's still not justice": Youth civic identity development amid distinct school and community contexts. *Teachers College Record, 109*(2), 499–481. https://doi.org/10.1177/016146810710900202

Sabzalian, L. (2019). The tensions between Indigenous sovereignty and multicultural citizenship education: Toward an anticolonial approach to civic education. *Theory & Research in Social Education, 47*(3), 311–346. https://doi.org/10.1080/00933104.2019.1639572

Sabzalian, L., Shear, S., & Snyder, J. (2021). Standardizing Indigenous erasure: A TribalCrit and QuantCrit analysis of K–12 U.S. civics and government standards. *Theory & Research in Social Education, 49*(3), 321–359. https://doi.org/10.1080/00933104.2021.1922322

Salinas, C., & Castro, A. (2010). Disrupting the official curriculum: Cultural biography and the curriculum decision making of Latino preservice teachers. *Theory & Research in Social Education, 38*(3), 428–463. https://doi.org/10.1080/00933104.2010.10473433

Tillet, S. (2012). *Sites of slavery: Citizenship and racial democracy in the post-civil rights imagination*. Duke University Press.

Thomas, D. (2022). "If I can help somebody": The civic-oriented thought and practices of Black male teacher-coaches. *Theory & Research in Social Education, 50*(3), 464–493. https://doi.org/10.1080/00933104.2022.2078258

Vickery, A. (2016). 'I know what you are about to enter': Lived experiences as the curricular foundation for teaching citizenship. *Gender and Education, 28*(6), 725–741. https://doi.org/10.1080/09540253.2016.1221890

Vickery, A. (2017) "You excluded us for so long and now you want us to be patriotic?": African American women teachers navigating the quandary of citizenship. *Theory & Research in Social Education, 45*(3), 318–348. https://doi.org/10.1080/00933104.2017.1282387

Westheimer, J., & Kahne, J. (2004). What kind of citizen? The politics of educating for democracy. *American Educational Research Journal, 41*(2), 237–269. https://doi.org/10.3102/00028312041002237

Woodson, A., (2016). We're just ordinary people: Messianic master narratives and Black youths' civic agency. *Theory & Research in Social Education, 44*(2), 184–211. https://doi.org/10.1080/00933104.2016.1170645

Woodson, A., & Love, B. (2019). Outstanding: Centering Black kids' enoughness in civic education research. *Multicultural Perspectives, 21*(2), 91–96. https://doi.org/10.1080/15210960.2019.1606631

Yoder, P. (2020). "He wants to get rid of all the Muslins": Mexican American and Muslin students' use of history regarding candidate Trump. *Theory & Research in Social Education, 48*(3), 346–374. https://doi.org/10.1080/00933104.2020.1773364

Civic Engagement in Communities of Color

Part I

CURRENT REALITIES OF CIVIC EDUCATION: PERSPECTIVES FROM THE MARGINS

Part I

CURRENT REALITIES OF CIVIC EDUCATION: PERSPECTIVES FROM THE MAKERS

CHAPTER 1

Emancipatory Civic Education for Black Students
An Action-Oriented Literature Review

Erica Kelley

Since the inception of our nation, the very idea of Black citizenship has been under attack. Compounding the modern attacks on voting rights and political activism is the way schools traditionally approach civic education, especially with Black students. Understanding and rectifying the flaws in traditional civic education with respect to Black students requires a critical examination of the racism and dedication to white supremacy inherent in social studies curriculum and instructional practices (Tillet, 2012). Social studies classes themselves can be emancipatory spaces in which Black students explore how structural and institutional racism impact their abilities to participate as change agents (Pinkney, 2016), and as Ladson-Billings (2003) notes, "The social studies can serve as a curricular home for unlearning the racism that has confounded us as a nation. Yet, we still find teachers continuing to tell us lies" (p. 8). Rather than revolutionizing instructional approaches to social studies, and, more specifically, civics content, the same whitewashed curricula, tone-deaf practices, and stale ideas are the standard for social studies education (Busey & Walker, 2017; Journell, 2016). Consequently, Black students are uniquely deprived of high-quality civic education in which the content and instructional practices support their particular cultural needs and encourage a critical examination of how race impacts civic participation and identity (Duncan, 2020). To tap into the transformational potential of social studies classrooms, scrutinizing elements of traditional civic education through the lens of critical race theory (CRT) provides not only a critique of the status quo but may also serve as a catalyst for systemic and micro-level change.

This chapter reviews literature on how traditional civic education negatively impacts the civic participation, engagement, and identities of Black students, as well as how high-quality civics instruction, grounded in critical race theory and culturally responsive pedagogy, can produce emancipatory outcomes (Duncan, 2020; Vickery, 2016). Research for this chapter was conducted in advance of an action research study in my own classroom after noticing how Black students both engaged with and seemed estranged from civic concepts; as such, other teachers might benefit from incorporating elements of the research into their own practices.

CRITICAL RACE THEORY AND PRAXIS

Concepts of citizenship and civic participation have been complicated from the very founding of the United States, bound in questions of what constitutes a full citizen and upon whom the full rights and privileges of citizenship should be bestowed. These questions were mired in issues of property rights, gender, and race; of those, property and race played and continue to play a key role in how Black people are written into (and out of) the narrative of U.S. citizenship (Ladson-Billings, 1998). The foundational document of the United States, the Constitution, declared an enslaved person to be three-fifths of a human being; the same document ensured that only property owners had voting rights (Ladson-Billings & Tate, 1995). Despite substantial legal changes since 1787, the interconnectedness of exclusion and dominance persists in the U.S. democratic system and influences how Black students develop their own civic identities (Tillet, 2012). CRT provides an appropriate lens through which to examine institutional racism and construct alternative ways to honor Black experiences and voices.

CRT, which began as a legal theory "committed to the struggle against racism, particularly as institutionalized in and by law" (Bell, 1995, p. 198), has become a popular tool for scholars to analyze and address the roles of race and racism in education. CRT in education, "like its antecedent in legal scholarship, is a radical critique of both the status quo and the purported reforms" (Ladson-Billings & Tate, 1995, p. 62). In practice, CRT evaluates and critiques how curriculum, policy, and instruction reflect institutional racism (Ledesma & Calderón, 2015). To even attempt to understand the educational experiences of students of Color and systemic educational inequity, race and racism must be central to any analysis.

Delgado and Stefancic (2017) isolate several key tenets of CRT, including the social construction of race, the non-aberrational endemic nature of racism, interest convergence, and intersectionality. Another key tenet of CRT—counter-narrative—is rooted in the "notion of a unique voice of color," highlighting the "presumed competence to speak about race and racism" minority status affords (Delgado & Stefancic, 2017, p. 11). CRT's reliance on counter-narratives illustrates "alternative epistemologies" (Ledesma & Calderón, 2015, p. 209) and resists objectivity, objective truth, and universality (Bell, 1995; Ladson-Billings & Tate, 1995). Because the accepted understandings of history, psychology, and education presented as objective truths are mired in racist ideology, CRT offers alternative means of conceptualizing facts and disrupting dominant ideologies.

This chapter focuses primarily on two CRT tenets—racism as endemic and counter-narratives—to review both the barriers to and emancipatory possibilities of civic education for Black students. Racism is deeply rooted in not only what students encounter in a civics classroom but also in how they encounter it; in its very ordinariness, racism too often goes unexamined or is dismissed as common, irrelevant, or even resolved (Delgado & Stefancic, 2017; Duncan, 2020; Woodson, 2016). It is vital to first examine the intentional and unintentional manifestations of racism in civic education before exploring how to challenge and reframe it in ways that are accessible and liberatory. Operationalizing CRT in the form of a critical race praxis, which includes making space for counter-narratives, problematizing traditional civic master narratives, and cultivating sociopolitical consciousness, can form the backbone of high-quality civic instruction that encourages students to become active civic participants (Duncan, 2020; Rodriguez, 2018; Vickery, 2016; Woodson, 2016).

Social studies education presents unique challenges to factual representation. Teaching history as objective truth not only whitewashes racial dominance and oppression but also normalizes it and fails to make room for critical inquiry and counter-narratives. Applying CRT to social studies is a way to confront the hidden curriculum and the absence of race in the field; by doing so with students, teachers can start to "address the disconnect between the artificial life of the classroom and [their] real lives" (Ladson-Billings, 2003, p. 10). Critical race scholarship in social studies education exposes and questions the United States' master narrative of racial dominance, the doctrine of authoritarian patriotism, and the construction of Black citizenship (Busey & Walker, 2017; Ender, 2019; Pinkney, 2016). For example, a history of Black people that focuses on enslavement and subjugation pays scant attention to their contributions beyond forced labor (Clay & Rubin, 2020; Tillet, 2012). Positive portrayals, if any, are of individual heroes and isolated movements rather than collective power or individual agency (Busey & Walker, 2017; Woodson, 2016). These versions of history reify white supremacy and complicate Black students' understandings of their own places within the narrative, constraining their conceptions of citizenship.

Critical race scholars and classroom teachers employ CRT not just to examine and analyze inequity and injustice but also to transform classrooms into emancipatory spaces for students to grapple with issues of race and its interplay with citizenship and agency (Duncan, 2020). This significant shift toward critical race *praxis* emerged in response to critics of CRT who argue that CRT highlights problems without providing solutions; Stovall (2016) writes, "in most of the CRT in education scholarship, praxis is still implied more than it is addressed directly. Invoking the work of critical pedagogy, our actions must remain reflexive if we are ever to improve the current condition" (pp. 281–282). Critical race praxis, in essence, puts CRT into practice to effect actual change within schools and communities (Su, 2007).

One of the most common forms of critical race praxis is culturally responsive pedagogy (Hayes & Juarez, 2012). Ladson-Billings (1995), who first discussed the application of CRT to education, envisioned culturally responsive pedagogy, originally culturally *relevant* pedagogy, as a framework for focusing on academic success, building cultural competence, and nurturing critical consciousness (see also Milner, 2014). Culturally responsive pedagogy in social studies and civic education includes purposeful teaching about the links among race, subjugation, and inequity, which manifests in challenging, open classroom discussions; investigation and creation of counter-narratives; critiques of accepted historical truths; and active participation by students and teachers as school and community change agents (Clay & Rubin, 2020; Epstein et al., 2011; Epstein & Gist, 2015).

BARRIERS TO HIGH-QUALITY CIVICS INSTRUCTION FOR BLACK STUDENTS

Despite the urgent need for dynamic civic engagement and participation among Black youth, schools still mired in "colorblind" or overtly racist curriculum and instructional practices are failing their students. Official curricula exhibit little to no effort to address the impact race and racism had and continue to have on our nation, so the historic denial of full citizenship on the basis of race goes unexamined and, by omission, is reinforced (Ladson-Billings, 1998; Pinkney, 2016). Though state history and civics standards have begun to include content on instances of Black history and civil rights movements, they are based in a messianic master narrative that privileges individual heroism over progressive change and the power of ordinary citizens (Woodson, 2016). Instead of learning about Black resistance and activism as ever-present in U.S. history, the civics curriculum is inundated with authoritarian patriotism, the imperious demand for blind allegiance and belief in American exceptionalism (Busey & Walker, 2017).

The way Black students encounter civics curriculum deepens its fundamental flaws. In terms of instructional practices, the one-size-fits-all approach to civic education uniquely inhibits the development of positive civic identities and likely civic participation among Black youth. Reliance on the traditional banking system of knowledge transmission, the promotion of authoritarian patriotism, skepticism and distrust of the government, and low civic expectations of Black students fail to make the idea of active citizenship approachable or even attractive (Busey & Walker, 2017; Littenberg-Tobias & Cohen, 2016; Tillet, 2012; Vickery, 2016). Instead of embedding into practice the means by which students may question the overt and hidden curriculum, educators all too often reinforce an already racist and exclusionary curriculum, such that Black students' experiences in civics classrooms have either no impact on their civic identities or, worse, drive them away from the idea of civic participation and engagement altogether (Pinkney, 2016; Rodriguez, 2018). Barriers to high-quality, meaningful civic education are multilayered and include not only what is taught but what goes untaught—not only how citizenship is conceptualized but how the traditional understanding of it goes unquestioned (Duncan, 2020; Woodson, 2016).

Curriculum

To the degree that social studies curriculum provides a foundation for students' understandings of history, its construction influences how students reconcile what they learn in school with what they experience and observe. Attempts to revise the official social studies curriculum to be more inclusive of Black history have been trivial or whitewashed, further entrenching white supremacy and leaving Black students conflicted about their place as citizens in the U.S. historical narrative (Duncan, 2020). The laser focus on standards, testing, and accountability in response to No Child Left Behind has created a shift toward compartmentalization and linear constructs, resulting in a litany of names, dates, and events that are easily digestible and testable; meanwhile, the words "race" or "racism" are notably absent or extremely rare in state standards (Busey & Walker, 2017; Heilig et al., 2012). Created in direct response to state standards and testing requirements, textbooks rarely reflect the nuances of actual history; failing to provide depth or context, they also distort and silence Black people's roles in U.S. and world history (Cummings, 2019; King, 2015).

Emerging from debates on how and what to include about Black history are historical representations that "purposefully made Black children into a Racial Other or subtly promoted ideas about race that removed white people's culpability with issues of race and racism" (Brown & Brown, 2015, p. 109). What students learn about Black people, especially in U.S. history standards, largely encompasses three main time periods: Black enslavement in the antebellum South, Reconstruction, and the civil rights movements of the 1960s (Busey & Walker, 2017; Tillet, 2012). The curriculum surrounding Black enslavement and Reconstruction emphasizes physical bondage, victimhood, and a lack of agency while whitewashing the codified and systematic dominance perpetuated for centuries by white hands (Tillet, 2012). Portrayals of the civil rights era, on the other hand, focus on the works of individuals, especially Martin Luther King and Rosa Parks, rather than emphasizing the sustained power of collective movements. Heilig et al. (2012) called the token incorporation of Black people in the history curriculum the "illusion of inclusion," suggesting relatively minor mentions of Black history satisfy the demands for inclusion but reinforce its tangential status to the dominant narrative (p. 403).

The heroification of a select few Black historical figures, known as the messianic master narrative, highlights their rarity and impairs students' senses of civic agency (Woodson, 2016). Instead of focusing on the power and agency of ordinary Black people as part of the traditional curriculum, students typically encounter only Black history heroes, a status they may view as unattainable; they may see the election of President Obama, the first Black president, as the work of one man rather than the work of millions of Black voters and activists (Woodson, 2016). When civil rights icons are presented in a curriculum steeped in whiteness and colonialism, the roles of activist and civic actor appear unattainable to Black students; they find themselves either unworthy or incapable of following in their heroes' footsteps (Woodson, 2016). Required history classes eschew myriad stories of everyday members and activists in the Black community, much less the histories of organizations like the Black Panthers or the Nation of Islam, in favor of the elusive Black hero (Busey & Walker, 2017).

An extensive analysis of K–5 standards across the 50 states found that not only was the Black messianic narrative the predominant means by which students engaged with Black history across the country, but that authoritarian patriotism was also prevalent in social studies curricula (Busey & Walker, 2017). Authoritarian patriotism exists in a curriculum that espouses U.S. exceptionalism and a dogmatic love of country. According to Busey and Walker (2017), the messianic narrative of Black history, in combination with authoritarian patriotism, diminishes the role of Black people in the national narrative and results in Black students' linking the very ideas of citizenship to either blind allegiance or unattainable heroics.

Civic Estrangement

Du Bois (1903/2018) described the "double consciousness" of Black Americans as "always looking at one's self through the eyes of others, of measuring one's soul by the tape of a world that looks on in amused contempt and pity" (p. 9). Over a century later, this sense of double consciousness still pervades conceptions of Black citizenship and identity, manifesting in *civic estrangement*. As Tillet (2012) explains, Black people's omission from civic myths, narratives, and visual history results in a citizen/noncitizen duality that leads to feelings of nonbelonging and disillusionment. In other words, while Black people have legal citizenship, the American master narrative of citizenship excludes and marginalizes their contributions and connection to civic life (Vickery, 2016).

Vickery (2017) distinguishes between citizenship as a "legal status that grants citizens certain rights, privileges, and freedoms that the government must protect" and its implications as "a social construct and discursive practice that has changed over time to exclude certain bodies from belonging and participating as legitimate members of the nation-state" (pp. 318–319).

As such, the very idea of citizenship is rooted in belonging and exclusion, emphasizing Black people's historic disconnection from full citizenship and the socially constructed rights and privileges of the U.S. civic community. Naturally, Black students' civic identity development, which is intimately tied to both a sense of membership and racialized citizenship, is impacted by their estrangement from the master narrative and the resulting feelings of being both citizen insiders and outsiders (Lannegrand-Willems et al., 2018; Myers et al., 2015).

Not only have Black students been asked to reconcile their double consciousness but they must also attempt to locate themselves as citizens in a political space that is at worst hostile and at best uninviting toward their active participation (Clay & Rubin, 2020; Duncan, 2020). Despite witnessing injustice run rampant around them and a world that seems balanced on a knife's edge, students encounter the same bland, whitewashed, clinical civics and social studies instruction that focuses on content knowledge about citizenship without context or calls to action (Journell, 2016). The dedication to avoiding controversy and adherence to authoritarian patriotism has rendered civics curriculum all but irrelevant for Black students; as a result, they are disconnected from content, concepts, and the potential of active citizenship (Cummings, 2019; Littenberg-Tobias & Cohen, 2016). Students' negative interactions with and perceptions of political structures perpetuate a "civic disjunction," which Clay and Rubin (2020) discuss as the disconnect between what Black students learn about the ideal of citizenship and the reality of their daily lives (p. 163). Whether termed double consciousness, civic estrangement, or civic disjunction, Black students face the daunting task of reconciling what they are learning about colorblind history and equal citizenship in school with their lived experiences of injustice and racism.

Lack of Connection

Continuing to ignore Black students' different needs and experiences related to citizenship fails to achieve the purported mission of civic education—to prepare all students to participate as active, engaged citizens. From a whitewashed social studies curriculum that minimizes race and racism to the dedication to exclusionary models of citizenship, Black students feel disconnected from the U.S. political system and the manners in which they typically encounter civic education in school. As Clay and Rubin (2020) point out, "students' daily experiences in a society marked by racial and socioeconomic inequalities become part of their evolving understandings of themselves as citizens—a lived, daily civics that is central to their civic learning and identity" (p. 163). By avoiding the realities of Black students' "lived, daily civics," traditional classroom-based civics instruction seems not only irrelevant but factually inaccurate in the face of their own experiences (Clay & Rubin, 2020, p. 163).

Because the curriculum has omitted or removed race and racism, engaging in honest dialogue about them becomes inappropriate or controversial; the dedication to noncontroversy and the avoidance of deep examination of injustice is one more reason many Black students find civics and history irrelevant to their own lives (Cummings, 2019; Heilig et al., 2012). Moreover, approaching the concept of citizenship in ways that imply singularity or continue to highlight an obsolete version of an ideal citizen alienates Black students who are not represented positively in the master narrative (Vickery, 2017).

OPPORTUNITIES FOR EMANCIPATORY CIVIC EDUCATION AND OUTCOMES

Despite the overt and covert attempts to reinforce racism and the noncitizen status of Black people, schools can counter the dominant narrative and promote civic engagement and positive civic identities. Academics and classroom teachers alike have been exploring critical race praxis, especially culturally responsive pedagogy as an approach to history and civics instruction (Epstein et al., 2011; Milner, 2014; Rodriguez, 2018; Stovall, 2016). Promising evidence indicates that engaging students in authentic discussions about race and racism, employing counter-narratives, and modeling critical patriotism can increase support for Black students (Ender, 2019; Epstein & Gist, 2015).

Critical Race Praxis

Putting CRT into classroom practice is nothing new, although attaching a name to it may be. Purposefully challenging white supremacy and developing citizen-activists was an open goal of institutions like freedom schools, citizenship schools, the Highlander Center, and all-Black schools during segregation (Pinkney, 2016). CRT, along with culturally responsive teaching, simply gave a name to what many teachers, particularly teachers of Color, have been doing for decades (Ladson-Billings, 1995; Ladson-Billings & Tate, 1995). The framework for culturally responsive pedagogy has guided teachers who want to encourage sociopolitical consciousness in students by challenging the dominant master narrative of citizenship, forging relationships and community partnerships, affirming and cultivating student agency and identity, and intentionally disrupting and complicating racialized citizenship (Milner, 2014; Vickery, 2016).

Student responses to culturally responsive history and civic education are promising: when teachers employ emancipatory methods, students are better equipped to demonstrate "sociopolitical consciousness, become critical consumers of information, and develop a positive racial identity" (Duncan, 2020, p. 177). Instruction that encourages students to critically examine racist curriculum and problematize racialized citizenship better prepares them to navigate their own civic identities (Vickery, 2016). Purposefully incorporating Black students' own cultures and experiences into instruction helps students understand how structural racism, agency, and identity influence one's own place within the U.S. master narrative (Epstein et al., 2011). By interrogating the traditional notions of citizenship and providing alternative conceptions of culturally diverse citizenship, teachers offer students a more appealing path to developing their own rich civic identities and senses of agency (Rodriguez, 2018).

Courageous Conversations

As Rodriguez (2018) noted, "schools are an ideal site to nurture broader understandings of citizenship" (p. 549), and what better place within that site than a social studies classroom, where preparing students to become active citizens is an espoused goal? One of the most powerful tools in the hands of emancipatory educators—open, honest, and often uncomfortable dialogue—enables teachers to address institutional racism, systemic injustice, and the power dynamics of racialized citizenship (Vickery, 2016). Engaging students in robust conversations that intentionally complicate race and citizenship, while making connections to students' lives, increases students' understanding of how to participate civically and aid in civic identity creation (Cummings, 2019; Duncan, 2020). Instead of avoiding controversy, social studies classrooms that incorporate and embrace it prepare students to engage in a contentious democracy, better equipped to recognize and respond to racism and injustice (Cummings, 2019, p. 291).

Parkhouse (2018) discusses the striking potential of a space where students can come to terms with the idealized version of the United States in comparison to their own lived experiences; awareness of such a "disjuncture" can result in "empowered—as opposed to discouraged—civic identities if they are in classrooms with candid discussions of power" (p. 303). Further, Parkhouse adds, this type of open discussion can help demystify the master narrative and challenge the dynamics of institutionalized racial oppression and dominance. In other words, when teachers create spaces for Black students to engage with and critically examine issues that impact their daily lives, those students can develop and deepen their understandings of the world and their places in it.

Counter-Narratives

Facing curriculum and traditional instructional practices that normalize and re-entrench white supremacy, counter-narratives complicate and disrupt common versions of both history and the present (Ender, 2019; Pinkney, 2016; Tillet, 2012). As stories that are not often told, especially those of and by marginalized people, counter-narratives are a fundamental facet of CRT and vital to social justice–oriented education (Ender, 2019; Ledesma & Calderón, 2015). Historical counter-narratives "contest the singularity of American civic myths to reconfigure a democratic aesthetic and praxis, and by extension write [African Americans] into the ultimate un-narrative of the United States" (Tillet, 2012, p. 10). Tillet argues that constructing counter-narratives can impact civic identity construction by challenging underlying assumptions about agency and power.

Because the master narrative has traditionally silenced Black voices, providing opportunities for students to read, discuss, and create alternative versions of what they have often been told is the "whole story" deepens and contextualizes their understandings of past, present, and their own future civic actions (Ender, 2019). Duncan (2020) suggests that encouraging Black students to tell their own counterstories in response to what they experience is itself a civic action, a form of active resistance that articulates the disjunction one feels between the master narrative of U.S. citizenship and one's own life.

Critical Civic Education

Tillet's (2012) exploration of counter-narratives includes a call to embrace critical patriotism, characterized by "dissidence and dissent," as opposed to "staunch allegiance and an inflexible attachment to the country" (p. 11). Similarly, Busey and Walker (2017) contrast authoritarian patriotism, which describes the dogmatic, blind loyalty to a flawed system, with democratic patriotism, which encourages dissent and questions even as it upholds the underlying principles and values of freedom, liberty, and civil rights. Moreover, they argue that Black critical patriotism has been an ever-present reality for Black people in the United States, even as the messianic narrative of Black history skews student perceptions of Black citizenship. Teaching students the historical contributions of Black intellectuals, freedom fighters, and ordinary citizens, as well as teaching them to critically interrogate the existing whitewashed curriculum, can transform their understandings of history and their own civic identities and activism (Busey & Walker, 2017; Woodson, 2016).

Beyond the representations of Black history in the U.S. master narrative, Black students also contend with the contradictions of racialized citizenship in their own lives. Clay and Rubin (2020) developed a concept called *critically relevant civics* that combines a critique of the traditional curriculum with the incorporation of students' lived experiences, skills, and resources to foster civic identities and support youth civic activism. Marginalized students' encounters outside of school, especially with state actors like the police, are civics lessons in themselves; contextualizing and openly interrogating those outside experiences in classroom civics instruction provides an opportunity to evaluate how social injustice impacts citizenship and civic action (Clay & Rubin, 2020).

CONCLUSION

Rather than addressing the needs and experiences of Black students, traditional civics curriculum and instructional practices uniquely harm them and contribute to negative attitudes toward civic participation and conflicted civic identities. The very idea of U.S. citizenship is mired in notions of white supremacy, exclusion, and non-membership, all of which infuse social studies and civic education. Encountering the realities of racist institutions and structures both inside and outside of school, Black students face a civic estrangement born from the disjunction between their lived experiences and the dominant narrative of freedom and equality.

However, teachers who want to counteract the messages of traditional civics instruction can take concrete actions. Incorporating critical race praxis in their classrooms can positively impact Black students' perceptions of their own civic identities and political agency. Including robust and candid discussions about race, racism, and current events, as well as providing and creating counter-narratives to enhance student understandings of Black history and citizenship, teaches students how to engage in critical patriotism. A critical stance that intentionally disrupts and complicates traditional notions of citizenship, patriotism, and political activism may result in the emancipatory outcomes and sociopolitical consciousness sought by culturally responsive educators.

REFERENCES

Bell, D. (1995). Who's afraid of critical race theory? *University of Illinois Law Review* (4), 893–910.

Brown, A. L., & Brown, K. D. (2015). The more things change, the more they stay the same: Excavating race and the enduring racisms in U.S. curriculum. *Teachers College Record, 117*(14), 103–130.

Busey, C., & Walker, I. (2017). A dream and a bus: Black critical patriotism in elementary social studies standards. *Theory & Research in Social Education, 45*(4), 456–488. http://doi.org/10.1080/00933104.2017.1320251

Clay, K., & Rubin, B. (2020). "I look deep into this stuff because it's a part of me": Toward a critically relevant civic education. *Theory & Research in Social Education, 48*(2), 161–181. https://doi.org/10.1080/00933104.2019.1680466

Cummings, R. (2019). Justice then and now: Engaging students in critical thinking about justice and history. *The Social Studies, 29*(1), 281–292. https://doi.org/10.1080/00377996.2019.1652140

Delgado, R., & Stefancic, J. (2017). *Critical race theory: An introduction* (3rd ed.). New York University Press.

Du Bois, W. E. B. (2018). *The souls of black folk* (P. H. Hinchey, Ed.). Myers Education Press. (Original work published in 1903)

Duncan, K. (2020). "What better tool do I have?": A critical race approach to teaching civics. *The High School Journal, 103*(3), 176–189. https://doi.org/10.1353/hsj.2020.0011

Ender, T. (2019). Counter-narratives as resistance: Creating critical social studies spaces with communities. *The Journal of Social Studies Research, 43*(2), 133–143. https://doi.org/10.1016/j.jssr.2018.11.002

Epstein, T., & Gist, C. (2015). Teaching racial literacy in secondary humanities classrooms: Challenging adolescents' of color concepts of race and racism. *Racial Ethnicity and Education, 18*(1), 40–60. https://doi.org/10.1080/13613324.2013.792800

Epstein, T., Mayorga, E., & Nelson, J. (2011). Teaching about race in an urban history class: The effects of culturally responsive teaching. *The Journal of Social Studies Research, 35*(1), 2–22.

Hayes, C., & Juarez, B. (2012). There is no culturally responsive teaching spoken here: A critical race perspective. *Democracy & Education, 20*(1), 1–14. https://democracyeducationjournal.org/home/vol20/iss1/1

Heilig, J., Brown, K. D., & Brown, A. L. (2012). The illusion of inclusion: A critical race theory textual analysis of race and standards. *Harvard Educational Review, 82*(3), 403–424.

Journell, W. (2016). Preface. In W. Journell (Ed.), *Reassessing the social studies curriculum: Promoting critical civic engagement in a politically polarized, post-9-11 world* (pp. xiii–xviii). Rowman & Littlefield.

King, L. (2015). "A narrative to the colored children in America": Lelia Amos Pendleton, African American history textbooks, and challenging personhood. *The Journal of Negro Education, 84*(4), 519–533. https://doi.org/10.7709/jnegroeducation.84.4.0519

Ladson-Billings, G. (1995). But that's just good teaching! The case for culturally relevant pedagogy. *Theory Into Practice, 34*(3), 159–165. https://doi.org/10.1080/00405849509543675

Ladson-Billings, G. (1998). Just what is critical race theory and what's it doing in a nice field like education? *International Journal of Qualitative Studies in Education, 11*(1), 7–24. https://doi.org/10.1080/095183998236863

Ladson-Billings, G. (Ed.) (2003). *Critical race theory perspectives on social studies: The profession, policies, and curriculum.* Information Ages Publishing, Inc.

Ladson-Billings, G., & Tate, W. F. (1995). Toward a critical race theory of education. *Teachers College Record, 97*(1), 47–68.

Lannegrand-Willems, L., Chevrier, B., Perchec, C., & Carrizales, A. (2018). How is civic engagement related to personal identity and social identity in late adolescents and emerging adults? A person oriented approach. *Journal of Youth and Adolescence, 47*, 731–748. https://doi.org/10.1007/s10964-018-0821-x

Ledesma, M. C., & Calderón, D. (2015). Critical race theory in education: A review of past literature and a look to the future. *Qualitative Inquiry, 21*(3), 206–222. https://doi.org/10.1177/1077800414557825

Littenberg-Tobias, J., & Cohen, A. K. (2016). Diverging paths: Understanding racial differences in civic engagement among white, African American, and Latina/o adolescents using structural equation modeling. *American Journal of Community Psychology*, 57(1–2), 102–117. https://doi.org/10.1002/ajcp.12027

Milner, H. R. (2014). Culturally relevant, purpose-driven learning & teaching in a middle school social studies classroom. *Multicultural Education* (Winter), 9–17.

Myers, J. P., McBride, C. E., & Anderson, M. (2015). Beyond knowledge and skills: Discursive construction of civic identity in the world history classroom. *Curriculum Inquiry*, 45(2), 198–218. https://doi.org/10.1080/03626784.2015.1011045

Parkhouse, H. (2018). Pedagogies of naming, questioning, and demystification: A study of two critical U.S. history classrooms. *Theory & Research in Social Education*, 46(2), 277–317. https://doi.org/10.1080/00933104.2017.1389327

Pinkney, A. (2016). The role of schools in educating black citizens: From the 1800s to the present. *Theory & Research in Social Education*, 44(1), 72–103. https://doi.org/10.1080/00933104.2015.1099486

Rodriguez, N. (2018). From margins to center: Developing cultural citizenship education through the teaching of Asian American history. *Theory & Research in Social Education*, 46(4), 528–573. https://doi.org/10.1080/00933104.2018.1432432

Stovall, D. (2016). Out of adolescence and into adulthood: Critical race theory, retrenchment, and the imperative of praxis. *Urban Education*, 51(3), 274–286.

Su, C. (2007). Crack silent codes: Critical race theory and education organizing. *Discourse: Studies in the Cultural Politics of Education*, 28(4), 531–548. https://doi.org/10.1080/01596300701625297

Tillet, S. (2012). *Sites of slavery: Citizenship and racial democracy in the post–civil rights imagination*. Duke University Press.

Vickery, A. (2016). "I know what you are about to enter": Lived experiences as the curricular foundation for teaching citizenship. *Gender and Education*, 28(6), 725–741. https://doi.org/10.1080/09540253.2016.1221890

Vickery, A. (2017). "You excluded us for so long and now you want us to be patriotic?": African American women teachers navigating the quandary of citizenship. *Theory & Research in Social Education*, 45(3), 318–348. https://doi.org/10.1080/00933104.2017.1282387

Woodson, A. (2016). We're just ordinary people: Messianic master narratives and black youths' civic agency. *Theory & Research in Social Education*, 44(2), 184–221. https://doi.org/10.1080/00933104.2016.1170645

CHAPTER 2

"Have We Been Civically Educated to Seize the Present Moment?"
Two Black Social Educators' Sense-Making of Civic Education

Carla-Ann Brown, Rasheeda West, and Elizabeth Yeager Washington

INTRODUCTION

This book created a new space for dialogue between us, a Black social studies practitioner-researcher and a Black literacy practitioner-researcher from very different backgrounds, who want to make sense of the civic education we received and our teachings of civics to Black students. Through this dialogue, we have become keenly aware that traditional civics as reflected in textbooks and curriculum standards—that is, focusing on the historical foundations, structures, and functions of U.S. democracy—is useless in the present moment of social and political conflict around race issues in the United States. It has taken both of us years to make sense of the connection between our civic disengagement and our communities' struggles. We experienced the angst of sitting in civics classrooms with white teachers, where we felt invisible and ill-prepared for our future as engaged citizens.

In this chapter, we share our dialogue on *the civic education we experienced in our schools and our communities*, the sense of "citizenship belonging" missing from our education, and what we learned about our civic identities and affinity with United States citizenship. We also discuss *what kind of civic education we want our Black students to have* that centers the lived experiences of Black people in ways that our schooling did not and our vision of the obligations we have as teachers of Black students. Finally, we discuss our re-imaginings, hopes, and fears as we go forward as Black social justice educators.

Navarro and Howard (2017) explain that:

> The quest for democratic citizenship is tied to the notion that individual differences ... are to be recognized, respected, understood, and embraced in a pluralistic society. Yet, history is replete with widespread accounts of how the "other" has been excluded and marginalized.... In many ways, pre-kindergarten through 12th-grade schools are the ideal setting to instill the appropriate knowledge, skills, and dispositions for living in a diverse and inclusive democracy. We would argue that one of the issues that have been most difficult for the nation to address is its history around issues tied to race and racism. Consequently, because of the nation's ambivalence around race, issues tied to race and racism have been largely absent from ... social studies education. (p. 209)

They also point out that "a democratic society must be willing to have the uncomfortable yet needed discussions about various marginalized populations ... who have been part of the very fabric of the United States since its inception" (p. 210).

As Black educators, we aim to teach for true and inclusive democratic citizenship and to help our students analyze critical issues around race and racism in the United States and the impact inequity has on authentic civic engagement. More broadly, we want our students to problematize the idea of what citizenship looks like in a diverse, inclusive democracy, including the issue of who gets to decide what being a "patriotic citizen" entails. We wonder, what conceptualizations of citizenship might there be beyond Westheimer and Kahne's (2004) categories of personally responsible, participatory, and justice-oriented citizens? How do we disrupt the traditional, status quo narratives that we have learned from our civic experiences and that keep getting reframed and repackaged? Most importantly, how can we seize the present moment of social and political injustice, and what should we do with that moment? What *can* we do?

WHO WE ARE

Now a middle school social studies teacher of 6th-grade World Cultures and a team leader, Carla-Ann is a practitioner-researcher with 10 years' experience. She began teaching in 2013 after graduating with her master's degree from the University of Florida and earning her EdD there in 2021. As chair of her school's equity task force, she advocates for culturally sustaining teaching and social justice–oriented equity pedagogies. Rasheeda, also a practitioner-researcher, who graduated from the University of Central Florida and earned her EdD in 2021 from the University of Florida, has 18 years in education and is a literacy specialist focusing on equity issues related to students' access to civics content through teachers' literacy practices in school districts throughout the state. Elizabeth is a University of Florida professor of social studies education who chaired Rasheeda's dissertation committee, worked with Carla-Ann on a social justice–oriented curriculum for her World Cultures class, and introduced Carla-Ann and Rasheeda to each other as Rasheeda focused her dissertation on critical civic education, with Carla-Ann as the participant in her case study.

The "present moment" to which we refer comprises two essential components. First, we are teaching in the wake of the 2020 murder of George Floyd by Minneapolis police officer Derek Chauvin, among other acts of police brutality that have mostly remained unchecked and without recourse for decades; the 2021 criminal trial of Chauvin that thankfully resulted in his conviction; and the ensuing Black Lives Matter protests around the country. Second, we are teaching within the national backlash to Black Lives Matter and the apparent fragility around calling out the foundations of racism that have plagued the United States. Within the last couple of years, this fragility has found a new "boogie man" for people unwilling to acknowledge this country's racist history and how it impacts the present (Ray & Gibbons, 2021) in the form of critical race theory (CRT). Ongoing efforts in over 28 states and counting, including Florida, focus on restricting teaching about racism, bias, systemic racism, white supremacy, and even the contributions of specific racial or ethnic groups to United States history (Stout & LeMee, 2021). Ongoing challenges to "anti-CRT" laws are playing out in courtrooms, as seen in the efforts of the NAACP, the NEA, and individual teachers, students, and businesses.

Our present moment also includes living and teaching in Florida, which is at the epicenter of these efforts. According to the Florida Board of Education:

> Examples of theories that distort historical events and are inconsistent with State Board approved standards include . . . the teaching of Critical Race Theory, meaning the theory that racism is not merely the product of prejudice, but that racism is embedded in American society and its legal systems to uphold the supremacy of white persons. Instruction may not utilize material from the 1619 Project and may not define American history as something other than the creation of a new nation based largely on universal principles stated in the Declaration of Independence. (Florida Board of Education, 2021)

The board further states that teachers "must not share their personal views or attempt to indoctrinate or persuade students to a particular point of view that is inconsistent with Florida curriculum standards" (Florida Board of Education, 2021). For us, as Black educators, the hypocrisy of the state legislature trying to erase the traumatizing experiences of living in Black and Brown skin, while at the same time exalting the perceived inclusivity and diversity of the state, is astounding. The "anti-CRT" legislation in Florida states:

> Classroom instruction will educate students on what it means to be a respectful and responsible citizen and encourage tolerance of diversity to protect democratic principles that our country is founded on. (Flgov.com, 2022).

At the same time, the legislation is intended to eliminate diversity, equity, and inclusion (DEI) initiatives in schools and to ensure that discussions of the impacts of systemic racism are suppressed, calling this "far-left indoctrination" and "Marxist" (Flgov.com, 2022). Among other things, Nikole Hannah-Jones's award-winning book, *The 1619 Project*, which is conceptualized to address the erasure of Black people from school textbooks, standards, and curricula, is specifically banned in Florida public schools. Hannah-Jones (2021) explains:

> [This erasure] is symbolic of how history is shaped by people who decide what's important and what's not. And that erasure is also a powerful statement. . . . The [1619] project argues that slavery is a foundational American institution. It is one of the oldest American institutions, and the legacy of the first 250 years of slavery still, of course, permeates throughout society in a variety of ways. (NPR, 2021)

THE CIVIC EDUCATION WE HAD

Question: How has civic education in its past and current forms contributed to the problem of a diluted and incomplete representation of civic engagement and responsibility?

Carla-Ann

My civic education consisted of learning about the societal rules and norms that are considered characteristics of contributing members of society. I grew up in a family that valued not causing problems or creating any strife outside of the home. There was a mindset that rules and laws were made for a reason, and responsible citizens do not go against the rules. The external image of the family and perception was important. My childhood experiences met the expectations of the dominant (white) society. I would later learn the compliance of my family helped maintain the barriers we found tensions with. As a family, we did not use civic engagement as a means to achieve justice; we were personally responsible and participatory citizens, not justice-oriented ones (Westheimer & Kahne, 2004). Civics in my schooling background consisted of a Eurocentric view of civic responsibilities, including traditional background information on the structure of the U.S. government and high praise of the United States as the greatest democracy in the world. As I reflect, I think about how my civic education consisted only of what I could do for the country, not how the country failed and continues to fail people who look like me.

Rasheeda

I grew up in Miami, Florida, in the 1980s and 1990s and was educated in one of the country's largest school districts. Like you, Carla-Ann, my civic education was grounded in conformity through character education and a focus on American patriotism. There were many reasons for this—one being the 1984 Miami-Dade Grand Jury Report that detailed the problems youth gangs posed in Miami-Dade County communities. Programs to put students on the path toward gainful employment and reduce the "cultural drift" and "culture of poverty" were established to remedy the issues mentioned in the report. Probably the most well-known of these is The Drug Abuse Resistance Education (DARE) program. The adults in my family would often talk about how impossible it was for Black people to get ahead, citing the gaps in progress between Black Miamians and everyone else. We understood many non-Black Miamians would simply continue to see the problem as a lack of effort or interest in progress instead of a systemic one supported by poor civic education. Indeed, my education did not provide me with the critical civic knowledge necessary to navigate local politics. I have to agree that my civic education prepared me to serve, not to have my rights met.

We identified some of the same missing elements in our civic education as we began our dialogue. First, we did not have a grounding sense of "citizenship belonging" in our living and learning spaces, despite growing up in tightly knit communities of Color. Ladson-Billings's (2004) assertion that whiteness is a criterion for full citizenship in a civics curriculum that privileges white, middle-class voices deeply resonated with us. Second, in both imagined and physical spaces, we had no experience with the idea of learning civics for critical consciousness of systemic racism and social injustice (Paris, 2012; Vickery, 2017), despite what we saw as urgent needs in our communities—for example, food insecurity and lack of affordable housing. Third, we received no encouragement or outlet to use our voices to advocate for social and political change. Quite the opposite was true; we lacked a sense of "enoughness," as we felt the low expectations of our teachers and communities (Woodson & Love, 2019). Our civic miseducation assumed we were "less than" citizens who might be able to fix superficial problems if we were "good" and "kind" enough (Boylorn, 2016; Salam, 2021).

So, what civic education did we have instead? In our school experiences, the realities of politics in the United States were withheld. Instead, we had to go out of our way to learn about them and saw too often that the democratic process did not include us. The implicit message was: Entrust democracy to the care of certain "others." As we grew into adulthood and became educators, we had to make efforts at problem solving to hold on to our dignity and ease the burden of suffering caused by systemic issues in our communities, even though we were taught both at school and home that civically engaged citizens should not confront the system. We also noticed how this form of civic education served to drive a wedge between people in Black communities, some of whom experienced modest successes within existing political structures. Undoubtedly, the message that people's struggles are their fault passed down through the generations; we were taught to blame each other, not the systemic issues that characterized our lived experiences, and that our education did not help us to notice. Had we noticed them better, could we have identified the structures that ensured our people could not advocate for justice?

THE CIVIC EDUCATION WE WISH WE HAD

Question: What theories and practices do you wish your teachers and/or families would have incorporated to prepare you as a Black student ready to engage in the democratic process?

Carla-Ann

Having learned that following the rules at all times as not to disrupt or cause negative attention is the accepted behavior of a productive member of society, I wish my family had more of an understanding of how the messaging at home fed into the indoctrination of society's dominant messaging. This would have helped me make sense of the everyday struggles people of Color endure and the structures put in place against them. I also wish my education provided me with more exposure to the diverse voices of American citizens through counter-narratives and prepared me with the tools to engage in pluralistic, critical conversations about civic participation. This type of education would have helped me to understand that being an active member of a community involved doing my part to ensure equitable access and living conditions for everyone. I wish I learned to ask: What are the structures that disenfranchise specific groups of people? How do we as a collective society (those with privilege and those with disadvantages) come together to fight for justice?

Rasheeda

I wish I had an education that acknowledged the diversity of my community, validated our experiences as minoritized people, and provided a foundation for understanding how the systems in this country work against us so we could navigate and change them. Had my teachers used critical literacy as a framework for engaging students with text and media, then confronting, interrogating, and extending ideas to the benefit of oneself and community likely would have been a common practice within my community. As an educated Black female adult watching the chaos of 2020 unfold, I felt inadequate in my attempts to explain the multiple system failures to others or determine how I could work to confront and change these systems. I was one of many adults living within a marginalized community who lacked the critical knowledge needed to change the community's social, political, and economic status. Critical race theory, Black feminist theory, critical multiculturalism, and participatory democracy are approaches to teaching and learning that would have prepared us all to confront the chaos, or perhaps even prevent it.

I needed an education that would prepare me to protect democracy and hold those who jeopardize it accountable. Access to civic education at this level would have changed how I viewed myself as a citizen and my community.

As we began to interrogate (consider) the civic education we wished we had growing up, we started to question how our educational background fell short. First, we wished we were provided with a civic education that prepared us to interact with the diverse communities and voices in a democratic society. Love (2019) asserts that civic education is charged with the responsibility of teaching students diverse attitudes, knowledge, and skills, including knowing "how to petition, protest, speak in public, [and] solve social issues" (p. 70) that will prepare them to be responsible and involved citizens. Second, we wished we were taught to understand the complexities of human nature and how lived experiences differ for individual people. Garcia et al. (2020) describe counterstories as the antithesis of the dominant narrative, functioning to interrogate incomplete and one-sided images of minority groups often perceived as reality. Unfortunately, the reality of our educational backgrounds encompassed the false realities of the dominant narrative. Third, we wished we had a better understanding of the fluid nature of civic identities. Democracy shifts as people grow and change; it is not static.

THE CIVIC EDUCATION WE WANT OUR STUDENTS TO HAVE

Question: What kind of civic education do Black students need to both navigate issues of inequitable democracy and racial injustice and work toward resolving them? How are the two issues related?

Carla-Ann

It does not make sense how easily adults fall for distorted and disillusioned realities of human experiences and existence. Are they that vulnerable? Are the lies that strong? Or are certain members of society so comfortable in a state of ignorance they cannot recognize they are being fed lies? Society's false narratives about anti-racist and democratic teaching since the 2020 Black Lives Matter demonstrations have been alarming, and they do not seem to be slowing down. Students must be equipped with the necessary tools to combat these false narratives and often outright lies that are constantly permeating news cycles, dialogue, and interactions.

Rasheeda

We seemed to be making progress in summer 2020 when race, justice, and politics were dominating conversations. In the months since, that momentum quickly faded. Black students need an education that keeps them at the center of the dialogue and reflects their lives. Democracy is fragile in the United States because we refuse to center race in conversations about freedom. Students are taught a race-neutral curriculum and then forced to endure the wrath of racism in policies and systems throughout their lives. They are unaware and unprepared to fend for themselves—to fight for their rights. We cannot continue to educate students about freedom and justice and act as if their positionalities do not exclude them from those freedoms. Students deserve an education that includes them. The majority of students in this country are Black and brown. The curriculum should reflect this new student body.

The 2020 U.S. Census report confirms the vast diversity of American society and the growth of minoritized groups over the past few decades. This demographic shift also represents the makeup of the students in our schools, 27% of whom are Hispanic/Latinx and 15% of whom are Black, as the shift continues in this direction (Schaeffer, 2021). Both of our educational backgrounds reflected a need to develop civic identities that would have prepared us for the democratic actions required of 2020 citizens in a free society. These same needs are crucial for students now and are even more urgent because we are trying to make sense of national trends that seem to indicate U.S. democracy is at a breaking point. Teachers must prioritize three things: teaching multiple perspectives, dismantling distortions, and making sense of the world.

Multiple Perspectives

Suppose students are only exposed to dominant voices and mainstream accounts of historical events and people. This instills an intentionally distorted perception of realities that minoritized groups face in America. As Black educators, we want to provide a space for our Black students to hear experiences and counterstories from marginalized groups who engage in civic participation and responsibility compared to dominant groups, particularly with regard to their navigation of multiple forms of racism and white supremacy in the United States (Duncan, 2020, 2022).

Providing students with diverse perspectives of history must also include local history. It has been our experience that students lack both broad and local historical perspectives, which moves them further away from civically engaging on local levels. Furthermore, we want students to confront issues in their communities. Having historical knowledge about their community provides them with a complete understanding of why issues exist.

Dismantling Distortions

Our civic education was centered on official narratives and authoritarian patriotism, including, for example, the idea of "true patriotism" only being accomplished through rigid conforming, a one-size-fits-all framework of citizenship, and the removal of individuals who push back against ingrained systems of democracy. In contrast, the civic education we want our students to have centers on democratic patriotism and justice-oriented citizenship. To us, this means creating spaces for students to grapple with the rights of citizens to question inequitable power imbalances and unjust structures and to counteract misuses of power in a society. We define critical patriotism as respect and admiration for the values and ideals of a country, while recognizing and questioning when those values and ideals fall short (Hawkman & Van Horn, 2019; Kissling, 2016). Making a shift to teaching civics in this way requires teachers and students to collectively work together to dismantle distortions about those of us who have historically and contemporarily existed in the outside margins of society.

Unfortunately, with traditional education practices, a focus on character education supports these distorted historical narratives. Character education focuses on students' character (morals, beliefs, behaviors) as a significant factor in how they experience life in America. This omits the impact of oppressive structures (which are maintained by distorted historical narratives) and promotes individualism over critical multiculturalism. Students seeing themselves as separate from other marginalized groups or their cultural group supports the distorted idea that character alone denotes good citizenship.

False representations of minoritized groups and disinformation are nothing new. Unless we acknowledge the role we all have to play in silencing certain voices, how can we change what students are exposed to in school? To gain the necessary tools to diminish these distorted narratives, students need to research and interrogate the skewed criteria for ideal citizenship that dominant voices and groups have created throughout history. Additionally, to extend this work, students must be able to map their misconceptions of citizenship onto the conditions of their communities and acknowledge the stakeholders involved in creating the inequitable conditions to confront the issues and make long-lasting changes. For instance, this could include providing students with opportunities to research how various strategies of critical patriotism through protests and collective movements have been used to fight against oppression and injustice and for systematic change and equity.

Making Sense of the World

We want students to receive a civic education that highlights the historical value of human voices, and the power people have in constructing an inclusive world. For example, having students engage in conversations about how the perception of civic participation, duty, and responsibility differ in various cultures is essential for them to recognize that democracy (the focus of civic education) is constantly evolving. It should reflect the needs of people, their communities, and their social circumstances across time.

Teachers can take specific actions to support students in making sense of the world through civic education. These actions include

- being intentional about pushing back on and "repurposing" existing civics standards that continue to cause harm;
- helping students to adjust the lens through which they view societal problems related to race;
- showing students how to peel back the layers of needs in their lives and communities to reveal policies, laws, and practices that stand in the way of progress toward racial justice;
- discussing current events directly related to racism and racial justice, with an eye toward helping students develop critical media literacy/critical race media literacy skills;
  » This can involve the intentional incorporation of literature written by historically marginalized authors who have personal firsthand accounts of historical events.
- talking with students about engaging in actionable problem-solving projects on issues that directly impact their lives; and
- guiding white students to realize that true equity does not mean they have to lose anything, and aiding them in conceptualizing what it means to be an ally.

SEIZING THE MOMENT

Teacher reflection and ongoing self-examination of their beliefs and biases are critical in the process of moving toward the type of civic education we want students to have. Continuous professional learning that is dynamic and contextualized must be included in this shift in practice. While sharing our dialogue, we surfaced the exhausting hypervigilance we feel must be maintained to challenge the status quo while being labeled "controversial" Black women because we are passionate about the teaching of history and the influence of racism and racial inequity. From what we have seen, those who have recognized racialized oppression have typically been portrayed as uncommon, radical, and on the path to "getting in trouble." Consequently, we gave a lot of thought to what does and does not make sense to us as we considered what civic education should look like in our classrooms. Alongside these considerations are the risk-taking actions that come with teaching for racial justice, the obstructions in our path, and our reasons for hope.

CONCLUSIONS

Carla-Ann

Since the Black Lives Matter protests of 2020 and the upheaval of current racial inequity in this country, I believe citizens are in a new place of critical awareness. The world is watching now. It feels reminiscent of interactions during the Civil Rights Movement. However, I wonder what will come of it. Republican politicians are terrified of this! Look at what happened with Stacey Abrams and voting campaigns and the fear white America has of what will happen to the "old America." The reality is that true equity does not mean one group has to lose something for others to gain. No matter how much those in power push this narrative, we do not exist in a zero-sum game. Today, in the face of climate change, student loan debt, the lack of affordable housing, and rising inflation, many young people from Gen Z have a "nothing to lose" mindset—so, let's speak out, believing that doing so is not a privilege but a necessity.

Rasheeda

I want to see students and families demand more from the educational systems in our country. Every social, political, and economic issue we have encountered since March of 2020 can be linked to how we educate our children. Adults who lack critical knowledge were once children who were not taught that knowledge. If we want democracy to be a reality in the United States, we must teach for it!

So, what, if anything, do we find useful in the traditional approach to civic education, as seen in textbooks, curriculum standards, and policy statements? Certainly, students need to understand how our government was created and know about the various structures and functions that are supposed to be in place for democracy to work. The traditional approach to civics provides a good starting point for dialogue about our histories, experiences, and needs to make democratic government viable.

However, traditional civic approaches are rendered useless when they do not provide Black students with actionable steps toward democracy, leaving nothing to do but comply with established norms. We reject the notion that democracy is a magic pill that will fix everything and the assumption that learning traditional civics content knowledge will motivate Black students to become civically engaged. Traditional civic education does not address all of the barriers this country has put in place. It ensures the maintenance of the status quo and the continuance of minoritized groups remaining marginalized. Additionally, traditional civic education neither addresses the human dimensions of democracy nor how discrimination and oppression can cripple a supposedly democratic society.

Going forward as Black civic educators, we challenge ourselves—and by extension, our students—to be mindful of certain questions that must be continuously revisited: In learning, what issues are affecting us the most right now? Who is served by the narratives we are hearing? Whose lens are we looking through? How do we get ourselves to notice the critical issues? How do we make sense of them? When we notice them, what are the underlying systemic issues and structures we can identify that need to be challenged in our world? Moreover, how can we add to Westheimer and Kahne's (2004) conceptualizations of citizenship to ask: What would an engaged citizen do in specific situations? What can civic engagement and patriotism look like in different contexts? What do our Black students, to whom we have a special obligation as Black teachers, need from us right now? What do they need in the present moment? How might they seize it?

There will always be pushback for social justice educators when it comes to challenging the master narratives of civic education. Undoubtedly, we fear political pressure from state officials and administrators; we fear that students will continue to get a watered-down version of what true democracy looks like; we fear the continuous cycle of misinformation that goes along with the political agenda of right-wing extremists. However, we want to use the pushback to our advantage, seeing it as an opportunity to help students understand the reality that democracy is fragile and not to simply assume it works for everyone. It is not a given; societies must constantly work to ensure that democratic institutions and spaces represent all people, not just the dominant groups who hold power. As Black civic educators, while we know whiteness has long been the primary criterion for full citizenship in the United States, we believe we must assert our "enoughness" to disrupt the idea of civics as a singular notion viewed only through one lens.

REFERENCES

Boylorn, R. M. (2016. Killing me softly or on the miseducation of (love and) hip hop: A Blackgirl authethnography. *Qualitative Inquiry, 22*, 785–789.

Duncan, K. E. (2020). "What better tool do I have?": A critical race approach to teaching civics. *High School Journal, 103*(3), 176–189.

Duncan, K. E. (2022). "That's my job": Black teachers' perspectives on helping Black students navigate white supremacy. *Race Ethnicity and Education, 25*(7), 1–19.

Flgov.com. (2022). Governor Ron DeSantis signs legislation to protect Floridians from discrimination and woke indoctrination. https://www.flgov.com/2022/04/22/governor-ron-desantis-signs-legislation-to-protect-floridians-from-discrimination-and-woke-indoctrination

Florida Board of Education. (2021). Rule 6A-1.094124, Required Instruction Planning and Reporting. https://www.flrules.org/gateway/ruleNo.asp?id=6A-1.094124

Garcia, P., Fernández, C. H., & Jackson, A. (2020). Counternarratives of youth participation among black girls. *Youth & Society, 52*(8), 1479–1500.

Hawkman, A. M., & Van Horn, S. E. (2019). What does it mean to be patriotic? Policing patriotism in sports and social studies education. *Social Studies, 110*(3), 105–121.

Kissling, M. T. (2016). How patriotism matters in U.S. social studies classrooms, fifteen years after 9/11. In W. Journell (Ed.), *Reassessing the social studies curriculum: Promoting critical civic engagement in a politically polarized, post-9/11 world* (pp. 41–54). Rowman & Littlefield.

Ladson-Billings, G. (2004). Culture versus citizenship: The challenge of racialized citizenship in the United States. In J. A. Banks (Ed.), *Diversity and citizenship education: Global perspectives* (pp. 99–126). Jossey-Bass.

Love, B. (2019). *We want to do more than survive: Abolitionist teaching and the pursuit of educational freedom*. Beacon Press.

Navarro, O., & Howard, T. (2017). A critical race theory analysis of social studies research, theory, and practice. In M. Manfra & C. Bolick (Eds.) *The Wiley handbook of social studies research* (pp. 209–226). John Wiley & Sons.

NPR.org. (2021). '1619 Project' journalist says Black people shouldn't be an asterisk in U.S. History. https://www.npr.org/2021/11/17/1056404654/nikole-hannah-jones-1619-project

Paris, D. (2012). Culturally sustaining pedagogy: A needed change in stance, terminology, and practice. *Educational Researcher, 41*(3), 93–97.

Salam, S. (2021). What is misogynoir? Unpacking the intersectional layers of racism and misogyny. https://feminisminindia.com/2021/12/06/what-is-misogynoir-unpacking-the-intersectional-layers-of-racism-and-misogyny

Schaeffer, K. (2021). U.S. public school students often go to schools where at least half of their peers are the same race or ethnicity. Pew Research Center. https://www.pewresearch.org/fact-tank/2021/12/15/u-s-public-school-students-often-go-to-schools-where-at-least-half-of-their-peers-are-the-same-race-or-ethnicity

Stout, C., & LeMee, G. L. (2021). Efforts to restrict teaching about racism and bias have multiplied across the U.S. https://www.chalkbeat.org/22525983/map-critical-race-theory-legislation-teaching-racism

Vickery, A. E. (2017). "You excluded us for so long and now you want us to be patriotic?": African American women teachers navigating the quandary of citizenship. *Theory & Research in Social Education*, *45*(3), 318–348.

Westheimer, J., & Kahne, J. (2004). What kind of citizen? The politics of educating for democracy. *American Educational Research Journal*, *41*(2), 237–269.

Woodson, A. N., & Love, B. L. (2019). Outstanding: Centering Black kids' enoughness in civic education research. *Multicultural Perspectives*, *21*(2), 91–96.

CHAPTER 3

Civics and Latinidad
Letters to the Past With Hopes for the Future

Jesús Tirado, Gabriel Rodriguez, Timothy Monreal, and Tommy Ender

Imagine an empty Zoom room. Only the host is visible; they are looking down as they are writing. The Zoom sound goes off. The host doesn't look up, but the pace of their writing increases. Another sound is quickly followed by another. The host dramatically puts down their pen and begins to let people in.

>*Jesús:* Hermanos! What's up?[1]
>*Tommy:* It is cold here.
>*Gabe:* Here too!
>*Tim:* Here too!
>*Gabe:* What's on everyone's mind? Where did we leave off?
>*Tim:* I've been thinking about this "sleeping giant narrative" about Latinxs community and voters?
>*Jesús:* Can you explain that a little more?
>*Tommy:* Is that about how our community is seen, as citizens in waiting?
>*Gabe:* Or about how we are all supposed to vote, act, be in one way?
>*Tim:* I think we should talk about all of that.
>*Jesús:* When we talk about citizens in waiting, do we mean how we are seen as constantly outside the political process? As newcomers to the political process?
>*Tommy:* Yes, I think that's a discussion we've had before,[2] and it's an important one. Latinx are more than just border and immigration issues.
>*Gabe:* Those are important too, but you are right—our community is so much more than just those issues.
>*Tim:* Right. There are activist groups in our community that are fighting for better health care, better schools, against

gentrification, and for better access to voting. Hell, they have been doing this work for over 100 years. Our community has groups where families are leading the charge, some that look more traditional, and then some in which the youth are taking up, even leading, activism.³

Gabe: I think folded within this is how we are seen as a monolithic community—we are all the same from coast to coast.

Tommy: Right, and we get punished when our different groups don't follow the narrative.

Tim: Right, like when Cubans and Venezuelans don't follow the narrative, or Tejanos, for that matter.

Jesús: Right, those comments are completely devoid of an understanding of the history that got those groups here or how history has shaped them.⁴ There's just this one narrative that everyone should act the same, do the same things, and participate the same way.

Tommy: Chris Busey⁵ has been doing some great writing about this, and I think we should, too. So, what's next in this conversation?

Gabe: I think we should think more about this and then come back together in a few weeks. How does that sound?

INTRO—WHAT WE ARE TRYING TO DO . . .

Our entry point into this chapter began with a free-flowing Zoom conversation between four of us: Jesús, Gabriel, Tim, and Tommy. During this initial platica (see also Fierros & Bernal, 2016; Monreal et al., 2023), we wanted to discuss how we might contribute to the aim of this book, in particular the invited question: What possibilities exist for civics taught using frameworks that center people of Color? In a next meeting, we took a deeper dive into how dominant discourse(s) about Latinx communities does little to nuance its intragroup diversity and how such flattening leads to limited understandings of Latinx civic participation. We began to think of our own experiences, particularly those when we were young students and now as researchers and tenure track faculty. What was it we wanted our past teachers to know? What would we want current teachers to know? Those questions became prompts for (our) "letters" to teachers. We envision this set of letters—part testimonio (see also Blanco, 2022) and part autoethnography—as a way for the four of us to launch a broader conversation into Latinx civics education by thinking together via personal and scholarly reflection.

While we believe it is significant to have this shared body of letters that speak to our individual and communal experiences of Latinx civic (mis) education, we must also acknowledge and think through what it means to be writing about Latinx civics as a group of cis, English-speaking, U.S.-citizen Latinx men, especially since the majority of us have ties to México. As a group, we were mindful of these positionalities, especially as current research has expanded (and critiqued) traditional and hegemonic categorizations of Latinidad (Aparicio et al., 2022; Flores, 2021). More specifically, we tried to be aware of the cultural and political leverage that Mexicans can yield over Latinidad (Busey & Silva, 2020) especially as Pew Research estimates that about 59% of the American Latinx population is of Mexican-origin (Krogstad et al., 2022). The fact that we are males changes how we relate to these questions and situates us in a specific way. We know that we are far from having a representative voice for Latinidad (if that is even possible), and we omit people, perspectives, and groups if we claim some universality in speaking for all the Latinx community. Still, given the paucity of Latinx-focused literature in the field of social studies education, we hope this chapter serves as an entry point for continued dialogue.

That said, our letters combine hopes for the future and lessons from our past(s). We wrote these letters hoping to pass on lessons that we are still struggling to learn ourselves. Letters that revolve around the imaginations of what the classroom can look like, of how we can value language and guard against the destructive narratives of our world, and find ways to live in nuance and toward better and deeper understandings of the world. Lessons that we think matter as we struggle to help define these futures for Latinx civics. We hope you read them as (our) invitations to do more and to engage in this work as well. Two of the authors (Jesús and Tim) recently held a workshop at a national conference for Latinx history. We found ourselves without a room, but with a group of patient teachers waiting and wanting to work with us. Their patience came from not only their enthusiasm but also from the fact that they knew we were the only ones presenting on Latinx History at this conference. We hope we never have room issues again or that we are the only presenters of our shared histories.

RODRIGUEZ LETTER

Dear Teachers,

In considering the possibilities for teaching civics using frameworks that center Latinx students, it is important to consider whether our vision aligns with their needs, desires, and questions. Put differently, I ask us to consider what it takes to support youth voice and recognize Latinx youth as stakeholders in their education. I ask educators to embrace an expansive understanding of civic education alongside more nuanced understandings of Latinx youth.

The study of civic education and Latinx education often takes on a language of crisis (Gándara & Contreras, 2009; Miles, 2021; Mirra & Garcia, 2017). This type of deficit framing obfuscates the multiple ways Latinx youth engage in their schooling and American polity. It is important not to lose sight of the micro-level ways inequality operates in the lives of Latinx youth and existing civic opportunity gaps (Gadsden et al., 2019; Kirshner, 2015; Levinson, 2012; Ochoa, 2013). A re-shift is required. Youth of Color witness "civic lessons" regularly through their lived experiences in schools (Clay & Rubin, 2020). Yet, as Rombalski (2020) argues, schools "often side-step student agency and change" (p. 29). When youth are engaged in issues they care about, seldom are they guided toward justice-oriented outcomes (Westheimer & Kahne, 2004). This speaks not to a problem with youth but with the constraints and fears educators possess. There is no question that teachers operate in a more polarized and partisan environment (Pollock & Yoshisato, 2021; Rogers et al., 2017), but the important task of promoting a healthy citizenry requires active engagement on the issues students care about, not evasive or middling approaches. Furthermore, when students express their grievances and participate in activism, it is important for educators to respond with acts of solidarity and not to work to ignore or undermine them.

Educators often engage in what Rios (2011) calls the "youth control complex." This deficit-orientation seeks compliance from students and, when applied to civic education, fosters an environment that encloses opportunities for youth to develop their sociopolitical identities. This is a missed opportunity. All too often Latinx youth are in classrooms that equivocate to white youth and status quo viewpoints that create a culture of false equivalencies that perpetuate fictions of fairness and neutral (Rodriguez & González Ybarra, 2022; Sánchez Loza, 2021).

To conclude, educators possess a great deal of power and expertise they could enact in support of Latinx youth. Latinxs are a complex ethno-racial community that continues to be misunderstood. Despite the long history of Latinx activism and civic participation, they continue to be discussed as a "sleeping giant." It is important to disrupt this homogenizing deficit investment. As Beltrán (2010) argues, "there is no sleeping giant—only political subjects whose variegated actions and intentions are obscured by this limited vision of Latino empowerment" (p. 9). Beltrán's argument reflects a critique of narrow, Eurocentric notions of what should count as participation in American polity. In helping nurture Latinx youth's sociopolitical identities and calls for justice in and out of school, it is important for educators to take action in ways that build on their cultural and linguistic assets.

MONREAL LETTER

Dear Teachers,

I start this letter with a vignette from my Central California high school experience in the early 2000s. I do this to show a visceral example of (1) the potential violences of "controversial issues" in civic discussions, (2) the subtle reproduction of dominant civic narratives, and (3) the complexity of the Latinx (civic) experience.

> *Sometime during my sophomore year of high school, the following question was up for debate in English class: "Should people have to learn English to be citizens in the United States?"*
>
> *In one moment's time, my present life evaporated in front of my eyes. I could not think about school. I was transported back to the packing shed where I spent my summers. I recalled my first day in the packing shed, a few weeks after my 13th birthday. I was lost. I was confused. I was nervous. I didn't know what to do. Between my anxiety and elementary Spanish, I couldn't communicate with anyone. I knew how it felt to not understand. It wasn't a reflection on my personal worth. It wasn't an indicator of my work ethic. My only goal was to prove my worth and earn an honest wage.*
>
> *I looked around the class. Hands were raised bitterly in an angry cloud of hate.*
>
> *"It's our country—learn our language!" shouted someone in front of me.*
>
> *Next, another student remarked, "If they don't like it here, no one is making them stay."*
>
> *"This is the United States of America, not the United States of Mexico."*
>
> *Ms. Williams, a tiny and gentle, white-haired veteran teacher, struggled to play the role of devil's advocate. She was painfully outnumbered. I raised my hand. Just as quickly I put it down, along with my head. I pretended to be asleep.*

In this vignette, racialized ideas about language stand in for matters of (il)legality. Thus, Latinx bodies and their freedom to move and belong in certain spaces become the *object* of school-sanctioned "debate" rather than living, human subjects. Especially important is how my school (and countless others) normalize(d) racialized claims about citizenship status in the name of open and *legitimate* discussion (Dabach, 2014; Dabach et al. 2018). Most often leveraged as a tool for engagement, so-called controversial issues have the potential to minimize and assuage violent and racist rhetoric in order to heed "both sides." Hence, following Dabach et al. (2018), it is vital that teachers do not play the devil's advocate, when dominant voices "make certain assertions that repeat common discourses that objectify, essentialize, and marginalize [Latinx] populations" (p. 308).

Although too scared to participate in this discussion, my internal conversations reinforced dominant civic narratives and frameworks, especially those of deservingness and the "good immigrant" (see Patler & Gonzales, 2015; Yukich, 2013). In other words, my internal scripts for legitimate residence and participation in the United States' democracy were tied to narrow idea(l)s of racialized "worthiness"—specifically, effort, resilience, and meritocracy. Such boundaries of inclusion require economic value to be a prerequisite of belonging and (re)produce a hierarchy of "citizens" based on one's employment. That is, lawyers and entrepreneurs, for example, need not prove their civic worth because of their perceived (and racialized) economic desirability.

Finally, my own experiences in the packing shed speak to the necessity for teachers to understand the complexity of the Latinx experience. While I did work in farm labor from an early age (because of my family's rootedness in migrant agricultural work and a continued precarious economic situation), I was not raised a "fluent" Spanish speaker. Following years of subtractive and racist education policies, my family saw English (only) proficiency as the path to success. Moreover, my mother is white and not Latinx, and she explicitly (re)enforced an assimilation narrative that has been the hallmark of the United States History curriculum. It was not until college that I was able to genuinely learn about my family's cultural wealth and proud history in the Central Valley. In sum, my genuine hope is that teachers today forward a radical, inclusive, and nuanced understanding of Latinx civics that furthers possibility and potential rather than shame and feigned sleep.

TIRADO LETTER

Dear Teachers,

This letter is supposed to be about the possibilities of Latinx civics, but before we can do that, I think we need to talk about who we are and start there. Back when I was teaching, a local mayor was asked, on air, if he was going to make any efforts to reach out to the growing Latinx constituents, and the politician responded that he was going to go home and make some tacos. The incident hit the news, and politicians, local organizations, and advocacy groups quickly responded, and at school, my colleagues and I wondered what the student response would be. A Latina student from that town was visibly upset and frustrated. She told a colleague that what was most upsetting to her was that most of the Latinx community in that town was mostly from El Salvador and that they don't eat tacos the way Mexicans do. As colleagues discussed how her response was odd due to the stereotyping of the comment, it reminded me that the Latino community extends beyond the first façade that one encounters to a multiplicity of worlds and comments.

LARGER THOUGHTS

In Sen's (2006) work on identity, Sen reveals that when people and groups are close to us, we know more about them, whereas the further away from us they are, the harder it is to know them. Monreal's letter brings up the perpetual foreignness that continues to keep our community at a distance, which means it is hard to get to know us and who we are. And despite the fact that our nations are all rich in histories, mythology, and culture, we have a surprisingly flat existence on the national stage. Busey and Silva (2020) state that even calling Latinx people Brown is problematic because it erases the Afro-Latinx presence. Stereotyping and masking constantly occur as our lack of knowledge becomes revealed. I am reminded that I had no knowledge of an entire nation's cuisine as we discussed Salvadorean cuisine together while teaching Salvadorean students. What other stories are we missing? What Indigenous and Black elements that run through our lands and stories are we missing? Where are the larger stories that have been lost to simplicity and oversimplification?

Takaki (2008) writes of the dangers of the master narrative that can limit and marginalize groups to the sidelines of American history and discourse so they can't participate in the stories and episodes of the master narrative. Worse yet, when that narrative keeps people as foreign, frames them as perpetual outsiders, and simplifies their differences to just a handful of experiences, that group can become increasingly disengaged and distanced. For Latinx, our civic future depends on us bringing the vast complexities of our communities to the discourses and help have them recognized. While it might take time for the majority of people to recognize the differences between us, we need to start making them know how the differences matter to us and how much our differences, as well as our similarities, define our future.

CONCLUDING THOUGHTS

While each letter and its corresponding author comes to the topic of Latinx civic engagement from a distinct vantage point, we are united in our focus and desire for educators to question their investments in respectability politics and simplistic understandings of political inclusion and participation. Moreover, as Latinx students continue to diversify classrooms across communities in the United States, educators also must have nuanced understandings that consider the ethno-racial diversity of this community. As educators cultivate more nuanced understandings on these topics we also maintain that working to empower Latinx students' civic identities entails an investment in solidarity. As researchers and schools espouse a commitment to youth voice, it is important that adults follow through not just in how they engage students in the classroom but in how they respond to their needs and desires.

REFERENCES

Aparicio, A., Bolivar, A., Chávez, A., Feliciano-Santos, S., Guerra, S. I., Pérez, G. M., Rosa, J., Rosas, G., Villarreal, A., & Zavella, P. (2022). Introduction. In A. Chávez & G. M. Pérez (Eds.), *Ethnographic refusals, unruly Latinidades* (pp. xiii–xxxvv). University of New Mexico Press.

Beltrán, C. (2010). *The trouble with unity: Latino politics and the creation of identity*. Oxford University Press.

Blanco, M. Y. (2022). *Testimonio as pedagogy of disruption: Central American teachers' engagement with youth testimonios about immigration and the effects of American Empire* (Publication No. 29255514) [Doctoral dissertation, Columbia University]. https://www.proquest.com/docview/2699954753/abstract/6B5A7724D6ED48CCPQ/1

Busey, C. L. (2019). Más que esclavos: A BlackCrit examination of the treatment of Afro-Latin@s in U.S. high school world history textbooks. *Journal of Latinos and Education, 18*(3), 197–214. https://doi.org/10.1080/15348431.2017.1386102

Busey, C. L. (2021). Theorizing AfroLatinx subjectivities, Afrolatinidades, and the racial politics of identity in education. In E. G. Murillo, Jr., D. Delgado Bernal, S. Morales, L. Urrieta, Jr., E. Ruiz Bybee, J. S. Muñoz, V. Sáenz, D. Villanueva, M. Machado-Casas, & K. Espinoza (Eds.), Handbook of Latinos and Education (2nd ed., pp. 146–156). Taylor Francis Group.

Busey, C. L., & Silva, C. (2020). Troubling the essentialist discourse of *Brown* in education: The anti-Black sociopolitical and sociohistorical etymology of Latinxs as a *Brown* monolith. *Educational Researcher, 50*(3), 176–186. https://doi.org/10.3102/0013189X20963582

Clay, K. L., & Rubin, B. C. (2020). "I look deep into this stuff because it's a part of me": Toward a critically relevant civics education. *Theory & Research in Social Education, 48*(2), 161–181.

Dabach, D. B. (2014). "You can't vote, right?": When language proficiency is a proxy for citizenship in a civics classroom. *Journal of International Social Studies, 4*(2), 7–56.

Dabach, D. B., Merchant, N. H., & Fones, A. K. (2018). Rethinking immigration as a controversy. *Social Education, 82*(6), 307–314.

Ender, T. (2021) Using counter-narratives to expand from the margins. *Curriculum Inquiry, 51*(4), 437–454, https://doi.org/10.1080/03626784.2021.1947733

Fernandez, J. S. (2021). *Growing up Latinx: Coming of age in a time of contested citizenship*. New York University Press.

Fierros, C. O., & Bernal, D. D. (2016). Vamos a pláticar: The contours of pláticas as Chicana/Latina feminist methodology. *Chicana/Latina Studies, 15*(2), 98–121.

Flores, T. (2021). "Latinidad is canceled": Confronting an anti-Black construct. *Latin American and Latinx Visual Culture*, *3*(3), 58–79. https://doi.org/10.1525/lavc.2021.3.3.58

Gadsden, V. L., Johnson, W. F., & Rahman, S. (2019). Civic knowledge, engagement, and participation narratives of youth of Color in urban schools. *Peabody Journal of Education*, *94*(1), 78–96.

Gándara, P. C., & Contreras, F. (2009). *The Latino education crisis: The consequences of failed social policies*. Harvard University Press.

Kirshner, B. (2015). *Youth activism in an era of education inequality*. New York University Press.

Krogstad, J. M., Passel, J. S., & Noe-Bustamante, L. (2022, September 23). *Key facts about U.S. Latinos for National Hispanic Heritage month*. Pew Research Center. https://www.pewresearch.org/fact-tank/2022/09/23/key-facts-about-u-s-latinos-for-national-hispanic-heritage-month

Levinson, M. (2012). *No citizen left behind*. Harvard University Press.

Miles, J. (2021). The ongoing crisis and promise of civic education. *Curriculum Inquiry*, *51*(4), 381–388.

Mirra, N., & Garcia, A. (2017). Civic participation reimagined: Youth interrogation and innovation in the multimodal public sphere. *Review of Research in Education*, *41*(1), 136–158.

Monreal, T., & Tirado, J. (2022). Don't call it The New (Latinx) South, estábamos aquí por años. In Y. Medina & M. Machado-Casas (Eds.), *Critical understandings of Latinx in global education* (pp. 100–125). Brill.

Monreal, T., Patiño-Longoria, F., & Herrera, M. (2023). Intergenerational pláticas as ethnic studies freedom dreaming in Kern County. *Ethnic Studies Pedagogies Journal*, *1*, 48–61.

Ochoa, G. (2013). *Academic profiling: Latinos, Asian Americans, and the achievement gap*. University of Minnesota Press.

Patler, C., & Gonzales, R. G. (2015). Framing citizenship: Media coverage of anti-deportation cases led by undocumented immigrant youth organisations. *Journal of Ethnic and Migration Studies*, *41*(9), 1453–1474. https://doi.org/10.1080/1369183X.2015.1021587

Pollock, M., & Yoshisato, M. (2021). What's going on: "Partisan" worries, and desires to discuss Trump-era events in school. *Teachers College Record*, *123*(10), 59–90.

Rios, V. M. (2011). *Punished: Policing the lives of Black and Latino boys*. New York University Press.

Rodriguez, G., & González Ybarra, M. (2022). "This is what I go through": Latinx youth facultades in suburban schools in the era of Trump. *Race Ethnicity and Education*, *25*(7), 922–938.

Rogers, J., Franke, M., Yun, J. E. E., Ishimoto, M., Diera, C., Geller, R. C., Berryman, A., & Brenes, T. (2017). Teaching and learning in the age of Trump: Increasing stress and hostility in America's high schools. *UCLA IDEA*.

Rombalski, A. (2020). I believe that we will win! Learning from youth activist pedagogies. *Curriculum Inquiry*, *50*(1), 28–53.

Sánchez Loza, D. (2021). Dear "good" schools: White supremacy and political education in predominantly white and affluent suburban schools. *Theory Into Practice*, *60*(4), 380–391.

Sen, A. (2006). *Identity and violence: The illusion of destiny*. W.W. Norton & Co.
Takaki, R. T. (2008). *A different mirror*. Little, Brown & Company.
Westheimer, J., & Kahne, J. (2004). What kind of citizen? The politics of educating for democracy. *American Educational Research Journal, 41*(2), 237–269.
Yukich, G. (2013). Constructing the model immigrant: Movement strategy and immigrant deservingness in the New Sanctuary Movement. *Social Problems, 60*(3), 302–320. https://doi.org/10.1525/sp.2013.60.3.302

CHAPTER 4

"I Understand Both of Them. But Nobody Understands Me!"
Civic Dissonances Among Arab-Palestinian Students in Israel

Aline Muff and Aviv Cohen

INTRODUCTION

Across countries, educational policies and curricula have become increasingly criticized for being informed by neoliberal and nationalistic ideologies that marginalize minority students' identities, cultures, and histories (Gillborn, 2014). Such policies disregard that civic learning is deeply embedded in particular social, political, historical, and economic contexts and fail to capture how citizenship is actually understood and practiced in different community contexts (Rubin, 2007; Rubin & Hayes, 2010).

Even though these policies and curricula do not sufficiently empower youth of Color, a growing body of research, mainly from North American contexts, testifies to civic activism and critical political awareness that these young people largely develop *outside* of school, countering assumptions of the persistence of so-called civic deficits and learning gaps among students of Color (Clay & Rubin, 2020; Gutiérrez, 2008; Moll & González, 1994; Rubin & Hayes, 2010).

This topic has been sparsely studied in other national settings. We argue that this line of research can provide essential insights into the context of diverse and conflict-affected societies like Israel, focusing on young Arab-Palestinian[1] citizens whose national identities are complex and torn. Arab-Palestinian citizens of Israel have been described as a "trapped minority," being marginalized within the Israeli state as well as by other Palestinian and Arab populations since both entities have questioned their loyalty *vis-à-vis* the Palestinian nation and the Israeli state (Rabinowitz, 2001).

Arab-Palestinians' legal status in Israel has been described as second-class citizenship since their *collective* rights as a national minority have been largely unrealized in practice (Jabareen, 2013), and their *individual* political and socioeconomic rights are compromised by discriminatory policies and racism in the public sphere (Abu-saad, 2004; Jamal, 2016). While individual citizenship rights such as formal equality, voting rights, access to courts, and the provision of educational opportunities are granted (Estreicher, 2018), some laws exclude Arab-Palestinians from the state's common good. For example, the Basic law, "Israel—The nation state of the Jewish people," which has constitutional status, established Israel as the historical homeland of the Jewish people, in which they are the only group with the right to national self-determination (Knesset, 2018). Discriminatory policies in the areas of housing (Shafir, 2018) and family unification (Boxerman, 2022) limit their individual citizenship rights *vis-à-vis* the majority population. They have become increasingly the target of racist incitement by the media and public political figures (Keren, 2021)—culminating in the success of extreme right-wing parties in the latest national election (Gotkine & Tal, 2022).

In this conflictual reality, obvious tensions exist within the theoretical concepts of citizenship and civic learning. Despite Arab-Palestinian citizens' marginalization, previous research demonstrated that they attach importance to both their legal identity as Israelis and their national identity as Palestinians (Amara & Schnell, 2004; Baum, 2010). This raises an important question as to how Arab-Palestinian students navigate these tensions in their civic learning. Exploring the civic experiences of students of Color in a context where national identity is stressed can strengthen our understanding of civic dissonances and expand theoretical framings of citizenship and civic learning in conflict-affected settings, and in general.

In this chapter we investigate Arab-Palestinian students' lived civic experiences and how these inform their evolving civic identities, drawing on data collected from interviews. We show that the students navigate a range of civic dissonances that are dynamic, stemming from their particular conflictual reality. We contend that such an understanding is crucial for the civic education process.

CONTEXTUAL BACKGROUND: ARAB-PALESTINIAN STUDENTS IN THE ISRAELI EDUCATIONAL SYSTEM

The outcome of the 1948 Arab–Israeli war was a defining event for both populations: For Jewish-Israelis, it led to the establishment of an independent nation-state that protects their collective identity and rights; whereas the state provided the remaining Arab-Palestinians with basic political and civil rights but constrained their access to the common good, offering only a "thin" form of citizenship (Shafir & Peled, 2002). Israel adopted a policy of divide and control toward its Arab minority to suppress the development of a national Palestinian and Arab consciousness that could potentially threaten the status quo of the Jewish state (Jabareen, 2006). Jabareen described the implications of this policy as systematic exclusion, which he links to the discrimination of Arab-Palestinian citizens in the areas of land dispossession and allocation, housing, labor market, practicing their language and culture, and political participation.

Regarding education, the Israeli government established separate public school sectors along the lines of religion and culture. Arab-Palestinian students usually attend schools in the Arab sector, where the main language of instruction is Arabic. The core curriculum is prescribed by the Ministry of Education, however, it has been argued that in practice each sector has some degree of autonomy in the implementation of the curriculum (Benavot & Resh, 2003). Nevertheless, inequalities in the education system remain regarding resource allocation, public funding, and lack of voice in educational policymaking and curriculum design (Abu-saad, 2004; Alayan, 2012).

Various studies have described how textbooks and curricula in Israel allow no room for Palestinian identity and history or the exploration of the Israeli–Palestinian conflict as a complex and multi-sided issue (Al-Haj, 2005; Mahamid, 2017). This is also the case with the civics curriculum and textbook. In 2009, following a political change of government, the textbook was revised, replacing an older version. The new education minister perceived the old curriculum as focusing too much on liberal and democratic notions of citizenship, while neglecting the Jewish character of the state (Cohen, 2019). An analysis of the revised textbook revealed that it prioritizes a nationalistic-religious discourse over democratic universal principles, undermines the rights and civic status of Arab-Palestinian citizens, and downplays their national identity and historical connection to the land (Pinson, 2020).

Pinson (2007, 2008) studied Arab-Palestinian students' civic experiences with the curriculum and how they negotiate their civic and national identities. She found that students drew on inclusionary and exclusionary discourses of citizenship in Israel: They defined inclusion to full citizenship as based on achieving equality of rights, and exclusion as based on their belonging to a different nationality (Palestinian or Arab), since, for them, full citizenship in Israel is reserved exclusively for Jews. Importantly, Pinson's findings indicate the dynamics of Arab-Palestinian students' complex civic reality, and we propose a further examination of their civic experiences, drawing on the theoretical framework of resource pedagogies, which we present below.

THEORETICAL FRAMEWORKS: CIVIC IDENTITIES AND PEDAGOGICAL RESOURCES IN CONFLICT-AFFECTED SOCIETIES

To better relate to the civic experiences of Arab-Palestinian students in Israel, we build on the theoretical framework that proposes that young people's lived daily experiences constitute important knowledge that can be summarized as *resource pedagogies*, including the concepts of funds of knowledge (González & Moll, 2002; Vélez-Ibáñez & Greenberg, 1992), third space (Gutiérrez, 2008; Moje et al., 2004), and culturally relevant or sustainable pedagogy (Ladson-Billings, 2014; Paris, 2012). These concepts suggest that education should draw on young people's cultural resources and knowledge from their homes and communities in addition to the knowledge they encounter at school in order to generate new knowledges and forms of literacy that are relevant for *all* students—including students of Color (Moje et al., 2004). This educational approach seeks to give credence to the multiplicity of students' cultures and identities while providing access to dominant cultural competence (Paris, 2012).

The framework of resource pedagogies is particularly relevant for civic education, as previous research has demonstrated that community resources and knowledge can provide a meaningful basis for students' evolving civic identities. Resource pedagogies can shape students' civic experiences as *disjuncture*—when students' experiences contrast with civic ideals, and *congruence*—when students perceive that their immediate civic institutions are working for their benefit (Rubin & Hayes, 2010). Scholars have defined civic identity as "a set of beliefs and emotions about oneself as a participant in civic life" (Hart et al., 2011, p. 773), as the establishment of *collective* and *individual* senses of social agency, responsibility for society, political moral awareness, and a sense of belonging to a larger polis (Youniss et al., 1997).

Research from conflict societies suggests that resource pedagogies can enhance students' civic learning by providing them with important alternative knowledge about local histories and critical analysis of these events (Barton & McCully, 2012; Rubin, 2016). Arab-Palestinian students study in an official, unified, and centralized educational system (Blass & Shavit, 2017) with a civic curriculum that marginalizes their Palestinian nationality (Cohen, 2019; Pinson, 2020). Given this conflictual context, we argue that the case of Arab-Palestinian students in Israel is worthy of exploration because their civic experiences may be complicated by the tensions between their Israeli citizenship and their belonging to the Palestinian nation.

METHODOLOGY

To explore how Arab-Palestinian students interpret their civic experiences and identities, we discuss data collected as part of a larger qualitative study about citizenship education in conflict-affected societies. In this chapter, we draw on the group interviews that were conducted with 10 high school students who participated in a civics course. The interviews were conducted in pairs of two or three, and one individual interview. The interviews were conducted in English by the first author who is originally from Germany and has lived in Israel for a few years; the second author, who is Jewish-Israeli, joined the data analysis stage. We are conscious about and have reflected on our position in relation to the research participants as members of the university and as coming from more privileged communities.

Our methodology was guided by critical theory, which locates social justice issues in the context of wider power structures and approaches the object of inquiry as "culturally inscribed and historically situated" (Kincheloe et al., 2018, p. 437). Therefore, we focused on authoring the voices of Palestinian youth in Israel and their understanding of civic issues.

These ontological and epistemological positions informed the choice of reflexive thematic analysis (Braun & Clarke, 2019) as a method. The coding and re-coding processes followed an open and organic approach that led to our initial theme development. These themes were then reviewed and interpreted through the lens of the theoretical framework of resource pedagogies and the research questions of how Arab-Palestinian students interpret their civic experiences, and how these inform their evolving civic identities.

The participants attended a school in a mixed (Jewish-Arab) city in Israel. The school has a Christian ethos and is attended by both Christian and Muslim students largely from middle-class backgrounds. The research was granted ethical approval, and we adhered to commitments to informed consent, voluntary participation, retrospective withdrawal, anonymity, and confidentiality. All names mentioned in the following are pseudonyms.

FINDINGS: CIVIC DISSONANCES AMONG ARAB-PALESTINIAN STUDENTS

In the interviews, the students described their civic experiences in terms of both disjuncture and congruence, reflecting their particular situation in the conflict-affected setting. To capture the complexity of their civic experiences, we organized them in themes of four civic dissonances, which we discuss along with the situations in which they occurred.

Official Versus Nonofficial Learning Resources

A first dissonance was described by students between the knowledge presented to them by official curricula—which largely omit Palestinian histories, culture, and perspectives on civic issues—and the knowledge they gained from their families or the internet. Students explained that official curricula present only a one-sided perspective on civic issues and the conflict in Israel, for example: "[T]he government controls the books, so we don't see the whole picture, we only see the side of the picture that we should see"

(Sada), and "It's [civics] an important subject, but what they teach most of the time doesn't reflect the truth" (Fahad).

Fahad's statement that civics is an important subject is notable because it indicates that although the students reject the official curriculum, they do not reject civics. One possible reason for the students' critical awareness of the civics content and their support for civics is the counter-knowledge that they learned from their homes and their community. For example, they explained how they learn about the 1948 war from their grandparents' personal experiences:

> *Daria:* There is important history that we should know, but they [the government and educational authorities] don't teach us everything. So, we should search our history. [. . .]
> *Yasmin:* You have to ask your grandmother or your grandfather. [. . .] We hear about what happened, but we don't feel what they [the Jewish-Israelis] feel. [. . .] My grandfather was in the [1948] war. [. . .] When they speak about this, some of them cry. It's hard for them—
> *Daria:* It's hard for them but maybe we can learn—
> *Rabia:* From their perspective.

While the students expressed disjuncture from the official curricula knowledge, this disjuncture is mediated through resource pedagogies from home, which equip them with counter-knowledge that seems to inform their critical political awareness. Perhaps since they are exposed to both "official" knowledge that reflects the dominant Jewish-Israeli narrative on the one hand and their community knowledge on the other, they are able to reclaim civics as an empowering subject—an argument that will be further elaborated on in the following sections.

Discrimination Versus Citizenship Rights

The students described another dissonance between discourses of discrimination and rights expressing both disjuncture and congruence with civics. Almost all students referred to experiences of racism and discrimination as encounters of disjuncture: "We are just second-class citizens" (Sada), or "I don't feel like a normal citizen in Israel. It's a very racist country . . . so, about citizenship, I'm not connected to [it], I don't feel it" (Fahad). They described this as a result of Israel's official definition as a Jewish and democratic state: "It's like democracy is all about equality and it's not happening here. [. . .] The country is saying 'We are a Jewish democratic country,' but you see you can't combine both" (Lina), or "We want and we expect from the country to treat everyone the same way! Not this because [someone] is Jewish" (Nadia).

Yet, the students also emphasized the importance of using their citizenship rights to fight social injustice and racism, thus reframing their limited citizenship as empowerment through *individual* rights and as a form of *congruence*: "It [citizenship] is important to learn and to know about our rights ... To know if I'm oppressed or not. Then I know how I can deal with the problem" (Kaira).

The civic dissonance between discrimination and rights seems to consist of both disjuncture and congruence—making students aware of injustices and feeling also empowered to address them. Yet, congruence and disjuncture can also lead students to be complacent or discouraged in their civic activism, which the next section shows.

Resistance Versus Acceptance of the Status Quo

A third mode of civic dissonance was students' positioning related to the Israeli–Palestinian conflict. In the following excerpt, Fahad described this dissonance within the Arab-Palestinian community in Israel, as acceptance of the status quo on the one hand, and problematizing the injustices that the community experiences on the other:

> A lot of the Arabs decided to accept the situation "OK, we have to live with it, we can't do anything about it." [. . .] [S]ome of them will say to you "we have it better than people in Egypt, we live better than people in Libya and in Syria." But if we live better, it doesn't mean that we live good. [. . .] you don't have to go very far to find the racism." (Fahad)

These two positions also emerged in the following exchange between Yasmin and Rabia:

> *Yasmin:* There are people who think that it's not enough what they give us, but I think that it's enough—for me. I study here, I have family—
> *Rabia:* Shall I tell you why you feel so good—because you compare yourself to the Arab countries where there is no study, no family. We should compare ourselves to a better place, not to a bad place. [. . .] You think our life here is perfect because you see it on the TV on the news [. . .]
> *Yasmin:* Yeah, compared to them we have a good life.
> *Rabia:* [. . .] But there [are] things you can't do, you can't say in the street whatever you want.

The position of accepting the status quo described by Yasmin refers to an *individual* and thin approach to citizenship of receiving basic rights and entitlements from the state. Other statements by Yasmin signaled that she's aware of injustices (for example: "We don't feel part of citizenship"), but at the same time she seems ready to accept this situation since it is better than living in a war zone. In contrast, Rabia and Fahad frame more *collective* forms of citizenship referring to collective experiences of discrimination and racism.

Arab-Palestinian students draw on both individual and collective discourses of citizenship; they might experience congruence with Israeli citizenship, based on individual discourses and disjuncture due to collective ones. These discourses seem to be rooted in their unique dual identity as both "Palestinian" and "Israeli," which we will discuss below.

Palestinian Versus Israeli Identity

The students were ambiguous about their identity as a form of belonging. In the following excerpt, Fahad explained that he identifies with both being Palestinian and Israeli. He is confused about his belonging—arguably because neither community fully accepts Arab-Palestinian citizens of Israel—expressing disjuncture and congruence toward both identities:

> I feel confused about who I am. Most Arabs in the country are confused about their identity. I don't know to which side I belong because both sides don't accept me. [. . .] I feel both of them [Israeli and Palestinian], I understand both of them. But nobody understands me!

Interestingly, the students described this disjuncture as particular to their generation. While their parents and grandparents were born and raised as Palestinians, this has changed among their generation, which identifies more as "Israeli," perhaps as a result of being socialized into Israeli nationality and culture and the geographical separation from other Palestinians:

> It's important to me to remember that my grandfather was a Palestinian, my father is a Palestinian. The situation is different now, I have to deal with it. I don't know how to identify myself, it's too confusing. (Fahad)

This issue was also raised by Kaira and Amira, who described Israeli as their legal citizenship identity and Palestinian as a nationality that they inherited:

> *Kaira:* Maybe that we are confused [causes difficulties about citizenship]. We don't know what our country is, what our nationality is. We are not sure about it. Sometimes we think we are Palestinians, and sometimes we are Israelis.
> *Amira:* Because we are born in Israel.
> *Kaira:* Because Palestine it is for our grandparents, and we grow up with "This is called Palestine," and then we have an Israeli passport so when we go to the airport, we are Israeli. So, we

don't know if we are Palestinians or Israelis. And when we go to another country and they ask us "Where are you from?," so we don't know if we have to say Palestinian or Israeli.

The students described these identities as highly politicized and make pragmatic and contextual use of how they identify themselves:

Amira: Because some countries hate the Jews [we can't identify ourselves as Israeli].
Kaira: When we go to Egypt and we say we are Palestinians they say "you mean Israel?," we say "No it's Palestine." [. . .] And sometimes you can't say that you are Palestinian, in some countries. [. . .] I think that if I will go there [to the USA or Europe], I will not say I'm from Palestine. And some people don't understand this and they think we don't have a nationality.

The students described the complexity of sharing a citizenship and national identity that others see as conflicting, while for them both identities are part of their reality, shaping their experiences of both civic disjuncture and congruence.

In sum, the Arab-Palestinian students in this study described complex civic experiences that are in tension with each other—exemplified by the four civic dissonances that result from the conflictual reality that they live in: official versus nonofficial learning resources, citizenship as an experience of discrimination versus the use of citizenship rights for empowerment, resistance versus accepting the status quo, and identifying as Israeli versus Palestinian. These dissonances seem to be informed by two major civic discourses: their official Israeli citizenship, as thin but granting them individual citizenship rights about which they learn in school as part of their civics lessons; and their Palestinian national identity, as thick and collective that informs their political awareness of injustices and motivates their civic activism, about which they learn from their homes and community.

DISCUSSION AND CONCLUSION

The main theoretical finding of this study is the students' descriptions of their lived civic experiences as both congruence and disjuncture (Rubin & Hayes, 2010). These experiences differ from studies that explored the civic experiences of students of Color in the United States, whose identities tended to be more static (Denney, 2021). This finding is likely a result of the particular context in which these students live, characterized by a national rift in a conflict-affected setting. The data show that the students constructed their civic identities as not clear-cut; rather, they shifted and changed among generations, stressing their pragmatic choices that depend on specific contexts and situations. This testifies to the argument that identities and cultures are not rigid but exist in relation to specific historical circumstances and contexts that are sensitive to change (Appiah, 2018).

Thus, this study regarding Arab-Palestinian students' civic experiences highlights two conclusions: First, the synergy of official curricula and out-of-school knowledge can inform students' "rich" civic identities that may enable the formation of a third space, where civic issues can be discussed from multiple sources and perspectives and generate new forms of knowledge (Gutiérrez, 2008; Moje et al., 2004). For example, in this case the students' exchanges about resistance versus accepting the status quo.

Second, the findings highlight the relevance of specific cultural contexts in shaping students' learning and understanding of their civic identities (Ladson-Billings, 2014). The students' comments about the changes in civic identities *vis-à-vis* previous generations demonstrate how civic identities are subject to contextual changes.

This has important implications for civic education in Israel—and worldwide. The Arab-Palestinian students' rich civic experiences testify to their "enoughness" in civic education (Woodson & Love, 2019) and show that meaningful civic learning is possible even in contexts where political efforts are invested to depoliticize minority students' civic learning. Still, there is a clear need for these students' home and community cultures to be validated in official curricula and public politics for civic education to be culturally sustainable and relevant (Ladson-Billings, 2014; Paris, 2012). This could not only make civic education more relevant for Arab-Palestinians students but also for students from the Jewish majority in Israel as they too could benefit from exposure to more dynamic, multi-sided, and balanced accounts of civic issues in Israel. An inclusive curriculum concerned with social justice issues and responsive to resource pedagogies is a crucial element for the civic education process.

REFERENCES

Abu-saad, I. (2004). Separate and unequal: The role of the state educational system in maintaining the subordination of Israel's Palestinian Arab citizens. *Social Identities*, 10(1), 101–127.

Alayan, S. (2012). Arab education in Israel: Lessons from positive learning experiences of Palestinian-Israelis. *Diaspora, Indigenous, and Minority Education*, 6(4), 214–229.

Al-Haj, M. (2005). National ethos, multicultural education, and the new history textbooks in Israel. *Curriculum Inquiry*, 35(1), 47–71.

Amara, M., & Schnell, I. (2004). Identity repertoires among Arabs in Israel. *Journal of Ethnic and Migration Studies*, 30(1), 175–193. https://doi.org/10.1080/13691830032000170222

Appiah, K. A. (2018). *The lies that bind: Rethinking identity*. Profile Books.
Barton, K. C., & McCully, A. W. (2012). Trying to "see things differently": Northern Ireland students' struggle to understand alternative historical perspectives. *Theory & Research in Social Education, 40*(4), 371–408. https://doi.org/10.1080/00933104.2012.710928
Baum, N. (2010). Standing tall: A look at the development of identity among Palestinian citizens of Israel. *Social Identities, 16*(1), 135–150. https://doi.org/10.1080/13504630903465969
Benavot, A., & Resh, N. (2003). Educational governance, school autonomy, and curriculum implementation: A comparative study of Arab and Jewish schools in Israel. *Journal of Curriculum Studies, 35*(2), 171–196. https://doi.org/10.1080/0022027022000022856
Blass, N., & Shavit, Y. (2017). *Israel's education system in recent years: An overview*. http://taubcenter.org.il/israels-education-system-in-recent-years-an-overview
Boxerman, A. (2022). *After coalition battle, Knesset reauthorizes ban on Palestinian family unification*. https://www.timesofisrael.com/after-coalition-battle-knesset-reauthorizes-ban-on-palestinian-family-unification
Braun, V., & Clarke, V. (2019). Reflecting on reflexive thematic analysis. *Qualitative Research in Sport, Exercise and Health, 11*(4), 589–597.
Clay, K. L., & Rubin, B. C. (2020). "I look deep into this stuff because it's a part of me": Toward a critically relevant civics education. *Theory & Research in Social Education, 48*(2), 161–181. https://doi.org/10.1080/00933104.2019.1680466
Cohen, A. (2019). Israel's civic education wars: A review of the literature and theoretical implications. *Educational Review, 71*(3), 287–305.
Denney, S. M. (2021). Student perceptions of support for civic identity development and identity exploration in a discussion-based U.S. government course. *The Journal of Social Studies Research*. https://doi.org/10.1016/j.jssr.2021.06.003
Estreicher, S. (2018). A Jewish state and a state for all of its citizens: Addressing the challenge of Israel's Arab citizens. *Public Affairs, 3*, 1–15.
Gillborn, D. (2014). Racism as policy: A critical race analysis of education reforms in the United States and England. *The Educational Forum, 78*(1), 26–41.
González, N., & Moll, L. C. (2002). Cruzando el puente: Building bridges to funds of knowledge. *Educational Policy, 16*(4), 623–641.
Gotkine, E., & Tal, A. (2022). Netanyahu to be invited to form government, paving way for return of Israel's longest-serving leader. *CNN*. https://www.cnn.com/2022/11/11/middleeast/benjamin-netanyahu-israel-government-intl/index.html
Gutiérrez, K. D. (2008). Developing a sociocritical literacy in the third space. *Reading Research Quarterly, 43*(2), 148–164.
Hart, D., Richardson, C., & Wilkenfeld, B. (2011). Civic identity. In S. Schwartz, K. Luyckx, & V. Vignoles (Eds.) *Handbook of identity theory and research* (pp. 771–787). Springer.
Jabareen, Y. T. (2006). Law and education: Critical perspectives on Arab Palestinian education in Israel. *American Behavioral Scientist, 49*(8), 1052–1074.
Jabareen, Y. T. (2013). The politics of equality: The limits of collective rights litigation and the case of the Palestinian-Arab minority in Israel. *Columbia Journal of Race & Law, 4*, 23.

Jamal, A. (2016). Constitutionalizing sophisticated racism: Israel's proposed nationality law. *Journal of Palestine Studies*, 45(3), 40–51.

Keren, M. (2021). Benjamin Netanyahu and online campaigning in Israel's 2019 and 2020 elections. In D. Taras & R. Davis (Eds.), *Electoral campaigns, media, and the new world of digital politics* (pp. 163–178). University of Michigan Press.

Kincheloe, J., McLaren, P., Steinberg, R., & Monzó, L. (2018). Critical pedagogy and qualitative research. *The SAGE Handbook of Qualitative Research*, 5, 235–260.

Knesset. (2018). *Basic Law: Israel—The nation state of the Jewish people.* https://main.knesset.gov.il/EN/activity/Documents/BasicLawsPDF/BasicLawNationState.pdf

Ladson-Billings, G. (2014). Culturally relevant pedagogy 2.0: Aka the remix. *Harvard Educational Review*, 84(1), 74–84.

Mahamid, H. (2017). History education for Arab Palestinian schools in Israel. *Journal of Education and Development*, 1(1), 37.

Moje, E. B., Ciechanowski, K. M., Kramer, K., Ellis, L., Carrillo, R., & Collazo, T. (2004). Working toward third space in content area literacy: An examination of everyday funds of knowledge and discourse. *Reading Research Quarterly*, 39(1), 38–70.

Moll, L. C., & González, N. (1994). Lessons from research with language-minority children. In *Journal of Reading Behavior*, 26(4), 439–456.

Paris, D. (2012). Culturally sustaining pedagogy: A needed change in stance, terminology, and practice. *Educational Researcher*, 41(3), 93–97.

Pinson, H. (2007). Inclusive curriculum? Challenges to the role of civic education in a Jewish and democratic state. *Curriculum Inquiry*, 37(4), 351–382.

Pinson, H. (2008). The excluded citizenship identity: Palestinian/Arab Israeli young people negotiating their political identities. *British Journal of Sociology of Education*, 29(2), 201–212.

Pinson, H. (2020). The new civics curriculum for high schools in Israel: The discursive construction of Palestinian identity and narratives. *Education, Citizenship and Social Justice*, 15(1), 22–34.

Rabinowitz, D. (2001). The Palestinian citizens of Israel, the concept of trapped minority and the discourse of transnationalism in anthropology. *Ethnic and Racial Studies*, 24(1), 64–85. https://doi.org/10.1080/014198701750052505

Rouhana, N. (1997). *Palestinian citizens in an ethnic Jewish state: Identities in conflict.* Yale University Press.

Rubin, B. C. (2007). "There's still not justice": Youth civic identity development amid distinct school and community contexts. *Teachers College Record*, 109(2), 449–481.

Rubin, B. C. (2016). We come to form ourselves bit by bit: Educating for citizenship in post-conflict Guatemala. *American Educational Research Journal*, 53(3), 639–672. https://doi.org/10.3102/0002831216646871

Rubin, B. C., & Hayes, B. (2010). "No Backpacks" versus "Drugs and Murder": The promise and complexity of youth civic action research. *Harvard Educational Review*, 80(3), 352–379.

Shafir, G. (2018). From overt to veiled segregation: Israel's Palestinian Arab citizens in the Galilee. *International Journal of Middle East Studies*, 50(1), 1–22. https://doi.org/10.1017/S0020743817000915

Shafir, G., & Peled, Y. (2002). *Being Israeli: The dynamics of multiple citizenship* (Vol. 16). Cambridge University Press.

Smooha, S. (1992). *Arabs and Jews in Israel: Change and continuity in mutual intolerance*. Westview Press.

Vélez-Ibáñez, C. G., & Greenberg, J. B. (1992). Formation and transformation of funds of knowledge among US–Mexican households. *Anthropology & Education Quarterly, 23*(4), 313–335.

Woodson, A. N., & Love, B. L. (2019). Outstanding: Centering Black kids' enoughness in civic education research. *Multicultural Perspectives, 21*(2), 91–96. https://doi.org/10.1080/15210960.2019.1606631

Youniss, J., McLellan, J. A., & Yates, M. (1997). What we know about engendering civic identity. *American Behavioral Scientist, 40*(5), 620–631.

Part II

CIVICS EMBODIED IN COMMUNITIES OF COLOR

Part II

CIVICS ENGODED IN
COMMUNITIES OF COLOR

CHAPTER 5

It's Been Here All Along
Integrating Local Stories of Struggle Into Civics Discourses

Asif Wilson, ArCasia D. James-Gallaway, and Sabryna Groves

INTRODUCTION

The ideological foundations of social studies and civic engagement (Boydston, 1980; Jones, 1906; Watkins, 2001) promote discourses that center whiteness and a violent supremacy across society and in schools (Banks, 2015; Brown et al., 2011; Busey & Dowie-Chin, 2021; Dilworth, 2004; Gordon, 1985; Vickery, 2015). These patterns have a long history in the United States and should be integral to, but are often absent from, social studies and civic education. Historian Robin D. G. Kelley reminds us of these violent, consequential acts and their connection to democracy and citizenship.

> The modern world . . . was built on the theft of humans, theft of land and water, indiscriminate murder, violation of customary rights, moral economy, enclosure of the commons, destruction of the planet. . . . and yet . . . the creators and perpetrators of this violence were also the inventors of "rights" and "citizenship." (Yancy, 2021, n.p.)

Thus, traditional civic education was, and continues to be, a pathway toward the embodiment of whiteness. As Ladson-Billings (2003) asserted, most social studies curricula make it seem as if "people of color are relatively insignificant to the growth and development of our democracy and our nation" (p. 4). We are troubled by this premise and the related pedagogical and curricular practices within schools, especially as they persist in social studies and civic education.

These fundamental and ubiquitous issues explain why contemporary pedagogical and curricular practices within classrooms often exclude local stories of struggle highlighting Black and Latinx communities. As we argue in this chapter, these local stories can make significant contributions to social studies and civic learning experiences within P–20 schools (primary through post-secondary settings), especially when paired with critical frameworks such as community cultural wealth (Yosso, 2005) and justice-centered educational praxis (Ayers et al., 2017). Deliberate inclusion of such perspectives can expose and problematize the hegemonic, racist basis that has historically constituted social studies education, and continues to do so. To support this contention, we provide a brief overview of two local stories of resistance against white supremacy. These examples—a historical example of Black student activism in Waco, Texas, and a contemporary example of students' political organizing in northwest Indiana—demonstrate how local stories of resistance against white supremacy and other interlocking systems of subjugation can enhance social studies and civics praxes in P–20 classrooms, bringing them into alignment with the realities of communities of Color and their enduring battles against oppression.

EMBRACING, CONTESTING, AND REDEFINING (FAILED) CITIZENSHIP

Historically, the relationship between Black people and citizenship has been fraught with paradox. Social studies scholars (Brown et al., 2011; Busey & Dowie-Chin, 2021; Dilworth, 2004; Ladson-Billings, 2004; Preston-Grimes, 2007) have revealed how traditional representations of citizenship are replete with notions of freedom, representation, and belonging that privilege whiteness and subordinate people of Color, particularly African Americans. Dilworth (2004) presents Carter G. Woodson's arguments against white sociologist Thomas Jesse Jones's post–Civil War civic education materials— that the content misrepresented African American history and encouraged Black learners to internalize a dehumanizing vision of citizenship with the ultimate goal of assimilation. Woodson's personal wartime experience echoed these tensions, as Black soldiers served a country that denied them the basic civil rights they were fighting to protect (Brown et al., 2011). This inconsistency was further illustrated in Preston-Grimes's (2007) analysis of education publications from 1930 to 1954 in Georgia. She detailed how the state promoted citizenship expectations for Black students that contradicted its concurrent erection and maintenance of systemic racial barriers that curtailed Black citizenship.

Examinations of more recent trends illustrate the persistence of this paradox. Banks (2015) coined the concept *failed citizenship* to articulate its influence on historically marginalized communities. *Failed citizenship* "occurs when the social, cultural, economic, and political systems within a nation-state prevent marginalized groups from attaining full structural inclusion into the nation" (p. 152). He argued that without inclusion, members of marginalized communities were alienated from the culture at large, pushing them to identify more readily with their community identities. Vickery's (2015) research supported Banks's contention. Black women social studies educators in Banks's study observed that society failed to recognize or treat Black people as citizens; their acknowledgment pushed them to dissociate from conventional conceptions of citizenship that their prescribed classroom curriculum expected them to teach. Ladson-Billings's (2004) research also characterized *failed citizenship*. She found that Black 8th-graders, despite their social studies curriculum exploring related topics, valued their racio-ethnic identity more than their nationality; they identified as African American, not American.

To interrupt *failed citizenship*, Banks (2015) recommended incorporating *transformative civic education practices* that enable students to preserve their community identity while still feeling structurally included and represented within their nation-state. This kind of recommendation is nothing new; Black educators and intellectuals have long resisted dominant citizenship narratives and promoted incorporating Black perspectives and figures into civic education curricula (Duncan, 2020; Gordon, 1985; Johnson, 2019; Preston-Grimes, 2007; Tyson, 2003; Vickery, 2015). To inspire new citizenship paradigms, Gordon (1985) conceptualized the emancipatory potential of pedagogy coupled with Black cultural knowledge, something Black educators in Georgia demonstrated in practice and publication (Preston-Grimes, 2007). Raising similar points, Duncan (2020), Tyson (2003), Johnson (2019), and Vickery (2015) have recommended the application of critical race theory (CRT) (Crenshaw et al., 1995) and related principles such as counter-narration to help bridge the culture–citizenship divide and center discussions of citizenship on the Black experience. Scholars (Bañales et al., 2020) outside the field of education have also explored these topics, recognizing the centrality and motivational capacity of cultural identity for people, including youth of Color relative to civic engagement. Adding to this work, this chapter considers how our research on local narratives engages with counter-hegemonic notions of citizenship that highlight the strengths and immaterial wealth of marginalized communities.

COMMUNITY CULTURAL WEALTH AND JUSTICE-CENTERED EDUCATIONAL PRAXIS

This section describes two interconnected theoretical frameworks—Yosso's (2005) community cultural wealth framework and Ayers et al.'s (2017) conceptualization of justice-centered education—to illustrate the civic strengths of communities of Color and the ways these strengths might be embodied as pedagogical practices in P–20 classroom spaces.

Widespread academic (mis)use of Bourdieu's (1986) cultural capital framework motivated Yosso (2005) to challenge how it positioned people of Color as deficient and incapable of sociocultural mobility. These views accentuated the inaccessibility of cultural capital, which privileged groups systematically hoarded and protected, to people of Color. Informed by CRT (Crenshaw et al., 1995), Yosso (2005) proposed community cultural wealth (CCW) to articulate six unique forms of capital that communities of Color use, and have used, to thrive and resist oppression. These include

- aspirational capital: the capacity to maintain hope in the face of social barriers;
- linguistic capital: the advantages that come with understanding more than one language or dialect;
- familial capital: the extended sense of family that is passed on within a cultural community through shared history and tradition;
- social capital: the support networks that familial capital affords historically marginalized individuals;
- navigational capital: the skills and knowledge acquired as one navigates social systems that exist to marginalize them; and
- resistant capital: the skills and knowledge that are promoted through cultural resistance to systems of inequality.

Focused on assets rather than perceived deficits, these forms of capital may facilitate more humanizing and joyous learning experiences and interactions between teachers and students. Yosso's (2005) framework, pedagogically and curricularly, positions students and communities of Color as sources of wealth, strength, and agency.

As of late, social justice teaching has emerged within a marketplace of neoliberal education reforms and the commercialization of pedagogical practices. As such, in many places, social justice educational teaching, as Ayers et al. (2017) argue, is more of "a popular buzzword . . . easily coopted and rendered toothless" (p. 91). These scholars, therefore, advocate for a shift from social justice teaching to justice-centered teaching, which

> opposes in the objectification of people for use and . . . lives out a kind of happy and hopeful opposition . . . that means living up to the demands of teaching in and for democracy . . . while embracing the idea that the full development of all is the essential condition for the development of each (and vice versa). (p. 92)

As the two case studies we detail next indicate, local stories of resistance demonstrate justice-centered pedagogical praxes (teaching and learning) and ways that CCW might be utilized as a pedagogical and curricular framework in P–20 classrooms. These concepts undergird ongoing citizenship battles that communities of Color have historically waged, conflicts with important lessons for social studies and civics research and practice.

CASE STUDIES

The two following case studies describe separate studies that coalesce around the importance of civics in underserved communities of Color. Both consider the aforementioned conceptual frameworks and serve as examples for how local histories of struggle can improve social studies' engagement with critical, counter-hegemonic conceptions of civics.

Resisting Dehumanization: A Black Student-Led Walkout in Waco, Texas, 1970

Centered on former Black student experience, ArCasia's study (James-Gallaway, 2020) employed a local, social history approach to examine the implementation of Texas school desegregation, rather than its legal history. ArCasia looked to the 1970s once school districts in and near Waco started to comply with federal mandates to dissolve racially separate schools. Evidence consisted primarily of oral history interviews with Black baby boomers born between 1946 and 1964 (Turner & James-Gallaway, 2022) and archival documents.

One portion of the larger project analyzed a Black student–led walkout at the start of the 1970–1971 school year. Throughout, Black students pointedly contested the school district's repeated violations of their citizenship. What follows briefly overviews this event, stressing its civic components. Two main factors led to the walkout and subsequent boycott. Days before the 1970 school year started, La Vega School District, a small district comprised of approximately 6,000 students that adjoins Waco to the northeast, surreptitiously and abruptly shuttered its only Black high school, George Washington Carver (Carver). This community institution had served as a vital, nurturing source of support for historically Black East Waco, a culturally rich but underinvested part of the city (James-Gallaway, 2022b). The district opened Carver in 1956—two years after the federal government outlawed school segregation—as an equalization school intended to quiet the Black community's pleas for higher-quality educational resources. Ongoing conversations with the federal government influenced the decision to close the school, and some reports suggest a district federal court judge approved it. Analysis of school board records and oral history interviews with former Black students, however, revealed that the district failed to publicly disclose the closure before the school year started. This clandestine activity led students to arrive at Carver for the first day of class, only to be informed of the school's closure and redirected to the district's white high school, LaVega High. Many narrators, a term oral historians use in reference to their interviewees, recollected this experience, noting how non-human (Wynter, 1994) it made them feel.[1]

In the 1970–1971 school year at LaVega High, Black students faced a racially hostile climate that had been ongoing since at least the first four Black students graduated in 1966. This environment reflected the tacit curriculum of Black intellectual ineptitude that pervaded the school desegregation process in Waco (James-Gallaway, 2022a). Part of this anti-Black malice stemmed from, according to narrators, the low-class status of the district's white students, who viewed new Black students as direct competition despite their socioeconomic background (Roediger, 1991). In tandem with white students and personnel at LaVega, the white community strived to clearly communicate their disdain, prohibiting Black students from entering their eateries during lunchtime. Black Waco's robust CCW (Yosso, 2005) supported students' navigation of this tumultuous climate.

Three disparate yet complementary stories explain the walkout's origins. One credited a small group of Black students with planning it the night before. Another attributed it to spontaneous combustion. The third indicated that a Black girl student, Erma Jean Laster, devised the entire scheme. These explanations converged around the following account. Tired of being treated like second-class citizens, LaVega High's new Black students clearly and politically displayed their displeasure. Their demonstration sparked pandemonium, which broke out across the school. From bathroom brawls to students jumping or being pushed out second-story windows, the scene reflected Black students' righteous indignation. Preemptively and spontaneously, Black LaVega students protested the closure of their beloved Carver High, marching out of class at 10 a.m. on September 14, 1970. From LaVega High, 50 to 60 Black students trekked the nearly 3-mile route back to Carver High. Many drew inspiration from political struggles such as the civil rights and Black Power movements. Some, like Willie Brown, chose to drive instead of walk, fearing white students or white community members might vandalize his car if he left without it. Because the walkout occurred on a Monday, many aggrieved Black students boycotted school for the rest of the week, continuing to express their frustration.

The actions of the white superintendent, Henry Cranfill, who oversaw this desegregation process, characterized the deep-seated anti-Blackness that permeated Black students' experiences in this new school. That summer, Cranfill had conspired with the LaVega school board to misinform and marginalize its only member of Color, a Black man named Rev. LaDell Thomas, about their plans to close Carver. During the walkout, local newspapers reported Cranfill's cries of bloodshed in reference to the Black students' demands for civic dignity. He chastised local government for their unwillingness to render aid from the National Guard, insisting Black students were uncontrollable and bloodthirsty. Seeking to legitimize stereotypes about Black people as unthinking and dangerous, Cranfill wrote letters of thanks to local law enforcement for their help with the rancor that ensued and the turbulent school year that followed. No evidence suggests he considered how his treatment of Black students or the policies or procedures he helped craft motivated their need to protest.

At graduation that spring, Black student Marshall Baldwin showed Cranfill precisely how he felt, declining to shake Cranfill's hand on stage. Baldwin reasoned that Cranfill had had myriad opportunities to improve the plight of Black students, and yet had refused. With a last name at the top of the alphabet, Baldwin set a trend that many, if not most, Black students followed. Explaining his civic impetus to his inquiring mother afterward, Baldwin noted: "Mama, you just don't know. . . . You were gone to work. . . . I'm out there living it. . . . You don't know what's happened in that school. . . . There were a whole lot of pitfalls in that school that you had to be aware of" (Baldwin, 2016, p. 43). While it is likely both Baldwin and his mother faced racial oppression at school and work, respectively, Baldwin's commentary underscores adults' tendency to discredit youth expressions of civic agency. Graduation gave Baldwin and his Black classmates a chance to courageously expose and contest the shortcomings of school desegregation they were forced to navigate. This final show of agency on the part of Black students portrayed their pronounced civic inclinations despite their school district's refusal to honor them as citizens.

This narrative about Black Waco student protest depicts just one way local history might enhance discussions around citizenship and the ways marginalized communities contest their oppression in drawing on their CCW (Yosso, 2005). Ultimately, this project argued that for Black Waco students, the school desegregation implementation process sustained white supremacy and anti-Blackness. It also illuminates the ways that Black students, like Baldwin, and their families resisted by refusing to capitulate to white supremacy or anti-Blackness. The examination's implications for social studies urge both practitioners and researchers to broaden their thinking around the utility of local history vis-á-vis popular topics such as civics. Doing so promises to deepen and expand social studies' inherent interdisciplinarity and its capacity to promote justice-centered educational praxis (Ayers et al., 2017; Wilson, 2021), something evident in more recent times as well.

Youth Organizing in the Shadows of Industry

For one year, Asif was employed as executive director at a youth organization in East Chicago, Indiana. While doing so, he also studied how the youth he worked alongside made sense of their agency and the pedagogical and curricular experiences that influenced these emergent identities (Wilson, 2018). The narrative that follows was constructed using interview data with the young people employed by the organization and analysis archival records detailing the curricular experiences that took place.

East Chicago, Indiana, sits in the northwest area of the state. When combined with the neighboring city of Gary, northwest Indiana is home to most of the state's Black and Latinx population (U.S. Census Bureau, 2020). Lake Michigan sits on the northern side of the city, which made it a prime area for industrial transportation. Incorporated in 1893, the city was originally named the Twin City. The Harbor and East Chicago were and continue to be divided by rail- and waterways, important geographic markers of the city's close ties to capital accumulation by way of industry. Once known for steel, and now for its large casino, East Chicago residents often find employment in one of the two main industries within the city. Underneath the city's post-racial ambience (multiracial political leadership and integrated working conditions) exists a long history of racialized oppression and struggle that is often excluded from the public discourse, especially the curricular content in local P–20 classrooms.

Embodying the problem-posing pedagogies of Paulo Freire (1970), Greenhouse Fellowship was a space for young people to critically read and (re)write the world around them. As part of their full-time responsibilities, each Fellow, as they were titled, spent 3 days per week at an East Chicago nonprofit agency supporting their day-to-day operations from a youth perspective. The remaining 2 days were spent attending seminars—educational spaces where the Fellows and invited guest speakers built critical capacities to read the world (Freire, 1970)—and working on community projects that the Fellows designed and implemented. Nine high school graduates started the program in August 2014, which compensated them at $25,000 plus benefits per year. Five Fellows completed the program the following July. The example that follows, detailing a community tour we developed, is an example of civic education centering CCW (Yosso, 2005) and justice-centered pedagogies (Ayers et al., 2017).

After several days of community-building exercises in the office at the start of the Fellowship, the associate director, Meghan, and Asif asked the Fellows to design a tour of their community. Each of them was asked to locate two places in East Chicago that were meaningful for them. One space was to be *an asset*—a place or event that represented a strength of their community. The other was *a delta*—a place or event that, in their opinion, could be transformed. After several days, the Fellows had constructed a tour route and associated narratives regarding each stop's significance. In a 15-passenger van borrowed from a local church, the Fellows led their peers and organizational staff on an exploration of their community, stopping at schools, community centers, housing developments, and other locations important to them. Those on the trip saw the parks where the Fellows celebrated important familial and community-based moments and other significant historical markers in the Fellows' lives, such as the church where Faith,[2] a Fellow, shared their families' deep ties to community activism.

This first stage of the community tour illuminated many things. The Fellows' individual and collective CCW emerged by positioning them as experts of their lives and their communities as curriculum. Meghan and Asif, the lead educators of the Fellowship, used the Fellows' CCW to construct future pedagogical and curricular interactions and learning experiences. The Fellows' emergent CCW was also used to agitate their critical capacities. Critical conversations surrounding the spaces and memories they were learning about encouraged them to consider how these spaces came to be over time and what systems and structures influenced them. This led to the second and third stages of the tour.

To add to the Fellows' historical knowledge of resistance in East Chicago, the organization connected with a local historian[3] named Mario—a Mexican crane operator at Inland Steel who held a plethora of knowledge related to the historical struggles of communities of Color in East Chicago. One rainy afternoon, Mario took us on a tour during which he detailed rich historical narratives that Meghan and Asif hoped would contribute to the Fellows' understanding of how their city was shaped over time. We learned about resistance, re-patriation, and other important historical structures and movements that shaped the Fellows' city. Following the tour, the Fellows teamed up with the local library's special collections and went on another educational journey. This located *historical events*, which were added to the tour, that happened in East Chicago and represented the city's identity. Asif and Meghan guided the Fellows into a critical analysis of their community and how it came to be shaped through systems over time. After learning more about the historical moments and movements that shaped their city, the Fellows went back to redesign their original tour. The revised version included new historical stops, like the site of a famous Latinx cultural house and a space known as "busy corner," where mill employees would make their home after work. The local stories that the Fellows discovered about their community detailed how systems and structures shaped it over time. Hearing these stories and discovering new information through archival study agitated their curiosities to learn more about their community and how they might shape it. They went on to continue studying their community and taking action for the remainder of their year as Fellows. Overall, the community tour created the learning conditions for the Fellows to develop critical questions to explore, make sense of, and take action to transform.

What started as an assignment to design and implement a tour of their community resulted in rich explorations of the past, critical explorations of the present, and actions that attempted to transform oppression in Fellows' lives. The pedagogy and the curriculum of Greenhouse Fellowship was bound in the community's rich curriculum and pedagogy—in their CCW (Yosso, 2005). The community and its rich stories provided the curricular starting points that were used to create teaching and learning experiences. The community also provided the critical contexts to support counter-hegemonic epistemological curiosities, what Freire (1998) referred to as, "a process of social and historical construction and reconstruction" (p. 38). The local stories created exploratory contexts, relevant to the Fellows' lives, that they had the freedom to explore educationally. Most importantly, the community provided the historical roadmaps and the contemporary openness (hooks, 2003) for the Fellows to act on their inquiries, attempting to transform the conditions that harmed them and their peoples (Ayers et al., 2017; Wilson, 2018).

TOWARD CRITICAL CIVICS EDUCATION AND PRACTICE

These case studies demonstrated regional and temporal narratives that converged to highlight the ongoing battle against racial and economic domination. These struggles, we posit, are crucial dimensions of critical civic education and practice. The historical account of the Black student–led walkout in Waco illustrated the limitations of school desegregation upon implementation, a process intended to further civic possibilities for Black Waco citizens; systemic racial oppression, however, sought to curtail such, something Black Waco students adamantly contested. The East Chicago instance portrayed an innovative program in which recent Black and Latinx high school graduates reimagined their dispossessed community, investigating its history, resources, needs, and promise; these actions led a group of young adults to rewrite their community's story and, arguably, shift the trajectory of its future. Together, these case studies depicted the oft-overlooked reservoirs of CCW (Yosso, 2005), considering them through a justice-centered educational praxis lens (Ayers et al., 2017). We merged these narratives to demonstrate how local histories of struggle can improve social studies learning. Additionally, they create a curricular roadmap for how social studies educators might access such local stories of resistance and support their students in investigating how they animate wider notions of civics. Both showed what small, unsuspecting places stand to teach us about civics and how marginalized communities adapt conventional frameworks to suit their needs. Including these considerations is crucial for progressing social studies broadly and civics in particular.

Like Yosso's (2005) CCW framework, justice-centered praxis (Ayers et al., 2017; Wilson, 2021) helps showcase the liberatory pedagogical and curricular possibilities of P–20 social studies and civics classrooms, as illustrated in this chapter. This perspective clarifies that virtually all communities have local stories of justice-centered struggle(s) that epitomize civics and social studies in unconventional ways. We argue for a recentering of these stories within civics teaching and learning experiences because these stories can serve as pedagogical and curricular resources for P–20 educators to explore the legacies of resistance to oppression present in their communities.

We hope that educators locate the local stories relevant to the geographies, cultures, and identities of their schools and students and utilize them to construct pedagogical and curricular learning experiences for their students. Given that many young Black and Latinx youth in dispossessed communities lack access to their local histories and traditional civic practices, local examples, such as the ones shared here, can act as civic starting points that provide roadmaps and foster freedom dreams (Kelley, 2002). In this sense, local stories can act as agentic catalysts for students, spotlighting relevant, curious, and critical pathways for students to explore their past(s) while also imagining their roles in reshaping their future(s).

What would it mean for local stories that surround school buildings to be a standard part of the curriculum and pedagogies in P–20 schools? What transformations might be possible within this pedagogical and curricular positioning, one that views Black and Latinx communities as full of civic wealth and that stresses justice-centered engagements? In civic education, what sort of world(s) might culturally sustaining and justice-centered praxes create for Black, Latinx, and other dispossessed students?

We raise a similar concern similar to Ayers et al. (2017) regarding the liberal and capitalistic contours of social justice teaching related to the harmful and exclusionary boundaries of social studies and civics educational praxes that claim to be bound in social justice. We advocate for, and put forward, a call for justice-centered social studies and civic educational praxes, ones that "engag[e] students, families, community members, and community organizers to study and research the goings-on right outside the schoolhouse door and to challenge through concrete initiatives the difficult, unjust realities of . . . education" (p. 96). Thus, if social studies takes social and racial justice seriously, it must move more urgently to expand civics frameworks. Doing so promises to better celebrate, humanize, and position as knowledge-bearing and knowledge-generating historically marginalized communities. These groups have much to teach academic and educational communities, who must seek out community resources in order to draw on their rich local legacies of struggle.

REFERENCES

Ayers, W., Kumashiro, K., Meiners, E., Quinn, T., & Stovall, D. (2017). *Teaching toward democracy: Educators as agents of change* (2nd ed.). Routledge.

Baldwin, M. (2016, June 24). Interview by S. Sutcliffe [audio recording and transcript]. Oral Memoirs of Marshall Baldwin, Baylor University Institute for Oral History, Waco, TX. https://digitalcollections-baylor.quartexcollections.com/documents?returning=true

Bañales, J., Hoffman, A. J., Rivas-Drake, R., & Jagers, R. J. (2020). The development of ethnic-racial identity process and its relation to civic beliefs among Latinx and Black American adolescents. *Journal of Youth and Adolescence, 49*, 2495–2508.

Banks, J. A. (2015). Failed citizenship, civic engagement, and education. *Kappa Delta Pi Record, 51*, 151–154.

Bourdieu, P. (1986). The forms of capital. In J. G. Richardson (Ed.), *Handbook of theory and research for the sociology of education* (pp. 241–258). Greenwood Press.

Boydston, J. A. (1980). The middle works of John Dewey, 1899–1924. *Philosophy and Phenomenological Research, 40*(3).

Brown, A. L., Crowley, R. M., & King, L. J. (2011). Black Civitas: An examination of Carter Woodson's contributions to teaching about race, citizenship, and the Black soldier. *Theory & Research in Social Education, 39*(2), 278–299.

Busey, C. L., & Dowie-Chin, T. (2021). The making of global Black anti-citizen/citizenship: Situating BlackCrit in global citizenship research and theory. *Theory & Research in Social Education, 49*(2), 153–175.

Crenshaw, K., Gotanda, N., Peller, G., & Thomas, K. (Eds.). (1995). *Critical race theory: The key writings that formed the movement*. The New Press.

Dilworth, P. P. (2004). Competing conceptions of citizenship education: Thomas Jesse Jones and Carter G. Woodson. *International Journal of Social Education, 18*(2), 1–10.

Duncan, K. E. (2020). "What better tool do I have?": A critical race approach to teaching civics. *The High School Journal, 103*(3), 176–189.

Freire, P. (1970). *Pedagogy of the oppressed*. Continuum.

Freire, P. (1998). *Pedagogy of freedom: Ethics, democracy, and civic courage*. Rowman & Littlefield.

Gordon, B. M. (1985). Toward emancipation in citizenship education: The case of African-American cultural knowledge. *Theory & Research in Social Education, 12*(4), 1–23. https://doi.org/10.1080/00933104.1985.10505485

hooks, b. (2003). *Teaching community: A pedagogy of hope*. Routledge.

James-Gallaway, A. D. (2020). More than race: Differentiating Black students' everyday experiences in Texas school desegregation, 1968–1978. Unpublished doctoral dissertation, University of Illinois, Urbana-Champaign.

James-Gallaway, A. D. (2022a). Tacit curriculum of Black intellectual ineptitude: Black girls and Texas school desegregation implementation in the 1970s. *History of Education Review, 51*(1), 81–95.

James-Gallaway, A. D. (2022b). What got them through: Community cultural wealth, Black students, and Texas school desegregation. *Race Ethnicity and Education, 25*(2), 173–191.

Johnson, M. W. (2019). Trump, Kaepernick, and MLK as "maybe citizens": Early elementary African American males' analysis of citizenship. *Theory & Research in Social Education, 47*(3), 374–395.

Jones, T. J. (1906). *Social studies in the Hampton curriculum*. Hampton Institute Press

Kelley, R. D. (2002). *Freedom dreams: The Black radical imagination*. Beacon Press.

Ladson-Billings, G. (2003). Lies my teacher still tells. In G. Ladson-Billings (Ed.) *Critical race theory perspectives on social studies: The profession, policies, and curriculum* (pp. 1–11). Information Age Publishing.

Ladson-Billings, G. (2004). Culture versus citizenship: The challenge of racialized citizenship in the United States. In J. A. Banks (Ed.), *Diversity in citizenship education* (pp. 99–126). Jossey-Bass.

Preston-Grimes, P. (2007). Teaching democracy before Brown: Civic education in Georgia's African American schools, 1930–1954. *Theory & Research in Social Education, 35*(1), 9–31.

Roediger, D. R. (1991). *The wages of whiteness: Race and the making of the American working class*. Verso.

Turner, F. F., & James-Gallaway, A. D. (2022). Black baby boomers, gender, and southern education: Navigating tensions in oral history methodology. *The Oral History Review, 49*(1), 77–96.

Tyson, C. A. (2003). A bridge over troubled water: Social studies, civic education, and critical race theory. In G. Ladson-Billings (Ed.) *Critical race theory perspectives on social studies: The profession, policies, and curriculum* (pp. 15–26). Information Age Publishing.

U.S. Census Bureau (2020). Quick facts: Indiana. https://www.census.gov/quickfacts/IN

Vickery, A. E. (2015). It was never meant for us: Towards a black feminist construct of citizenship in social studies. *The Journal of Social Studies Research, 39*(3), 163–172.

Watkins, W. H. (2001). *The white architects of Black education: Ideology and power in America, 1865–1954*. Teachers College Press.

Wilson, A. (2018). *Winter in America: Exploring epistemologies of youth activism in the 21st century* (Doctoral dissertation, University of Illinois at Chicago). https://www.proquest.com/dissertations-theses/winter-america-exploring-epistemologies-youth/docview/2085291385/se-2

Wilson, A. (2021). Curricularizing social movements: The election of Chicago's first Black mayor as content, pedagogy, and futurities. *Journal of Curriculum Theorizing, 36*(2), 32–42.

Wynter, S. (1994). No humans involved: An open letter to my colleagues. *Forum N.H.I. Knowledge for the 21st Century, Knowledge on Trial, 1*(1), 42–71.

Yancy, G. (2021, June 1). *Robin D. G. Kelley: The Tulsa race massacre went way beyond "Black Wall Street."* Truthout. https://truthout.org/articles/robin-kelley-business-interests-fomented-tulsa-massacre-as-pretext-to-take-land

Yosso, T. J. (2005). Whose culture has capital? A critical race theory discussion of community cultural wealth. *Race Ethnicity and Education, 8*(1), 69–91.

CHAPTER 6

#FreeThemAll
Civic Action Through Southeast Asian Community Defense Digital Toolkits

Van Anh Tran

As of this writing, over 2,000 SEA (Southeast Asian) community members have been deported from the United States (Southeast Asia Resource Action Center, 2020b, p. 73). These deportations are a part of an ongoing cycle of violence and are a result of this country's violent carceral system. After surviving war, genocide, and violence at the hands of U.S. imperialism, SEA refugees were resettled in systematically underresourced and criminalized communities in the United States where they were funneled into a pipeline from incarceration to deportation (Asian American Resource Workshop, n.d.; Chow, 2005). Now, decades later, the state continues to perpetrate violence against SEA communities. Seventeen thousand refugees and immigrants from Cambodia, Laos, and Vietnam have removal orders based on past criminal convictions (Southeast Asia Resource Action Center, 2020a, p. 73).

Aligning with the demands of other liberation movements, community organizations locally and nationally have come together to build the capacity of SEA communities and beyond to organize against the injustices of incarceration and deportation. This chapter will engage with digital toolkits developed by local and national grassroots, SEA community organizations, and coalitions as a case study of how communities of Color have approached and enacted civics. To pursue this inquiry, I will engage in a comparative analysis of a selection of toolkits produced between the last quarter of 2020 and the first quarter of 2021 that focus on SEA deportation defense campaigns ranging from amplifying the cases of community members at risk of state-sanctioned violence to strategies to mobilize elected officials. This chapter seeks to understand the ways that SEA communities enact civics by asking:

- How do SEA deportation community defense toolkits addressing different needs in the community compare?

- How do the toolkits' content and structure invite active participation to resist systems of oppression within and beyond the fight against SEA deportation?

With the objective of engaging individuals, advocates, community members, and more who want to organize against detentions and deportations, these toolkits are a powerful site of analysis that offer valuable insight to how communities of Color conceive and practice civics.

NEGOTIATING SEA CITIZENSHIP

This exploration recognizes the ways that migration and displacement interact with notions of citizenship (Castro & Knowles, 2017; Knight Abowitz & Harnish, 2006; Rosaldo & Flores; 1997) and carcerality (Buenavista, 2018; Kuoch, 2020). Situated within critical civic education (Falkner & Payne, 2021; Wheeler-Bell, 2014), this analysis centers resources developed by and for SEA community members. Uplifting the community cultural wealth (Yosso, 2005) and counter-narratives (Solórzano & Yosso, 2002) that sit within the ways of knowing and being of SEA communities, the selection of resources developed by community organizations in this chapter demonstrate a critical approach to enacting of civics (Au, 2012; Freire, 1970; hooks, 2014).

Cultural Citizenship

Though beyond the scope of this chapter, it is important to note that the experiences, political identities, and racialization of SEA communities in the United States are intimately entangled with the broader Asian American community. Rodríguez (2018) explains:

> Asian American immigration history in relation to U.S. citizenship was distinct from other migrant or racialized groups as Asians were the only group for whom legislation was crafted to exclude their entry into the United States (e.g., Page Act of 1875, Chinese Exclusion Act of 1882). (p. 530)

The specific exclusion of Asian people as "aliens ineligible to citizenship" (Parker, 1925, p. 26) textures an understanding of current struggles against SEA deportation and emphasizes the need for Asian American and SEA stories in the teaching and learning of citizenship in the United States (Rodríguez, 2018).

SEA communities in the United States constantly negotiate their transnational positions. Um (2015) conceives of diaspora as "not only in terms of the dispersal of communities from one source to many sites but also the enduring connections to the ancestral source" (p. 199). As such, Levinson (2011) reminds us, "citizenship was never as stable, uncomplicated, or territorial bound as we might have thought" (p. 284). Conceiving citizenship as an "ontological problem that is both a crisis of meaning and a crisis of belonging" (Rodríguez, 2018, p. 536), cultural citizenship is a helpful frame to understand the ways that SEA communities take up and enact civics due to the way it "builds on multiple cultural communities' histories of negotiating and sustaining civic membership and claiming space" (Falkner & Payne, 2021, p. 82). Rosaldo and Flores (1997) describe cultural citizenship as a way of "claiming membership in, and remaking America" (p. 58). Recognizing the ways that communities of Color and institutionally marginalized communities draw from their roots, wisdom, and values to resist systemic oppression (Castro & Knowles, 2017; Knight Abowitz & Harnish, 2006), cultural citizenship "emphasizes the agency in marginalized groups in establishing and asserting human, social, and cultural rights to enfranchise themselves" (Rodríguez, 2018, p. 536). The histories and experiences of SEA communities in the United States and their struggles against detention and deportations demonstrate the relationships between migration, displacement, citizenship, power, and oppression.

Carcerality

Engaging with SEA deportation is necessarily engaging with the ways that legacies of U.S. imperialism and militarism (Vang, 2016) manifest in state-imposed criminalization (Buenavista, 2018; Kuoch, 2020). Carcerality involves "social and political systems that formally and informally promote the discipline, punishment, and incarceration of individuals" (Buenavista, 2018, p. 80). Carcerality exposes the power dynamics that undergird the relationship between criminalization and capitalism (Buenavista, 2018; Lawston & Escobar, 2009–2010). Over the course of the last century, the relationship between the U.S. criminal legal system and the immigration system has constructed the phenomenon of "illegal" immigration (Buenavista, 2018; Lawston & Escobar 2009–2010; Ngai 2004). Between the passage of the Immigration Act of 1924—which enacted quotas and barred the entry of migrants from the so-called "Asiatic Barred Zone" (Department of State, n.d.; Ngai, 2004; Rodríguez, 2018)—and the Immigration and Nationality Act of 1965—which eased former restrictions (Cohn, 2015; Ludden, 2006; Ngai, 2004)—legislation in the United States explicitly conveyed a preference for white, European migrants, while institutionalizing the undesirability of migrants of Color. Buenavista (2018) explains:

> Undocumented status and deportability became inextricably linked through the ability of the federal government to remove humans deemed undesirable; as such, undocumented status equated to criminal activity. (p. 81)

Mass deportations surface the intimate relationship between the U.S. criminal legal system and immigration system that streamlines the process of continued displacement. In Kuoch's (2020) critique of the intersection between U.S. imperialism and the carceral state through the figure of the "deportable-refugee," they uplift the ways that "exploring Southeast Asian [community organizing] reveals possibilities of abolitionist imaginaries at this very same intersection" (p. 26).

SOUTHEAST ASIAN DEPORTATION COMMUNITY DEFENSE: AN OVERVIEW

To date, SEA refugees are the largest refugee community to be resettled in the United States (Kuoch, 2020; Southeast Asia Resource Action Center, 2020a, p. 76). A common refrain in SEA deportation community defense events and rallies is "We are here because you were there." As a result of U.S. imperialism and militarism in Southeast Asia between the 1950s and 1970s and the destructive and overwhelming impact on those who called Cambodia, Laos, and Vietnam home, many SEA refugees were forcibly displaced and subsequently resettled in the United States (Vang, 2016). The U.S. government was heavily involved in the region during this time to combat the spread of communism. For the purposes of this chapter, Southeast Asia is a political and social organizing identity that encompasses those who are impacted and displaced by the legacies of war and genocide in Cambodia, Laos, and Vietnam. While grouped together in this way, it is important to recognize the heterogeneity of these communities based on culture, educational experience, ethnicity, language, socioeconomic status, and more.

The purported "War on Drugs" of the 1970s in the United States and following "tough on crime" legislation resulted in the over-policing of communities of Color (Bui, 2018; Kuoch, 2020; Stumpf, 2006; Truong, 2021). Years later, many SEA community members with prior convictions are at risk of deportation. The impact of SEA deportations extends beyond the individuals themselves and deeply affects the families and communities from which they are separated. While deportations occurred under the Bush and Obama administrations (Gramlich, 2020; Simanski, 2014; Wong, 2014), they particularly intensified under the Trump administration (Northeast Region Pardons Project, n.d.). When Joe Biden was inaugurated following the 2020 presidential election, he issued a memorandum that indicated that the Department of Homeland Security (2021) would temporarily pause "removals for certain noncitizens ordered deported to ensure we have a fair and immigration enforcement system" (para. 2). In addition to pausing deportations, however, this memorandum directed ICE to continue detaining and arresting those who were newly released from incarceration and those who have "aggravated felonies." This directive and the deep connectedness of the U.S. immigration and criminal legal systems imply that community members continue to be vulnerable to deportations.

My Commitments

I came to this project as a community member, and later a board member, with the Asian American Resource Workshop (AARW), which is a member-led, community organization that serves pan-Asian communities in the Greater Boston area. Through my involvement with AARW, I began organizing against SEA deportations alongside community organizers and impacted community members—all of whom extended an incredible amount of love and care to me and allowed me to find a political home during my time in Boston. Born and raised in the Little Saigon ethnic enclave in Southern California, I sought connection and community in Dorchester—a neighborhood in Boston that I knew had a large Vietnamese community. I acknowledge that my identities, positionalities, and experiences influence how I understand, interpret, and analyze the resources shared in this chapter. Although I did not contribute to the development of the specific toolkits highlighted in this chapter, I have utilized many of them as a community member and organizer and have participated in the calls to action presented. It is impossible for me to disconnect my experiences from my analyses. Understanding my perspective and values makes visible my commitment to SEA communities and impacted community members.

SEA Digital Toolkits From 2020-2021

Local, statewide, and national SEA anti-deportation coalitions have convened under the assumption that organizing efforts should center those most impacted (Asian American Resource Workshop, n.d.; SEAFN, n.d.). Organizing amidst a pandemic and global uprisings against anti-Blackness and police brutality, SEA community organizations produced and distributed digital toolkits in response to a variety of injustices immediately facing the community. Whether to amplify the cases of specific community members who were at risk of harm or to influence elected officials, this selection of digital toolkits demonstrates the ways that SEA communities have approached and enacted civics.

This investigation of six digital toolkits created by SEA organizations across the United States will explore invitations to resist systems of oppression within and beyond the fight against SEA deportation. To narrow my analysis, I limited the timeframe of selected toolkits to those produced between the last quarter of 2020 to the beginning quarter of 2021, as this period also coincided with a political transition in U.S. electoral politics. The toolkits that I selected for this chapter were based on the following criteria:

- Accessibility: Is this toolkit publicly available? Is it easy to access?
- Authorship: Is the toolkit developed by a SEA grassroots, community organization? Is it developed by a coalition of organizations fighting for justice and liberation?

- Purpose: Is the toolkit designed with a specific end goal? Is this purpose explicit?
- Call to Action: Does the toolkit provide clear action items for the reader? Are there concrete ways for the reader to engage with the issue around which the toolkit was developed?

It should be noted that due to the nontransparent nature of detention centers, immigration enforcement agencies, government policies, and institutional machinations, community organizations rapidly responded to shifting circumstances by updating campaign objectives and strategies. Thus, multiple digital toolkits in the following selection were updated over time. Moreover, some toolkits highlighted in this chapter may have been formerly included in other toolkits or were synthesized into their current form due to updated messaging or shifting political targets. What I will be engaging with is the most up-to-date toolkits as of this writing, but the contents may change again depending on the needs of the various campaigns. Using my own SEA community networks, I identified the following selection of toolkits. While not a comprehensive or complete list of toolkits developed by SEA community organizations between 2020 and 2021, Table 6.1 provides insight to the different ways that the SEA community enacts civics.

Analysis

My analysis of the toolkits is grounded in a critical qualitative inquiry that calls for "[examining] the relationship between personal and community troubles, and the public policies and public institutions that have been created to address those issues" (Denzin, 2015, p. 33). My analysis process consisted of a recursive four-round cycle: (1) reading and re-reading within and across the six toolkits; (2) initial coding (Saldaña, 2013) of each toolkit and reflective processing; (3) axial coding (Saldaña, 2013) and reflective processing; and (4) establishing interpretations, revisiting earlier reflective processing, and re-reading. Guided by my first inquiry question, my initial coding process allowed me to look across my toolkit selection to identify their major components, explore commonalities, and engage their unique contents. My second inquiry question in concert with critical qualitative inquiry's commitment to "expose and critique the forms of inequality and discrimination that operate in daily life" (Denzin, 2015, p. 32) guides my later round of coding, revision, and interpretation so that I can focus on the ways that the toolkits facilitate and nurture resistance. Moreover, the overarching and intersecting frames of cultural citizenship and carcerality supported my axial coding so that I could "strategically reassemble" the details that were splintered during initial coding (Saldaña, 2013, p. 218). Through this process of identifying larger themes and categories, I began to establish interpretations to consider the ways that SEA engage and enact civics.

SEA Civic Action

Although variations related to components such as design, extent of background information shared, amount of external resources provided, level of power targeted, and calls to action prioritized occurred across the selected toolkits, their common elements illustrate the ways that SEA communities negotiate, construct, and claim citizenship (Kang, 2010). Falkner and Payne (2021) remind us that "civic practices are embedded at all levels of society and are deeply related to everyday civic culture practiced within a community" (p. 83). The following themes across the selection of six toolkits illustrate the collective, interwoven knowledges from which SEA communities draw and the intentional ways that they enact civics.

Know History, Know Self, Know Each Other

With a rich tradition in Black, Indigenous communities of Color, storytelling is an embodied practice that "invokes reclamation, resistance, and hope" (Kawano, 2019, p. 36; Tuhiwai Smith, 2013). Nearly every toolkit in this selection included a section that details the context of the campaign in the form of a narrative. Although varying amount of detail is included, nearly all the toolkits include a brief history that informs the campaign and narrates the current lived impacts on community members. Particularly in the toolkits that aimed to amplify the deportation cases of specific community members, such as #FreeSaelee and #DefendBoun, SEA communities were able to offer counterstories or counter-narratives to open "a window into ignored or alternative realities" (Delgado & Stefancic, 2001, p. 39) for readers who may be less familiar with the SEA experience. Falkner and Payne (2021) explain that "cultural citizenship recognizes the multiple identities that impact civic communities" (p. 83). Similarly, the toolkits make visible multiple aspects of who the community members of focus are—beyond their identities as formerly incarcerated and at-risk for deportation. For example, a reader could learn that "Boun Keoun is a Khmu refugee from Laos who served as an incarcerated firefighter" who was injured while fighting the California wildfires in late 2020 (#DefendBoun, 2020). A reader may gain insight to Nancy Nguyen, "Executive Director at VietLead, a mother of two and longtime Vietnamese community advocate and organizer," who was arrested for protesting the then director of ICE, Tony Pham (Drop the Charges, 2020). Through the context sections of the toolkits, SEA communities employ counter-narratives.

hooks (1989) discusses the importance of not only speaking to but also speaking *with*—having a dialogue. hooks (1989) uplifts the relationship between storytellers and listeners and speaks to the way that sharing space and stories provides a way to recognize each other's presences (hooks, 1994). The toolkit that did not necessarily include a narrative, "Stop Trump's Ban on Work Permits," still recognized the presences of not only the reader or

Table 6.1. *Sample of SEA Digital Toolkits, 2020-2021*

Campaign & Launch Period	Link	Authorship	Purpose
#FreeSaelee October 2020	bit.ly/FreeSaelee	Advocates for Iu Mien - California (facebook.com/AdvocatesforIuMien)	Putting pressure on ICE to release Kao Saelee from detention.
Drop the Charges October 2020	bit.ly/DTCShannon	VietLead & coalition of partner organizations (vietlead.org)	This is a follow-up to the rapid response "Action for VietLead #FreeNancy" toolkit and campaign developed after the arrest of VietLead's Executive Director Nancy Nguyen to drop her charges.
#DefendBoun November 2020	bit.ly/DefendBoun	Asian Law Caucus (advancingjustice-alc.org) Asian Prisoner Support Committee (asianprisonersupport.com, 2021)	Demand that Governor Newsom pardon both Boun and Kao (from earlier toolkit) to prevent their deportation and to stop turning Californians over to ICE.
Stop Trump's Ban on Work Permits December 2020	tiny.cc/ProtectWorkPermits https://tinyurl.com/ProtectWorkPermits	Northeast Region Pardons Project (nepardonproject.org, 2020)	Make public comments to oppose Trump's ban on work permits to slow the administration's efforts.

Campaign	Link	Organizations	Description
#BringHieuHome November 2020 (campaign and toolkit updated in March 2021 to reflect most recent circumstances)	bit.ly/ BringHieuHome	Mekong NYC (mekongnyc.org) Southeast Asian Defense Project (seadefense.org) VietLead (vietlead.org)	Initially, the purpose of the toolkit was to demand the immediate release of Hieu Huynh and the 400 immigrants and refugees who were detained by ICE at the Essex County Correctional Facility in Newark, New Jersey. By March 2021, updates to the toolkit indicated that Huynh had been transferred and would be boarding a deportation flight. The target of the toolkit, then, became the White House—demanding President Biden and Vice President Harris "ground the plane."
			This toolkit is also closely associated with the #FreeTien (bit.ly/FreeTien) toolkit, developed for the purpose of demanding the release of Tien Pham from a facility on the West Coast. Campaigns on both coasts joined together when community organizers and members learned that both Huynh and Pham were slated to be on the same deportation flight to Vietnam.
STOP ANTI ASIAN VIOLENCE: URGE THE BIDEN ADMINISTRATION TO STOP THE DEPORTATION OF VIETNAMESE REFUGEES March 2021	bit.ly/Ground ThePlane	Asian Prisoner Support Committee (asianprisonersupport .com, 2021)	This toolkit synthesizes the cases of both Hieu Huynh and Tien Pham to demand that President Biden immediately stop the upcoming March 2021 deportation flight to Vietnam and affirm his support of SEA refugees.
			The Ground the Plane toolkit follows not only #BringHieuHome and #FreeTien but also the #StopICETransfers (bit.ly/StopICETransfers) toolkit—that includes information on #DefendBoun and formerly included #FreeTien before it became a separate toolkit.

"listener" but also the impacted community members. While the toolkit did not include an explicit narrative, it contained a fact sheet—translated to Vietnamese, Khmer, Lao, and Hmong—that explained the impact of banning work permits on the community and what readers could do to advocate for SEA communities. This acknowledgment of the potential needs of the reader (level of context, language, etc.) demonstrates a recognition of and desire for relationship with the reader. The dialogue between toolkit design and reader further develops in the way that the toolkits are both in conversation with each other and consistently updated to reflect current and changing circumstances. There is a responsiveness in the toolkits—given their form and their serious subject matter. "#BringHieuHome," for example, no longer includes the material that it contained in its original form when first developed in November 2020. Currently, the #BringHieuHome toolkit reflects the most recent updates to Hieu Huynh's case—including multiple transfers and notifications that a deportation flight to Vietnam had been scheduled for March 2021. The updated toolkit contains calls to action and events that SEA coordinating organizations planned and hosted to prevent Hieu's deportation. Through Hieu's toolkit, the dialogue among toolkits is acute. Similarly, the "#DefendBoun" toolkit directly references the earlier "#FreeSaelee" toolkit and advocates for Cao Saelee, in addition to Boun Keoun—the focus of the toolkit. The "#DefendBoun" (2020) toolkit indicates:

> Weeks earlier, Governor Newsom also handed Kao Saelee, another refugee and incarcerated firefighter over to ICE and has ignored calls from hundreds of thousands of people to pardon him and halt transfers (toolkit: bit.ly/FreeSaelee). Kao and Boun are just two of hundreds of Californians turned over to ICE by CDCR during the COVID-19 pandemic. Demand that Gov. Newsom pardon Boun and Kao to prevent their deportation and stop turning Californians over to ICE!

The changing toolkits reflect the continual, dialectical relationship between community members—those who develop the toolkits and those who utilize and share them. The histories and storytelling that emerge from the toolkits serve not only to convey the ways that legacies of U.S. imperialism and militarism continue to impact the lives of SEA community members in the current day but also to uplift the identities and agency that these community members have. Further, the toolkits actively engage with the reader—not only through offering resources for more information and concrete action steps to exercise their agency, but also through the intentional design of the toolkits to be accessible on multiple levels (language, visual complements, image descriptions, etc.). As cultural citizenship attends to people's multiple identities, "the way society responds to these identities either binds people to or alienates them from the civic culture" (Ladson-Billings, 2004, p. 112). The creation and distribution of these toolkits that center actions that have critical and immediate impacts, however, show how SEA communities are civically engaging through their identities (Ladson-Billings, 2004).

Sustaining the Movement and the Moment

Flores (1997) explains that cultural citizenship involves "self-definition, affirmation, and empowerment" (p. 262). Moreover, cultural citizenship underscores "the affirmation of citizen identity through participation in one's community" (Falkner & Payne, 2021, p. 87). The content and structure across the toolkits center accessibility, broad community engagement, and choice. Not only did the SEA community organizations who developed the toolkits' contents claim their space within the movement, they also designed the toolkits to make space for others within and beyond their communities to participate as well. While each toolkit focused on specific, time-bound objectives with concrete action items to reach those distinct goals, the format was consistent across all toolkits to ensure that others would be able to continually engage in the ways that would work best for them.

In addition to the opening context and background narratives (or initial fact sheet in the case of the "Stop Trump's Ban on Work Permits" toolkit), each toolkit contained the following:

- A graphically designed image that synthesized the campaign and contained pertinent information (including, but not limited to: toolkit link, campaign hashtag(s), and the campaign title, ask, and/or objectives)
- Hashtags (some unique to the specific campaign, others utilized by broader justice movements)
- Campaign objectives, ask, and/or main target (which often was elected officials)
- Scripts for calls and emails; examples of social media posts
- Additional graphically designed images that synthesize the campaign that can be included in social media posts across platforms

The attention to accessibility is clear throughout this selection of toolkits. Not only were the toolkit links and language concise and easily shareable, but each image within the toolkits contained detailed descriptions. This care and intentionality affirm the ways that the SEA coordinating organizations sustain current and future movements against incarceration and deportation. In lowering the barrier for entry to engage with the toolkit materials and in designing the toolkit to be accessible across different abilities, knowledges, and experiences, SEA communities can encourage active participation and engagement in current campaigns and invite interest and participation in future campaigns. All resources required to act were included in the toolkits, including examples of social media posts and scripts to call or email targets (with their contact information). Moreover, the graphically designed images served multiple purposes. The images serve as an accessible anchor for the toolkit and as a way for those engaging with the toolkit to share the resources even more widely in a way that may be more likely to catch the attention of a larger number of people on social media (see Figure 6.1). In fact, all the toolkits included in this sample, except for the earliest—"#SaveSaelee"—included multiple versions of graphics, with the intention that they could be shared more easily across different social media platforms (see Figure 6.2).

Figure 6.1. *Main Graphics for "#DefendBoun" and "#BringHieuHome" Toolkits*

In fact, the social media graphics detailed the calls to action and included information that anyone engaging with the social media posts would need to act, without necessarily having to go through the toolkit first (see Figure 6.2). The "STOP ANTI-ASIAN VIOLENCE" social media graphics, for example, highlighted the target and its contact information (the White House Switchboard phone number) and contained the call script that readers would need to take up the call to action. In being able to share the contents of the toolkit widely, in multiple forms, SEA communities can build connections and capacity with a wider community. Similarly, the hashtags allow those who may or may not be in movement-building spaces to engage and participate in campaigns organized for SEA deportation community defense.

Figure 6.2. *Social Media Graphics for "Drop the Charges" and "STOP ANTI ASIAN VIOLENCE" Toolkit*

Figure 6.2. *(continued)*

Call Script to Henrico Commonwealth Attorney Shannon L. Taylor

Calling directions: (804) 501-4218 x Dial 0

"**Hi my name is** [name] **and I represent** [organization, or city/county of where you live]. **I'm calling to demand that ALL** charges be dropped against community organizers who are being targeted by Tony Pham, ICE director. At least nine community members, leaders, activists, and organizers from Philadelphia, Pennsylvania and Charlotte, North Carolina have been issued warrants of arrest for misdemeanor charges that amount to trespassing and littering. It's clear that these actions are intended to punish and intimidate organizers for speaking out against ICE and its human rights abuses. I am outraged that community leaders and organizers are being detained and extradited for peacefully assembling, especially in the middle of a pandemic.

Henrico Commonwealth Attorney Shannon Taylor has historically run on a progressive platform in Henrico County since 2011, so we call on her to continue to strengthen her commitment to progressive politics. Can we depend on C.A. Shannon Taylor to drop the charges against Nancy and the other community organizers from the September 8th action, and stand against the political retaliation taken against community organizers?"

#DropTheChargesShannon

Within the digital space, people within and beyond the SEA community can share and engage with the content of the toolkits. Moreover, they are able to immediately act to reach the identified objectives within the toolkits. SEA coordinating organizations who developed this selection of toolkits incorporated different tiers of action that readers can take, depending on their comfort level, ability, needs, and more. The "#FreeSaelee" toolkit and the "#DefendBoun," structured in similar ways, show one example of the different calls to action presented by SEA communities. For example, a reader has the option of joining an online community (Facebook group) to learn more about defense organizing updates and receive updates, donate to a reentry fund, sign a petition, call Governor Newsom, submit support letters, and/or tweet at Governor Newsom. Within each of these options are resources that set readers up for success, including

Figure 6.2. (continued)

links, contact information, letter templates, and call scripts. This level of choice—and the resources needed to engage readily available—creates the possibilities of different community members being able to convey their interests and assert their creativity. Feeling a sense of belonging to the movement for the safety and well-being of SEA communities, as well as broader movements for social justice, allow those within and beyond the SEA community to step into their power and enact civics in critical and meaningful ways. Thus, the toolkits' accessibility, flexibility and responsiveness, and potential for broader reach invite active and sustained participation from those who engage with their materials. The grassroots, community-led organizations who designed the toolkit make clear their commitment to building relationships with those who engage with them (whether through the toolkits or beyond), recognizing the complex and intersecting identities

Figure 6.2. (continued)

of community members, and focusing on the overarching goal of justice and liberation for all communities.

Community as Civics

Community is not only an organizing tool for grassroots organizations (Ishizuka & Chang, 2016), such as the ones who developed the toolkits in this chapter; it also extends beyond geographic space and becomes a way for theories of citizenship to be put into practice. The calls to action presented in the toolkits did not occur in a vacuum; often, the toolkits served as a complement to other community building and organizing efforts. The findings from the toolkit analyses emphasize the interconnected nature of

Figure 6.2. *(continued)*

> #FreeThemAll #GroundthePlane
>
> ## STOP ANTI-ASIAN VIOLENCE
>
> **Call the White House Switchboard: 202-456-1414**
>
> Hi, my name is ____ and I represent ____ (organization, or city/county where you live). I am calling in strong support of Tien Pham, Hieu Huynh, and 31 other Vietnamese refugees, scheduled to be on a deportation flight this coming Monday, March 15th. This deportation is shameful, and it tears apart families and communities. To deport Hieu, Tien, and all those who are scheduled to board this flight is to sustain Trump's long standing white supremacist legacy. We demand you do everything in your power to ground the plane so that Hieu, Tien, and the 31 other community members can be reunited with their families and loved ones!

the specific campaigns and of the carceral systems in which we are fighting against. The creation and distribution of the toolkits (and their responsive contents and form) indicate that this work cannot be done alone. Although reactive in the way that each toolkit responded to events, the design of the toolkits was also proactive to encourage broad and continued engagement.

SEA deportation community defense emphasizes the agency that we have as individuals and as collectives, providing opportunities for those of us committed to struggles for liberation to situate ourselves within broader contexts and recognize and exercise our power. Exploring the strategies that SEA communities have enacted to combat injustice demonstrate the connections between patterns of migration and displacement, belonging and citizenship, and the influence of power dynamics and carcerality on lived experiences. As we continue to expand the ways we conceive civics and civic engagement, the case of SEA deportation community defense demonstrates the ways that unjust policies have resulted in real, lived consequences—not only on the directly impacted people but on the communities to which they are connected (and the broader institutionally marginalized communities impacted by those very same structures). Through a recognition of the humanity of all community members, however, we can combat injustice through individual and collective action. In remembering our histories, learning the histories of other oppressed peoples, and intentionally and responsively developing multiple, accessible ways for people to engage, we move closer toward shared liberation.

REFERENCES

#BringHieuHome. (2020, November). Mekong NYC, Southeast Asian Defense Project, & VietLead. https://bit.ly/BringHieuHome

#DefendBoun. (2020, November). Asian Law Caucus and Asian Prisoner Support Committee. https://bit.ly/DefendBoun#*FreeSaelee*

Advocates for Iu Mien—California. https://bit.ly/FreeSaelee

Asian American Resource Workshop. (n.d.). *Community Defense Against Southeast Asian Deportation*. AARW. https://www.aarw.org/fighting-southeast-asian-deportation

Asian Prisoner Support Committee. (2021, March). STOP ANTI-ASIAN VIOLENCE: Urge the Biden administration to stop the deportation of Vietnamese refugees. https://bit.ly/GroundThePlane

Au, W. (2012). *Critical curriculum studies: Education, consciousness, and the politics of knowing*. Routledge.

Buenavista, T. L. (2018). Model (undocumented) minorities and "illegal" immigrants: Centering Asian Americans and US carcerality in undocumented student discourse. *Race Ethnicity and Education, 21*(1), 78–91.

Bui, T. (2018, June 13). Refugee to detainee: How the U.S. is deporting those seeking a safe haven. The Nib. https://thenib.com/refugee-to-detainee-how-the-u-s-is-deporting-those-seeking-a-safe-haven

Castro, A. J., & Knowles, R. T. (2017). Democratic citizenship education: Research across multiple landscapes and contexts. In M. M. Manfra & C. M. Bolick (Eds.), *The Wiley handbook of social studies research* (pp. 287–318). John Wiley & Sons, Inc.

Chow, G. K. (2005). Exiled once again: Consequences of the congressional expansion of deportable offenses on the Southeast Asian refugee community. *Asian American Law Journal, 12*, 103–136.

Cohn, D. (2015, September 30). How U.S. immigration laws and rules have changed through history. Pew Research Center. https://www.pewresearch.org/fact-tank/2015/09/30/how-u-s-immigration-laws-and-rules-have-changed-through-history

Delgado, R., & Stefancic, J. (2001). *Critical race theory: An introduction*. New York University Press.

Denzin, N. (2015). What is critical qualitative inquiry? In G. S. Cannella, M. S. Pérez, & P. A. Pasque (Eds.), *Critical qualitative inquiry: Foundations and futures* (pp. 31–50). Routledge.

Department of Homeland Security. (2021). *Acting Secretary of DHS Directs a Review of Immigration Enforcement Practices and Policies*. https://www.dhs.gov/news/2021/01/20/acting-secretary-dhs-directs-review-immigration-enforcement-practices-and-policies

Department of State. (n.d.). *MILESTONES: 1921–1936 The Immigration Act of 1924 (The Johnson-Reed Act)*. Office of the Historian. https://history.state.gov/milestones/1921-1936/immigration-act

Drop the Charges. (2020, October). VietLead. https://bit.ly/DTCShannon

Falkner, A., & Payne, K.A. (2021). "Courage to take on the bull": Cultural citizenship in fifth-grade social studies. *Theory & Research in Social Education, 49*(1), 78–106.

Flores, W. V. (1997). Citizens vs. citizenry: Undocumented immigrants and Latino cultural citizenship. In W. V. Flores & R. Benmayor (Eds.), *Latino cultural citizenship: Claiming identity, space, and rights* (pp. 255–277). Beacon Press.

Freire, P. (1970). *Pedagogy of the oppressed*. Continuum.

Gramlich, J. (2020, March 2). How border apprehensions, ICE arrests and deportations have changed under Trump. Pew Research Center. https://www.pewresearch.org/fact-tank/2020/03/02/how-border-apprehensions-ice-arrests-and-deportations-have-changed-under-trump

hooks, b. (1989). *Talking back: Thinking feminist, thinking Black*. Sheba Feminist Publishers.

hooks, b. (1994). *Teaching to transgress: Education as the practice of freedom*. Routledge.

hooks, b. (2014). *Teaching to transgress*. Routledge.

Ishizuka, K. L., & Chang, J. (2016). *Serve the people: Making Asian America in the long sixties*. Verso Books.

Kang, H.-K. S. (2010). *Cultural citizenship and immigrant community identity: Constructing a multi-ethnic Asian American community*. Lfb Scholarly Pub Llc.

Kawano, Y. (2019). *Storytelling of Indigenous and racialized women in the academy in Toronto: Implications for building counter-narrative learning spaces* [Unpublished doctoral dissertation]. University of Toronto.

Knight Abowitz, K., & Harnish, J. (2006). Contemporary discourses of citizenship. *Review of Educational Research, 76*(4), 653–690.

Kuoch, J. (2020). *"Deportable-refugees": Oral histories of the Southeast Asian Freedom Network (SEAFN)* [Unpublished master thesis]. University of California, Los Angeles.

Ladson-Billings, G. (2004). Culture versus citizenship: The challenge of racialized citizenship in the United States. In J. A. Banks (Ed.), *Diversity and citizenship education: Global perspectives* (pp. 99–126). Jossey-Bass.

Lawston, J. M., & Escobar, M. (2009–2010). Policing, detention, deportation, and resistance: Situating immigrant justice and carcerality in the 21st century. *Social Justice, 36*(2), 1–6.

Levinson, B. A. (2011). Toward an anthropology of (democratic) citizenship education. In B. A. Levinson & M. Pollock (Eds.), *A Companion to the anthropology of education* (pp. 279–298). Wiley Blackwell.

Ludden, J. (2006, May 9). *1965 Immigration law changed face of America. NPR: All Things Considered.* https://www.npr.org/templates/story/story.php?storyId=5391395

Ngai, M. (2004). *Impossible subjects: Illegal aliens and the making of modern America.* Princeton University Press.

Northeast Region Pardons Project. (n.d.). *History of Southeast Asian deportations.* www.nepardonproject.org/history-of-southeast-asian-deportations

Northeast Region Pardons Project. (2020, December). *Stop Trump's ban on work permits.* tiny.cc/ProtectWorkPermits

Parker, A. W. (1925). The ineligible to citizenship provisions of the Immigration Act of 1924. *The American Journal of International Law, 19,* 23–47.

Rodríguez, N. N. (2018). From margins to center: Developing cultural citizenship education through the teaching of Asian American history. *Theory & Research in Social Education, 46*(4), 528–573.

Rosaldo, R., & Flores, W. V. (1997). Identity, conflict, and evolving Latino communities: Cultural citizenship in San Jose, California. In W. V. Flores & R. Benmayor (Eds.), *Latino cultural citizenship: Claiming identity, space, and rights* (pp. 57–96). Beacon Press.

Saldaña, J. (2013). *The coding manual for qualitative researchers* (2nd ed.). Sage.

SEAFN (n.d.). Southeast Asian Freedom Network. https://seafn.org

Simanski, J. F. (2014). *Immigration enforcement actions: 2013.* Department of Homeland Security Office of Immigration Statistics.

Solórzano, D. G., & Yosso, T. J. (2002). Critical race methodology: Counter-storytelling as an analytical framework for education research. *Qualitative Inquiry, 8*(1), 23-44.

Southeast Asia Resource Action Center. (2020a, January 14). Asian American Organizations Denounce Deportations of over 30 Cambodian Americans at Beginning of 2020. SEARAC. https://www.searac.org/immigration/asian-american-organizations-denounce-deportations-of-over-30-cambodian-americans-at-beginning-of-2020/

Southeast Asia Resource Action Center. (2020b, August 7). Southeast Asian organizations denounce deportation of 30 Vietnamese Americans. SEARAC. https://www.searac.org/immigration/southeast-asian-organizations-denounce-deportation-of-30-vietnamese-americans/?fbclid=IwAR17jNZUSy2ZY5si7ESMzYDaTgtyGip3yIiOrS-kn7F_WV1Xw_tjbyl8xTU

Stumpf, J. (2006). The Crimmigration crisis: Immigrants, crime, and sovereign power. *American Law Review, 56*(2), 367–419.

Tuhiwai Smith, L. (2013). *Decolonizing methodologies: Research and Indigenous peoples.* Zed Books Ltd.

Truong, T. (2021). *Trinh v. Homan*: The indefinite detention of Vietnamese refugees in the 21st century. *Review of Law and Social Justice, 30*(3), 415–452.

Um, K. (2015). Crossing borders: Citizenship, identity and transnational activism in the Cambodian diaspora. In K. Um & S. Gaspar (Eds.), *Southeast Asian migration: People on the move in search of work, refuge, and belonging* (pp. 198–214). Sussex Academic Press.

Vang, C. Y. (2016). Southeast Asian Americans. In D. K. Yoo & E. Azuma (Eds.), *The Oxford handbook of Asian American history* (pp. 88–103). Oxford University Press.

Wheeler-Bell, Q. (2014). Educating the spirit of activism: A "critical" civic education. *Educational Policy, 28*(3), 463–486.

Wong, T. K. (2014). Nation of immigrants, or deportation nation? Analyzing deportations and returns in the United States, 1892–2010. In J. S. W. Park & S. Gleeson (Eds.), *The nation and its peoples: Citizens, denizens, migrants* (pp. 264–278). Routledge.

Yosso, T. J. (2005). Whose culture has capital? A critical race theory discussion of community cultural wealth. *Race Ethnicity and Education, 8*(1), 69–91.

CHAPTER 7

More Than Talk
Youth Poets' Civic Action and How Youth Spoken Word Prepares Minoritized Youths as Civic Actors

Camea Davis

> *Though, I am just one pin in a balloon named injustice*
> *One pebble in an ocean of systemic oppression*
> *One small kid*
> *Without privilege to leave a nation that hunts bodies like mine*
> *I speak*
> *and*
> *Act.*
>
> —*Research Poem by Author*

Minoritized youth poets are not only literary leaders, experts of their lived experiences, and radical truth-tellers that narrate a generation surviving America's urban cities and schools; many minoritized youth poets are also bold civic actors. They speak and act. They armor themselves with their voices and do civic actions that liberate.

I start with the story of minoritized youth poets' presence as civic actors to foreground their agency and action in the context of systemic intersecting oppressions they are forced to traverse. Evidence of the maltreatment forced upon this youth population is apparent in every comparative statistical analysis that compares their lives and learning to their white, middle-class peers. While useful to outline disparities, those measures have missed the brilliance and power minoritized youth employ to transform their worlds. I ground this work in a different starting place: youth spoken word (YSW) spaces in urban city centers. These spaces are exemplar locations of minoritized youth leading civic action and building political consciousness.

The objective of this chapter is to explain how minoritized youth poets ages 18 to 21 are civically active and their rationales for civic action. This research expands the knowledge of YSW communities as tools of literacy development, personal empowerment, and youth identity development to include how YSW can transform minoritized youths' civic lifeworlds. This study responds to Woodson and Love's (2019) call to rethink what civic empowerment should mean in studies of Black kids' civic sufficiency by inviting minoritized youth to self-define their civic actions and rationales.

IT ALL STARTED WITH THE WORD: DEFINING YOUTH SPOKEN WORD AND ITS USE

Spoken word, as used in this study, refers to the fusion of written poetry, acting techniques, and oratory to bring the poetic alive in performance (Weinstein & West, 2012). Spoken-word poets participate in the historical oral traditions of the African griot and later African American storytellers, who preserved history through orally presenting folktales, family stories, and ancestry (Fisher, 2003). Youth spoken word (YSW) is a vital youth culture within the broader hip hop culture that follows activist traditions of the civil rights movement and the Black Power Movement to amplify the voices and resistances of Black people (Petchauer, 2015).

Today, spoken word is engaged by many racial groups and featured in varied venues from street corners to United States presidential inaugurations. The purpose of YSW is typically to amplify youth voice. Numerous studies have substantiated youth voice through YSW as a powerful tool for youth empowerment, agency, and engagement in schooling (Fisher, 2005; Hill, 2009; Kim, 2013; Low, 2011; Winn, 2016). Additionally, youth poets' conceptions of citizenship (Fiore, 2015), politics (Cohen, 2006; Cohen & Kahne, 2011) and pedagogies for civic education (Kuttner, 2016) have been documented, yet there remains a need for research on the *civic actions* youth poets engage in.

CIVIC EDUCATION FOR MINORITIZED YOUTH

Much research on African American youth's civic engagement is mostly descriptive and comparative, detailing African American youth civic behaviors relative to other races; these studies provide no explanation for differences (Lopez, 2002; Sánchez-Jankowski, 2002). Scholars seeking to document accurate illustrations of minoritized youth civic engagement call for a conception of civic engagement specifically for minoritized youth due to the mischaracterization of this population as apathetic, deviant, and disengaged

(Woodson & Love, 2019). Cohen (2006) argued that methodologists that attempt to capture African American civic engagement may be employing flawed methods that are historically and culturally irrelevant to this population.

Civic education is significant for African American youth because, as Hope and Jagers (2014) found, African American youth were more engaged when they had a broad structural understanding of the inequities that exist; thus, African American youth who were exposed to civic education were more civically engaged. Collective responses to injustice are documented as effective in urban communities (Ginwright et al., 2005; Kim & Sherman, 2006). Related, Kirshner and Pozzoboni (2011) employed an asset-based youth development model to explore how youth respond to school closures in their communities and found that youth took meaningful actions toward school reform. Similarly, Checkoway (2013) studied youth who were civically active through community-based programs in economically disinvested and racially segregated areas to make a positive civic change in their communities. Checkoway cited youth-led community level acts as a model for a new civic education for minoritized youth.

DOCUMENTING THE CIVIC POWER OF THE POEM

Youth poets are civically adept. By identifying students' poems that expressed notions of active, transformative, and cultural versions of citizenship, Pellegrino et al. (2014) found that youth poets have civic knowledge and concerns. Similarly, Fiore (2015) argued that spoken word has a unique position to effect social change by providing students with a platform from which to question the conditions of their lives. Likewise, Ingalls (2012) analyzed the rhetoric of spoken word as one way to inspire civic action. Winn (2016) wrote: "Poetry writing invites youth to become civic actors in their homes, communities, and beyond by sharing their work" (p. 28), thus positioning youth poets as capable civic actors. There remains a need to understand the specific actions that youth poets accomplish.

Scholars have also studied YSW as a literary activism; activism is one enactment of civic engagement. For example, Vajra Watson (2016) argued that a literate citizenry is the foundation of democracy and found that YSW spaces equipped youth to be civically and politically conscious. Additionally, Muhammad and Gonzalez (2016) found that poetry performance provided youth a form of visible activism where they could see themselves as change agents. Scholars have made it apparent that YSW can equip youth with civic literacies and even inspire youth to take civic action, yet there remains a gap in documenting the specific civic actions youth poets execute outside of the writing and performance acts. This study fills this gap at the intersection of civic education and youth spoken-word literacy research to explain how minoritized youth poets ages 18 to 21 are civically active and why they take civic actions.

As a Black woman, former youth poet, current YSW organization leader, and poet-researcher, my research explored the following questions: How are youth poets civically active and why? How does spoken-word literacy equip youth poets to execute civic actions?

THEORETICAL FRAMEWORK

The theoretical framework begins with Dewey's (1916) conception of democratic education as capable of preparing an informed citizenry capable of fully realizing the benefits of the democratic society. Due to the failures of U.S. American democratic society evidenced by systemic oppressions, I add Freire's (1972) liberationism to understand transformation within a flawed democratic system. Freire's liberationism is one tool to better prepare citizens for a *just* democracy. Freire posits that human liberation, and consequently transforming society, requires a praxis of reflection *and action*. For Freire, reflection without action was mere chatter; action void of reflection was dangerous and uncritical activism. YSW poetry writing is an example of reflection that creates adequate space for action. The reflection on social issues and injustices is evidenced by the advanced political commentary in the poems that youths write (Hall, 2007; Jocson, 2006; Stovall, 2006); Yet, in a Freirean definition, voice alone is not sufficient to achieve liberation. Liberation requires action.

The writing and performance acts in YSW literacy are significant civic contributions, but the work cannot stop there. This research explores what other civic actions are inspired by engagement with YSW communities. During the research design, this conceptual framework was employed to select a methodology capable of practicing liberationist research by amplifying participant perceptions and experiences as an expert and allowing youth to self-define their civic actions.

CRITICAL POETIC INQUIRY METHODOLOGY

Critical Poetic Inquiry (CPI) (Davis, 2019; Davis & McTier, 2023) was employed as a methodology capable of practicing liberationist research by amplifying participant perceptions. CPI analysis amplifies participants' voices and synthesizes transcript themes to the most salient points through poetic re-presentation. The CPI process begins with collecting qualitative research data in the form of interview transcripts or written texts. The data are not initially in poetic form. The poet-researcher uses participant data as the raw material of the interpretive analytic process of poetry construction.

I conducted inductive coding of each transcript individually, followed by a thematic analysis of prevalent themes across all transcripts (Braun & Clarke, 2006). During each phase, I also wrote free-verse poetry as research memos to interpret the data. Last, themes about how participants collectively constructed meanings of specific codes such as "civic actions taken" or "rationales for civic actions" were synthesized into research poetry. In the research poems, all of the ideas and images are from the transcripts, but the poems are not constructed with direct quotes.

The critical aspect of this methodology probes whose voice is dominant, whose voice is subjugated, and why. I argue that CPI functions as a culturally relevant method that (1) produces trustworthy research findings, (2) uses cultural competence as a sense-making tool, and (3) develops research that can critique and address social inequity (Davis, 2019). Additionally, CPI allowed this research to construct counterstories (Solórzano & Yosso, 2002) of minoritized youth civic action and present the research findings as a form of protest to deficit-based gap studies of minoritized youth civic actions (Woodson & Love, 2019).

I conducted semi-structured interviews with 12 participants who earned the title of Youth Poet Laureates (YPL) in 2016–2017, were ages 18 to 21, and who identified as racially minoritized. The YPL program provided access to exemplary participants for this study because the program has a culture rooted in spoken word and a mission focused on identifying youth who are civically active.

FINDINGS

More Than Talk: Youth Poets Engage in Personal, Nontraditional, Diverse Civic Actions

Participants' activism was concentrated primarily on youth's local community contexts, which included neighborhoods where they live and attend school, as well as the local government. Participants discussed how the need to recognize themselves as members of the community inspired them to act because the work was contributing to people and places they valued. Freire's dialogic for liberation helps identify youths' focus on the self, first, and then in dialogue with the local contexts significant to a liberation strategy. Participants noted that as community members, their civic acts for the community benefited them as well. Participants responded to the specific urgent needs of their community, which required an acute awareness and involvement in the local community. Among the determined needs, participants prioritized urgent needs.

Furthermore, this study found that minoritized youth civic action is also personal because it is a response to individual youth's personal experiences with injustices or trauma. They understand the personal as a part of the systemic injustice.

For example, Brittany, an African American woman, college student, and resident of a low-income community, explained:

> It makes me think about the phrase the personal is political I think a young person who's civically active realizes that everything personal to them is also political . . . sometimes it's simple as waking up in the morning. Like how do you wake up? That's like a political act and a radical act depending on how you identify rather its Black, Mexican, Muslim, anything, Vietnamese.

Participants cited experiences such as being harassed by the police, being sexually assaulted, being racially profiled, or being attacked for religious affiliations as instances that inspired them to take civic action in their communities. Participants noted that their specific types of civic action required vulnerability. To be prepared as civic agents, youth noted interpersonal interactions were a mandatory.

For example, Dayonna described:

> I had brothers and an older sister and we all lived in this house and it was a lot of things happening in the house at the time. I was very timid. I didn't really know how to express myself in any kind of way. And I was in a house that had a lot of domestic violence happening all the time. I was like, yo I need some way to cope, and so writing seemed to be the best way. And then when I got to the teen center, I was like, yo it's a million other kids out here that are like me! Some are worst. It's like I need to be able to help them to help myself.

Participants intentionally engaged in civic actions that allowed them to positively contribute to communities that share their experiences.

A significant finding of this research is that minoritized youth participants in this study demonstrated a record of diverse types of civic actions that included traditional actions—those readily accepted and celebrated in Eurocentric paradigms of civic actions, such as engaging with electoral politics: lobbying, phone banking, working polls, campaigning, voting, canvassing, petitioning, fundraising, donating money to civic causes, community organizing, nonprofit leadership, providing resources to the needy (food, services, etc.), awareness raising, educating, community service, volunteering, natural disaster relief, and internships at civic organizations. Participants also engaged in nontraditional actions—those more pluralistic, diverse civic actions informed by participants' politicized identities and the roles those identities play in their sociopolitical contexts, such as, promoting literacy among struggling readers, creating safe places for minoritized persons counter to public protests, being a role model, self-care and self-love in the context of identity-based oppressions, performing poetry in political and civic spaces, digital community and coalition building, engaging in discussions, and encouraging and correcting in contexts of opposition and oppression. For example, Alya explained:

> Lately, I think self-care is choosing how I'm going to be an activist today. And that being an activist is something that I can take on and take off. But being a person in this world in the identities that I carry, I can't take those off. And if I have to protect myself by not being vocal once, then I will. But if I have to protect myself by being an activist in that moment, I will. And it's all about safety still.

Ayla's words demonstrate a nuance to Freire's (1972) action-reflection dialogic in which she is negotiating when action is safe or unsafe, and choosing reflection in the unsafe moments while being willing to take outward action when feeling safe to do so.

Also, Ninel, a Jamaican American entrepreneur, organizer, and multifaceted artist from a low-income community in a major urban city explained:

> So, I do things here because we need it. If I don't, then who will? So, it's sacrifice but at the same time, I'm learning to love myself regardless of all of the ugly things in the world. That's the hardest struggle for me right now is learning to love myself through the depression. Through the friends having their issues. Through the world being as chaotic and as it is through the names that get released in the press every couple of weeks, like through all of that stuff I still have to love myself. And that's been the biggest lesson to learn.

In these quotes, participants explain that caring for themselves prepares them to best serve and care for others in healthy ways and allows them to nurture their own self-efficacy. Most important, several participants identified that self-care is an essential act that allows them to survive the exhaustion of the more traditional civic actions.

To continue, minoritized youth participated in actions they felt they had access to and could yield. This is mediated by their holistic cultural identities, which include but are not limited to age, race, class, socioeconomic status, geographic location, country of origin, and religion. Due to systemic barriers, such as poverty, some actions were not accessible to participants. Also, participants had to evaluate the personal, financial, physical, and emotional risks as minoritized people in taking certain actions depending on their holistic, cultural identities. For example, participants living and working on college campuses had to evaluate if certain actions would jeopardize their financial aid and if they could literally afford to take such an action. For example, Brittany explained the thing with protesting here on campus is it's a PWI, predominately white institution, and then for me, it's just like I'm a first-generation college student. I'm here on scholarship and things like that so I'm not going to walk out of class. Then the time it happened . . . I was like darn it's right when class starts.

Likewise, work–life balance was a concern. These youth are people with full lives and competing priorities, not always afforded the unlimited time, resources, or other privileges to participate in civic action.

It's Personal: Why Youth Poets Take Civic Action

Table 7.1 presents participants names, ethnic identities, and rationes for their civic actions evidenced by one direct quote from each of their transcripts. These quotes demonstrate a personal connection toward civic actions that youth characterize as spiritual, intuitive, and ancestral.

Table 7.1. Participants' Chosen Names, Ethnic Identities, and Rationales for Civic Actions.

	Participant Name	Ethnic Identity	Rationale for Actions
1	Ayla	Multiracial; Black, Chinese, Vietnamese	"Because I believe in my ancestors that this is a right and a blessing that I have to protect: being an activist."
2	Brittany	African American/Black	"I can't keep it in, and I feel like this is part of who I am."
3	Dayonna	African American/Black	"When I realized that my voice mattered, I realized that is the reason why I do what I do."
4	Dominique	African American/Black	"It's just innate. . . . It brings me joy. It feels like a purpose; it feels like my purpose."
5	Hajjar	Afghan-Kurdish	"People are worth it. . . . If I am to care for people, I have to fight for them too."
6	Hannah	Sierra Leonean American	"I've been silent for too long. . . . Basically, I realized that I shoot back with my tongue."
7	Kenny	African American/Black	"It's important to stick up for family and friends, and I've been trying to do a better job of it cause I'm not the best, but that's why the civic work we do is so important and that's what keeps me doing it."

Table 7.1. (continued)

	Participant Name	Ethnic Identity	Rationale for Actions
8	Muhammed	Guinean American	"Because I want to create a change within this world."
9	Nijahn	African American	"You get fed up. You sit there and you're like, dang, so who's going to fix this problem? Then you realize that could be you, and you're like, 'Oh, OK. I can do something about this.' And I think once you do it, the thing that really motivates me is the fact that once you do it, somebody is going to be behind you."
10	Ninel	Jamaican American and African American/Black	"If I don't touch these people, then I will be leaving a demographic untouched."
11	Ogechi	Nigerian American	"I have something that the world needs, and I have the capabilities. I have the tenacity and the determination to make all of them happen."
12	Sharon	Fujianese American	"I want to make a positive impact on the world."

Some names are pseudonyms, and some are participants' legal names that they requested be used.

COMMUNITY EXPECTATION—LIBERATIONIST PRAXIS OF YSW REQUIRED ACTION

Youth poets in this study explained rationales for civic action that include community responsibility and the YSW community's expectation that youth poets take actions that align with themes in their poetry performance. Participants described taking civic actions because their mentors helped them identify their civic power and agency in the present moment as youth. It's important to note that all participants had engaged in the YSW community for numerous years prior to participating in this research. For example, Ogechi stated, "My mentors really did open my eyes in the sense of what I could actually do right now, not even like 5 years down the line or 10 years when I'm an adult but what I can physically do right now." Similarly, Dayonna explained, "Coming to [the teen center] there were things I didn't know I could do as a youth that they opened me up to. Like there's a whole different spectrum of things that I experienced. That's whether it was walking in the community. Whether it was teaching camps." YSW mentors also modeled civic actions and invited youth to engage with them. Brittany described her YSW mentors: "They are both very active in the community and the poetry scene and so seeing them made me realize I should do this. They were role models, and they're very encouraging, too." Ayla commented: "We have a lot of really good connections with the whole city because all of our coaches are also activists. We always got to be in different activist spaces and learn from each other." Participants in this research modeled their civic actions after their mentors, who were civic leaders present in their local communities.

Participants overwhelmingly explained that they took civic actions because civic action was an expectation in the YSW community. As a result, their slam poetry coaches, mentors, and peers all expected them to engage in purposeful actions related to themes they wrote about in their poetry. For example, Dayonna explained: "One thing about where I'm from and my city, we don't just spit poems. We activists too." Similarly, Ogechi described that "the civic engagement that we do there was just like a part of being on the team. You didn't really see it as another project." These quotes illustrate how participants understood civic action as a mandatory element of being leaders in the YSW community. Kenny explained: "I feel like [civic action] is very necessary as a performance poet, and it separates the people who are just gaining something from this oppression and those who are working to stop it." Kenny's comment demonstrates that youth are keenly aware of the broader sociopolitical context in which their literary work exists and feel obligated not only to speak about social issues but also to take civic action to address them.

Mentors in YSW programs prepared participants to engage in civic action by explicitly teaching them the language, skills, mindsets, and effective organizing strategies needed to engage in civic action. For example, Ogehci discussed attending workshops on how to lobby for juvenile justice rights in her community. Additionally, Nijahn discussed at his YSW organization how he was explicitly taught how to engage with white police officers and know his citizen rights. As an example, he helped organize and lead a "solidarity meeting" between Black youth in his community and the local police department.

DISCUSSION

The purpose of this research was to describe what civic actions minoritized youth poets took and why they took them. Youth Poet Laureates served as an exemplar subset of minoritized youth as participants for this research due to their demonstrated concern for civic issues. This research amplified these minoritized youth civic actions as a counter-narrative to the prevailing idea that minoritized youth are civically inept.

This research found that minoritized youth poets were civic leaders who engaged in a robust list of civic actions, including forms of arts activism, raising awareness through education and social media, protesting, community organizing, and electoral politics. This population viewed civic action as a personal and political project through which their intersectional identities were mediated. Participants demonstrated that the process of reflecting through YSW writing and performing was tethered to their desire and preparedness to take civic action.

The repeated presence of arts activism as a form of civic action affirmed former research citing YSW as activism (Kim, 2013; Muhammad & Gonzalez, 2016; Watson, 2016). Significant is that participants understood YSW literacy and civic action as the same project committed to social justice. Participants put their YSW in nonpoetic, often political, spaces and used it as one form of civic action. At the same time, participants discussed being mentored by poetry coaches who were also activists to learn the language and strategies to engage in effective civic acts. These findings demonstrate the power of adult-to-youth mentoring relationships characterized by shared respect, autonomy, and modeling of civic action.

Important civic education is taking place in YSW spaces that expands the use beyond literacy education into civic education that equips youth to engage in civic actions. Centering minoritized youths' communities as assets and adults in those same communities as civic education experts can address the civic debt, "where systemic political inequities accumulate and manifest in civic performance gaps" (Lo, 2019, p. 114). The civic education in YSW spaces can address the lack of racial dialogue in the classroom and the normative teaching of Eurocentric political philosophy (Lo, 2019) because YSW mentors teach using critical liberationist theory. Thus, there is an added civic significance to YSW.

Further, this research aligns with Woodson and Love's (2019) argument for centering Black kids' "enoughness" in civic education research. While not all participants in this research were Black, they were all from minoritized racial identities, and thus their self-reported and defined civic actions affirm minoritized youths' civic sufficiency. This study responds to Woodson and Love's call to rethink what civic empowerment should mean in studies of Black kids' civic sufficiency by inviting minoritized youth to self-define their civic actions and their rationales for practicing them. Equally, this research broadens definitions of what counts as civic action to include the significance of arts-based and personal civic actions. Including arts alongside traditional civic acts resists the erasure of these youths' actions from the civic education literature.

IMPLICATIONS

This research cautions YSW practitioners not to leave the civic agency piece out or allow it to stop at the performance and written level. To center youth stories and not their social subjugation in the civic world, nor give them access to make a civic change, is violent. Youths' humanity is compromised as merely performative. In turn, performance poetry can become a type of blackface in which minoritized youth bodies are placed as props to signal a shallow inclusivity. Youth deserve more.

Civic education practitioners can create more space in curricula to center art, social justice, and racial identity development, and to be intentional in teaching critical political theory as routes to civic action. Educators could invite youth to boardrooms to make decisions concerning their lives, learning, and communities. Civic educators could also consider inviting community-based mentors who are experts on preparing youth for civic action into learning spaces as experts and illuminating the YSW spaces as assets in minoritized communities. They should also understand and engage with YSW spaces as civic centers leading critically relevant democratic education.

REFERENCES

Braun, V., & Clarke, V. (2006). Using thematic analysis in psychology. *Qualitative Research in Psychology, 3*(2), 77–101.

Checkoway, B. (2013). Education for democracy by young people in community-based organizations. *Youth & Society, 45*(3), 389–403.

Cohen, C. (2006). African American youth: Broadening our understanding of politics, civic engagement and activism. Youth Activism. Social Science Research Council.

Cohen, C. J., & Kahne, J. (2011). Participatory politics. New media and youth political action. http://ictlogy.net/bibliography/reports/projects.php?idp=2180&lang=es

Davis, C. (2019). Sampling poetry, pedagogy, and protest to build methodology: Critical poetic inquiry as cultural relevant method. *Qualitative Inquiry, 27*(1), 114–124. https://doi.org/10.1177/1077800419884978

Davis, C., & McTier, S. A. (2023). A call & response critical poetic inquiry of resistance ideologies among teachers and Black youth. *International Journal of Qualitative Studies in Education, 36*(5), 759–773. https://doi.org/10.1080/09518398.2022.2025469

Dewey, J. (1916) *Democracy and education: An introduction to the philosophy of education.* Macmillan.

Fiore, M. (2015). Pedagogy for liberation: Spoken word poetry in urban schools. *Education and Urban Society, 47*(7), 813–829.

Fisher, M. T. (2003). Choosing literacy: African diaspora participatory literacy communities. https://elibrary.ru/item.asp?id=8828349

Fisher, M. T. (2005). Literocracy: Liberating language and creating possibilities: An introduction. *English Education, 37*(2), 92–95.

Freire, P. (1972). *Pedagogy of the oppressed.* Translated by Myra Bergman Ramos. Herder. https://pdfs.semanticscholar.org/64a7/9f89a714dc4d2d845597bb342a72443ace71.pdf

Ginwright, S., Cammarota, J., & Noguera, P. (2005). Youth, social justice, and communities: Toward a theory of urban youth policy. *Social Justice, 32*(3 (101), 24–40.

Hall, H. R. (2007). Poetic expressions: Students of color express resiliency through metaphors and similes. *Journal of Advanced Academics, 18*(2), 216–244.

Hill, M. L. (2009). *Beats, rhymes, and classroom life: Hip-Hop pedagogy and the politics of identity*. Teachers College Press.

Hope, E. C., & Jagers, R. J. (2014). The role of sociopolitical attitudes and civic education in the civic engagement of Black youth. *Journal of Research on Adolescence, 24*(3), 460–470. http://doi.org/10.1111/jora.12117

Ingalls, R. (2012). "Stealing the air": The poet-citizens of youth spoken-word. *Journal of Popular Culture, 45*(1), 99–117.

Jocson, K. (2006). There's a better word: Urban youth rewriting their social worlds through poetry. *Journal of Adolescent & Adult Literacy, 49*(8), 700–709.

Kim, J., & Sherman, R. F. (2006). Youth as important civic actors: From the margins to the center. *National Civic Review, 95*(1), 3–6.

Kim, R. (2013). "Never knew literacy could get at my soul": On how words matter for youth, or notes toward decolonizing literacy. *The Review of Education/Pedagogy/Cultural Studies, 35*. https://doi.org/10.1080/10714413.2013.842868

Kirshner, B., & Pozzoboni, K. M. (2011). Student interpretations of a school closure: Implications for student voice in equity-based school reform. *Teachers College Record, 113*(8), 1633–1667.

Kuttner, P. J. (2016). Hip-hop citizens: Arts-based, culturally sustaining civic engagement pedagogy. *Harvard Educational Review, 86*(4), 527–555.

Lo, J. (2019) The role of civic debt in democratic education. *Multicultural Perspectives, 21*(2), 112–118.

Lopez, M. H. (2002). Civic engagement among minority youth. CIRCLE.

Low, B. (2011). *Slam school: Learning through conflict in the hip-hop and spoken word classroom*. Stanford University Press.

Muhammad, G., & Gonzalez, L. (2016). Slam poetry: An artistic resistance toward identity, agency, and activism. Equity & Excellence in Education. *University of Massachusetts School of Education Journal, 49*(4), 440–453.

Pellegrino, A. M., Zenkov, K., & Aponte-Martinez, G. (2014). Middle school students, slam poetry and the notion of citizenship. *Journal of Educational Controversy, 8*(1), 8.

Petchauer, E. (2015). Starting with style: toward a second wave of hip-hop education research and practice. *Urban Education, 50*(1), 78–105. https://doi.org/10.1177/0042085914563181

Sánchez-Jankowski, M. (2002). Minority youth and civic engagement: the impact of group relations. *Applied Developmental Science, 6*(4), 237–245. doi:10.1207/S1532480XADS0604_11

Solórzano, D. G., & Yosso, T. J. (2002). Critical race methodology: Counter-storytelling as an analytical framework for education research. *Qualitative Inquiry, 8*(1), 23–44. https://doi.org/10.1177/107780040200800103

Stovall, D. (2006). Urban poetics: Poetry, social justice and critical pedagogy in education. *Urban Review, 38*(1), 63–80. https://doi.org/10.1007/s11256-006-0027-5

Watson, V. M. (2016). Literacy is a civil write: The art, science, and soul of transformative classrooms. In R. Papa, D. M. Eadens, & D. W. Eadens (Eds.), *Social justice instruction: Empowerment on the chalkboard* (pp. 307–323). Springer International Publishing.

Weinstein, S., & West, A. (2012). Call and responsibility: Critical questions for youth spoken word poetry. *Harvard Educational Review, 82*(2), 282–302.

Winn, M. T. (2016). Still writing in rhythm: Youth poets at work. *Urban Education*, 1–37.

Woodson, A., & Love, B. (2019). Outstanding: Centering Black kids' enoughness in civic education research. *Multicultural Perspectives, 21*(2), 91–96.

Part III

POSSIBILITIES FOR CIVIC EDUCATION

CHAPTER 8

Black Feminist Pedagogy for Anti-Racist Civics

Tiffany Mitchell Patterson, Natasha C. Murray-Everett, and Crystal Simmons

> Black women have had to develop a larger vision of our society than perhaps any other group. They have had to understand white men, white women, and Black men. And they have had to understand themselves. When Black women win victories, it is a boost for virtually every segment of society.
>
> —Angela Davis

In the field of social studies, the mission and goal is to prepare future citizens who are well-informed, engaged, and effective participants for a globalized world. Scholars within the discipline have researched and discussed the implications of civics-based instruction in social studies classrooms. However, civic education as originally conceptualized is rooted in racist assimilation notions that have long been critiqued by scholars of Color (Howard, 2003; Ladson-Billings, 2003; Marshall, 2003; Tyson, 2003). Even the term "citizen" and who is viewed as a citizen is widely contested. More specifically, citizenship and race have long been inextricably connected. For example, while Black people may legally possess rights as citizens with the passage of the Fourteenth Amendment (1868), Fifteenth Amendment (1870), Civil Rights Act (1964), and Voting Rights Act (VRA; 1965), the uptick in anti-Black racism and racial violence is a reminder that Black Americans do not reap the full benefits of citizenship (Vickery, 2017). We view this as problematic given many of the civil rights gained by various groups in this country are the result of Black Americans' efforts, and more specifically, the result of Black women whose marginalized and intersectional identities (as both Black and women) give them a unique purview of what citizenship means for some and what it doesn't mean for others.

Renewed interest in civic education and anti-racism from the political right and the left provide an important window of opportunity for how to (re)conceptualize civics and what it means to teach for a democracy that is racially and socially just. More recently, the concept of anti-racism has reemerged in the wake of COVID-19, rampant anti-Black racism, and racial violence toward Black bodies at the hands of the police. Following the 2020 presidential election cycle, we saw numerous headlines referencing the role of Black women in saving American democracy—"Black women are heroes" (Brewton-Johnson, 2021); "Black women are the backbone of American democracy" (Stevens, 2020, para. 31)—and noting how Black women have always been at the forefront of nearly every progressive social movement in the United States. These are not falsehoods by any means. Although we are the first to show up, we are the last to be saved.

At the heart of anti-racism is a call to action to push back on and confront the systemic racism that is entrenched in society. Anti-racist teaching, practice, and education is justice-oriented and political. It is a part of a broader understanding of racial justice. According to Cynthia Tyson (2003), "Social studies education with a strong civic education component would include lessons about power, about intellectual frameworks that are analytical, critical, and action-oriented" (p. 20). One of the frameworks often utilized to critique and analyze social studies and civic education is critical race theory (CRT). CRT scholars in social studies have examined the ways curriculum, the profession, and policies continue to support and create racial inequities in classrooms. As Ladson-Billings (2003) argues: "CRT can serve as an analytic tool to explain the systematic omissions, distortions, and lies that plague the field" (p. 9). A singular approach to understanding oppression may not take into account the multifaceted ways in which oppressions overlap with one another. Coles and Pasek (2020) note:

> Considering that large-scale social justice movements are often framed around single specific axes of identity or oppression (e.g., feminism, antiracism), the intersectional invisibility of Black women may hinder these movements' abilities to address Black women's unique concerns. At a time when both feminist and antiracist movements face criticism for not adequately addressing the needs of Black women (Grzanka, 2019), we must develop a deeper understanding of what leads to Black women's invisibility. (p. 2)

This chapter utilizes Black feminist pedagogy to recenter the civic knowledge, scholarship, and activism of Black women in disrupting hegemonic and oppressive systems rooted in capitalism, sexism, and racism as it relates to the classroom (Henry, 2005; Omolade, 1987). Black women have developed strategies and practices to combat white supremacy and patriarchy. The historical evolution or waves of Black feminism is evident in U.S. and global movements for liberation as Black women have continually offered a political paradigm for progressive agendas (Berry & Gross, 2020; Jones, 2020; Taylor, 1998).

This work is not an exhaustive list or approach and builds upon the historical legacy of Black women activists. Furthermore, it may be helpful for educators who have already engaged in the historical knowledge of race and racism and have a recognition of how civics needs to include the contributions of Black women who have played a crucial role in saving American democracy. This could also serve as an entry point to educators seeking to glean lessons on Black feminist pedagogies that can foster anti-racist civics. This is also for educators who are asking the questions, "What's next?" and "How do we do this work with students?"

We will discuss civic education briefly, and then explore how Black women problematize civics and engage in Black feminist pedagogy. We offer a framework, RESPECT, as the crux of this chapter, which will provide social studies teachers with a blueprint for how to authentically implement anti-racist work of Black women by centering their lived experiences and activism. We conclude the chapter with a call to action for social studies educators to engage in anti-racist civics.

BLACK WOMEN PROBLEMATIZING CIVICS

Historically, the inception of traditional civic curriculum is largely rooted in white supremacist notions of assimilation, much of which persists today. For example, absent are the ways Black women participate in maintaining, strengthening, and improving communities and society. Learning civics from within the experiences and knowledge of Black women can help us to achieve these goals more fully. When we think about the field of social studies and how we have theorized and problematized civic education, we do not always value or privilege the knowledge, the lived experiences, or the activism of Black women in our discussions. Groups in the margins of U.S. society have been the conscience of America and the main sites for struggles to close the gap between American democratic ideals and institutionalized racism and discrimination (Banks, 2008). Black women educators and social studies scholars (Duncan, 2020; Ladson-Billings, 2003; Marshall, 2003; Preston-Grimes, 2007; Tyson, 2003; Vickery, 2017) have long problematized traditional civic education, from a critical race theoretical lens to honoring Black education pedagogies that enact an intersectional and anti-racist lived civics. In both the theoretical and practical sense, Black women educators have unique insight to the omission and distortion of Black women and their civic agency (Vickery, 2017) and offer a perspective to challenge the limitations of traditional civic education.

Throughout the Black Freedom Struggle, African Americans have theorized and written about the complexities of democracy and advocated for the importance of an informed citizenry to achieve equity and justice

(Preston-Grimes, 2007). Activist educator Nannie Helen Burroughs (2019) captures this sentiment in the following statement:

> Education and justice are democracy's only life insurance. Without these mere armourment is so much junk and high preachments about democracy. We talk much about making America safe for democracy. The only way to make America safe for democracy is to make her what she is supposed to be in matters of justice and equality of opportunity for all her citizens. (p. 124)

Similarly, Dr. Anna Julia Cooper, often referred to as the mother of Black feminism, believed that the access to an equitable education for Black youth rooted in dismantling racially embedded systems of power are the key for youth to be prepared for the realities of society they will face (Johnson, 2009). Black women educators have continuously advocated for an antiracist civic education to disrupt systems of oppression. Through critical race theory (CRT), Black women education scholars extended conceptualizations of civic education by utilizing CRT to bring to light the ways in which race/ism is deeply embedded within social studies (Ladson-Billings, 2003; Tyson, 2003). The lens, curricula, and instructional delivery through which civic education is understood has a profound impact on how it is taught. Marshall (2003) notes that "the agenda for citizenship education can never be deracialized and at the same time, be democratic, dynamic, and in step with the actuality of life in these United States" (p. 93). In sum, Black women teachers have attempted to foster a critical citizenry in which students are taught to read the word and the world around them (Freire, 1987). Black women educator experiences inform Black feminist pedagogy as an emancipatory endeavor that asserts the need for an intersectional approach to liberation in education. Therefore, social studies educators must take heed of the practices of Black women teachers and scholars in order to inspire students as future citizens to use their voices and take action to help create a more equitable community and society (Vickery, 2017).

BLACK FEMINIST PEDAGOGY

Black feminism is an outgrowth of the "broader antiracist project of African American social and political thought" (Collins, 2000 p. 96). Black women have historically advocated for multifaceted freedoms based on their intersectional lived experiences in racist, classist, and patriarchal societies. Black feminist thought emerges from the viewpoint that Black women's collective historical experiences with overlapping oppressions may stimulate a self-defined Black women's standpoint that in turn can foster Black women's activism (Collins, 2000). Thus, Black feminism is expansive with many tensions and conceptualizations. However, Collins (2000) has identified core themes of Black feminist thought, which include (1) analyzing Black women's work (paid and unpaid), (2) challenging stereotypical and controlling images through self-definition, (3) intersectionality and sex politics, and (4) intellectual and social activism. At the core of Black feminism is Black women's organizing and activism, which continues to offer a political paradigm for progressive agendas. Yet, the work of Black women and girls as sociopolitical change agents in society and in racial justice work in schools continues to be marginalized (Kelly, 2020). A Black feminist pedagogy "sets forth learning strategies informed by Black women's historical experience with race, gender, class bias and the consequences of marginality and isolation" (Omolade, 1987, p. 31). Black feminist pedagogy can be a powerful lens to engage in anti-racist civic education. The core tenets of Black feminist pedagogy (Henry, 2005; Omolade, 1987) are rooted in activism and social change, which include (1) providing critical analysis and interpretations of society through Black women's experiences, (2) a critical lens to interrogate and dismantle power relationships in the classroom, and (3) allowing for alternative ways to teach and to understand oneself and the complexities of the world. In the next section we will discuss our RESPECT framework that centers the anti-racist work of Black women through their lived experiences and activism.

RESPECT: A FRAMEWORK FOR ANTI-RACIST CIVICS

Utilizing the underpinnings of Black feminist pedagogy, we wanted to create a framework and guide for teaching and embracing the civic knowledge, scholarship, and activism of Black women who have and continue to model for the nation and the world what it means to be a global citizen. As Vickery (2017) has encouraged teacher educators to think about their role in the fight for humanity and citizenship, we have created a mnemonic grounded in a Black Feminist perspective. Given that Black women deserve respect in the foundation of this work we utilized the Queen of Soul Aretha Franklin's song "RESPECT" to identify the following seven tenets: R–Revolutionary, E–Epistemology, S–Self-Determination, P–Political and Social Activism, E–Emancipatory, C–Collectivism, and T–Truth-Telling. Each section is guided by popular phrases and quotes from Black women scholars and activists. It is our hope that this framework will be used and implemented in social studies methods courses and classrooms as a way to include and frame the transformational work of Black women in the pursuit of and fight for citizenship.

Revolutionary

> Revolution is a serious thing, the most serious thing about a revolutionary's life. When one commits oneself to the struggle, it must be for a lifetime.
>
> —A. Y. Davis (1972)

Black feminist scholar Joy James (1999) defines the term *revolutionary* as "dynamic movement rather than fixed stasis within a political praxis relevant to changing material conditions and social consciousness" (pp. 19–20). For Black women, the fight for liberation is longstanding. Despite this long and historical narrative of oppression, Black women have had to adjust, adopt, and utilize new strategies and methods to counter the racial injustices of their times. For example, the methods and strategies employed by Black women abolitionists to destroy the institution of slavery are vastly different from the grassroots organizing of Black women during the height of Jim Crow. Regardless, Black women have been, and continue to be, revolutionary whether they are fighting on the front lines organizing or protesting, serving in a political capacity, serving their communities, or protecting their families and children. Black women participate in and advocate for democracy even when they are systematically excluded from reaping its benefits.

In more recent times, Black women's political participation has proven to be instrumental in the pursuit of "saving democracy." As mentioned earlier, a general Google search of Black women during the 2016 and 2020 election cycles would reveal numerous news headlines declaring Black women as "heroes" and the "backbone" of democracy. More specifically, the work of Stacey Abrams in Georgia and her community organization Fair Fight were responsible for turning the state blue for the first time in 30 years and electing its first Black and Jewish senators. These revolutionary acts of Black women like Abrams who led grassroots efforts in mobilizing and registering the Black and Brown vote, despite broken and failed promises by the very democracy we fight for, are necessary for our own liberation. By acknowledging these acts, we can critically examine the hypocrisy that undergirds our democracy.

Epistemology

> Radical black feminists have never confined their vision to just Black emancipation of Black women or women in general, or all black people for that matter. Rather they are the theorists and proponents of a radical humanism committed to liberating humanity and reconstructing social relations across the board.
>
> —R.D.G. Kelley (2002, p. 137)

In many ways, Black feminist thought is more than a definition or theory, it is a way of knowing, being, and advocating for the full liberation of Black women and others. The unique vantage point of Black women has allowed us to advocate for liberation in totality not in part. Patricia Hill Collins (2000) has argued that epistemology determines not only what and how knowledge is used but why people believe what they believe to be true. Furthermore, Collins (2009) articulates that "power relations shape who is believed and why" (p. 328). As a result, Black women have had to validate each other and affirm universal truths. Collins has thus identified four dimensions of Black feminist epistemology: (1) lived experiences to constitute meaning, (2) use of dialogue, (3) ethics of personal accountability, and (4) the ethic of caring (p. 328). Through these four dimensions (and others) Black women have explained and analyzed the multiple ways in which their identities have been impacted by the interlocking forms of oppression. More importantly, they have demonstrated how the knowledge they have constructed has led to their fight for justice and empowerment.

Self-Determination

> I will not have my life narrowed down. I will not bow down to somebody else's whim or to someone else's ignorance.
>
> —b. hooks (Angelou & hooks, 1998, para. 20)

Black women are determined and resolute to change the oppressive structures that hold them back. They are agents of their own change. Despite the stereotypical narratives and controlling images that exist as it relates to Black women in society, we stand in our power. At the core of Black feminism is Black women's organizing and activism, which continue to offer a political paradigm for progressive agendas. Barbara Smith (2000) reminds us that Black women have long worked to challenge heteronormative, racist, sexist, classist, and oppressive structures. Black women have engaged in numerous forms of activism both privately and publicly. Freedom waits on no one, and Black women are acutely aware of this. Yet, they have asked no one for permission to work toward that freedom. In fact, their self-determination is an act of liberation. Black women have proven this, whether it was Harriet Tubman and her revolutionary stance against the institution of slavery; Sojourner Truth demanding that the rights of Black women be included in the struggle for women's suffrage; Madame C. J. Walker, determined to be a self-made entrepreneur and millionaire; or Fannie Lou Hamer demanding a seat and representation in the pursuit for democracy. Countless Black women continue to be self-determined in their recognition and demands for racial, social, political, and economic justice.

Political and Social Activism

> Black women have always demanded and done more.
>
> —C. Carruthers (2018, p. 38)

One of the earliest examples of political and social activism by Black women was during the anti-slavery movement. However, within the narrative and discussion of abolitionism, the contributions and anti-racist work of Black women often take a back seat to the work of William Lloyd Garrison and Frederick Douglass. Black women abolitionists are also overshadowed by the zealous efforts of white women abolitionists. Black women such as Maria Stewart, Frances Harper, Elizabeth Freeman, Sarah Parker Redmon, Mary Prince, Sarah Forten, and Charlotte L. Forten Grimke, to name a few, often go nameless in the historiography of abolitionism. However, through their brave and daring work, these women paved the way and stage for Black women and male activists to come. For example, Maria Stewart, in the 1830s, was the first woman to make public anti-slavery, political, and feminist speeches to racially integrated crowds. As scholar Marilyn Richardson noted:

> A bold and militant orator, she called on Black women to develop their highest intellectual capacities, to enter into all spheres of the life of the mind, and to participate in all activities within their community, from religion and education to politics and business, without apology to notions of female subservience. Her original synthesis of religious, abolitionist, and feminist concerns places her squarely in the forefront of Black female activist and literary tradition only now beginning to be acknowledged as of integral significance to the understanding of the history of Black thought and culture in America. (Stewart & Richardson, 1987, pp. xiii–xiv)

Following in the groundbreaking work of these Black women abolitionists, leaders of the 19th and 20th centuries such as Ida B. Wells Barnett, Amy Ashwood Garvey, Mittie Maude Lena Gordon, Ella Baker, Rosa Parks, Claudette Colvin, and many others continued their political and social advocacy. Keisha Blain (2020) discusses how women like Garvey and Gordon worked to promote liberation abroad as well. In Blain's (2020) analysis of these 20th-century Black-nationalist women, "individuals who advocated for black liberation, economic self-sufficiency, racial pride, unity, and self-determination" (para. 2), she cites Amy Ashwood Garvey, co-founder of the Universal Negro Improvement Association (UNIA) and wife of Marcus Garvey. According to Amy Ashwood Garvey, "The Negro question is no longer a local one. But of the Negroes of the world, joining hands and fighting for one common cause" (para. 4). For Blain, Garvey broadened the plight for liberation to include the struggles of peoples of African descent globally. Black women understand that freedom is not limited to the national stage. The fight for liberation must be global. As we see in more contemporary times, Black women continue to do this work through political and social activism.

Emancipatory

> The women of the Combahee River Collective believed that another world was possible, one in which Black women, and thus all of humanity, were freed from systems of oppression and exploitation, as the result of a collective struggle that reached down to the roots of the problems we face.
>
> —K.-Y. Taylor (2020, para. 22)

As discussed in the social and political activism of Black women, the quest for freedom—socially, economically, and politically—has and continues to be the primary goal. However, the interlocking systems of oppression (racial, sexual, heterosexual, and class oppression) create barriers that prevent true emancipation and liberation. Black women understand and can attest to the ways they are targeted and impacted by these oppressions. Through their experiences, Black women's politicization and radicalization emerged, hence the creation of the term identity politics by the Combahee River Collective. The Combahee River Collective (1977) was a group of Black feminists who worked together to address the oppressions that all women of Color experienced. By focusing on their identities and how they came to understand their oppression, Black women became active politically and socially, thus forming strategies to combat and challenge these multiple levels of domination. Black women know that if they are free, then everyone will be free, since their liberation would mean a destruction of these oppressive systems. Through this we can analyze the ways a destruction of these systems leads to a democracy that is racially and socially just.

Collectivism

> We realize that the only people who care enough about us to work consistently for our liberation are us. Our politics evolve from a healthy love for ourselves, our sisters and our community which allows us to continue our struggle and work.
>
> —Combahee River Collective (1977 para. 9)

To follow with the idea of emancipation, the Combahee River Collective (1977) also understood the importance of solidarity and coalition building. As noted in the quote above, the only people who care enough about

Black women consistently for their liberation are Black women. There are many historical and contemporary examples of collective organizing, which remains a longstanding tradition of Black women. As we think back to Black women abolitionists—the Atlanta washerwomen of 1881, the National Association of Colored Women, the National Council for Negro Women, the Student Nonviolent Coordinating Committee, the Women's Political Council, Fair Fight, and the Movement for Black Lives, just to name a few—we are reminded that Black women abolitionists were active members of anti-slavery organizations, in which Yee (1992) finds that "community building, political organizing, and forging a network of personal and professional friendships as activists" (p. 2) were central. With growing collective action and labor-related efforts in the Reconstruction era, Atlanta domestic workers formed the Washing Society in 1881 and launched a successful labor strike that organized thousands, resulting in higher wages (Hunter, 1997). A group of Black professional women had a record of organizing as the Women's Political Council (WPC) of Montgomery, Alabama, and had already planned a citywide boycott prior to the well-known Montgomery Bus Boycott. The organizing prowess of the WPC was instrumental in the boycott's long-term success (King Encyclopedia, n.d.). Further, domestic workers were a large percentage of boycotters, as Davis (2016) eloquently described: "Even though we may not know the names of all of those women who refused to ride the bus from poor Black communities to affluent white communities in Montgomery, Alabama, it seems that we should at least acknowledge their collective accomplishment. That boycott would not have been successful without their refusals, without their critical refusals" (p. 58). Through these examples of collectivism, we come to understand that systemic change requires more than just one person, but rather the collective action of everyday people—in this case, Black women.

Truth-Telling

The way to right wrongs is to turn the light of truth upon them.

—I. B. Wells-Barnett (1895)

Black women have always been radical truth-tellers because they had to be. In the words of Barbara Smith (2020), "if nothing else Black feminism deals in home truths in analysis and in practice" (p. 37). Liberation requires truth, and so does anti-racism. Consequences are often associated with truth-telling efforts, but Black women have been willing to risk their lives for the sake of freedom and liberation. Be it through their words, music, art, dance, writings, teaching, politics, activism, care, or love, the truth has been at the heart of Black women's civic knowledge and participation. This truth is unapologetic, speaks truth to power, and centers the full humanity of Black women—and as a byproduct, the full humanity of everyone. As Ida B. Wells-Barnett emphasizes, the dismantling of oppressive systems and the revealing of injustices requires the truth of how they operate, who they benefit, and who they target. Throughout history, we have seen many efforts to undermine and whitewash the truth of white supremacy. Even now, many school boards and state legislators are working tirelessly to revise or eliminate the truth of racialized experiences in this country by stroking fear of critical race theory. Through the truth-telling efforts of Black women's histories and activism, we can create the foundation of a more complete transformative civic education.

CONCLUSION

It is our hope that our RESPECT framework builds on the historical tradition of Black women and their civic knowledge and pedagogy. We offer this blueprint to social studies educators as a guide for how they may engage in anti-racist civics—by centering the lived experiences and anti-racist work of Black women. The way we get there is through diverse and expansive political and social activism. We believe that by teaching and centering the knowledge, experiences, and collective work of Black women in (anti-racist) civic education we can all get to a more just and equitable society—a society that in essence will liberate and free us all.

Each tenet from the RESPECT framework informs one another, and thus the tenets overlap. For example, you cannot separate *political and social activism* from *collectivism* and the coalition building that Black women engage in, nor can you isolate *truth-telling* from *self-determination*. Truth-telling demands self-determination, a willingness to be vulnerable and challenge stereotypical narratives. The tenets of Black feminist thought and pedagogy are not linear and should be engaged more holistically.

As we consider the questions presented in the introduction of the chapter—*What's next? How do we do this work with students?*—we must first recognize that this approach requires a reframing of civic education that is rooted in dismantling systemic oppression. It is not just about traditional civic behaviors such as voting but also about unpacking the -isms. Engaging in anti-oppressive work, more specifically in anti-racist work, requires a divestment from white supremacy and patriarchy. For some, this may seem anti-patriotic. When we take stock of the curriculum, it notably does not include the perspectives of Black women and does not articulate who they are or their civic knowledge. It is for this reason that we encourage not only a representation of "more Black women" but rather lean into the expansive ideas that Black women offer when implementing civics that are more robust and justice oriented.

The tenets of the RESPECT framework can be incorporated through the use of essential questions that can guide lessons and unit plans. Below are examples of potential essential questions that can be used as a starting point to engage students in an understanding of civics through a broader lens of Black women's activism.

R—Revolutionary

- In what ways do Black women's revolutionary acts benefit democracy writ large?

E—Epistemology

- How are the knowledge and lived experiences of Black women valued and/or incorporated within the historical context?

S—Self-Determination

- How has self-determination played a role in Black women's quest for liberation?

P—Political and Social Activism

- What methods have Black women utilized to engage in political and social actions?

E—Emancipatory

- How and why do Black women participate and advocate for democracy even when they are systematically excluded from reaping its benefits?
- How have Black women defined freedom?

C—Collectivism

- In what ways, have Black women worked together in both informal and formal ways to fight for justice?

T—Truth-Telling

- What sacrifices have Black women endured as a result of telling the truth?

While we have offered examples of Black women in this chapter who have engaged in anti-racist civics, we urge teachers and teacher educators to learn their histories. We encourage you to locate your knowledge gaps of Black women and their civic knowledge and contributions. We ask that you engage in research on these women to explore their activist work and what they did to help shape our democracy for the betterment of us all. Liberation is about love. We must have hope and joy in the movement, and those stories must also be taught so that the next generation has the tools to dismantle interlocking systems of oppression. This work is sustained through our hope, joy, and love, as well as the belief that our society will and can be better. Dillard (2021) succinctly reminds us to (re)member the spirit of the work of Black women educators:

> But if you listen carefully and really want to learn from the power and humanity of Black women, you will find lessons that you need to know to be the teachers that Black students deserve, and all students need. (p. 179)

REFERENCES

Angelou, M., & hooks, b. (1998). Interview with Maya Angelou and bell hooks. Shambhala. http://www.hartford-hwp.com/archives/45a/249.html

Banks, J. A. (2008). Diversity, group identity, and citizenship education in a global age. *Educational Researcher*, 37(3), 129–139. http://doi.org/10.3102/0013189X08317501

Berry, D. R., & Gross, K. N. (2020). *A Black women's history of the United States*. Beacon Press.

Blain, K. N. (2020, June 9). The Black women who paved the way for this moment: Today's protests build on a long tradition of activism. *The Atlantic*. https://www.theatlantic.com/ideas/archive/2020/06/pioneering-black-women-who-paved-way-moment/612838

Brewton-Johnson, M. (2021, February 8). Once again, Black women are heroes. It's time to pay up. *Cognoscenti*. https://www.wbur.org/cognoscenti/2021/02/08/black-women-stacey-abrams-kamala-harris-morgan-brewton-johnson

Burroughs, N. H. (2019). *Nannie Helen Burroughs: A documentary portrait of an early civil rights pioneer, 1900–1959* (K. B. Graves, Ed.). University of Notre Dame Press.

Carruthers, C. (2018). *Unapologetic: A Black, queer, and feminist mandate for radical movements*. Beacon Press.

Coles, S. C., & Pasek, J. (2020) Intersectional invisibility revisited: How group prototypes lead to the erasure and exclusion of Black women. *Translational Issues in Psychological Sciences*, 6(4), 314–324.

Collins, P. H. (2000). *Black feminist thought: Knowledge, consciousness, and the politics of empowerment*. Routledge.

Combahee River Collective. (1977). *The Combahee River Collective Statement*. Library of Congress. https://www.loc.gov/item/lcwaN0028151

Davis, A. Y. (1972, June 20). Interview with Angela Davis (No. 67). In *Black Journal*. WNET; American Archive of Public Broadcasting (GBH and the Library of Congress). http://americanarchive.org/catalog/cpb-aacip-512-1v5bc3tn06

Davis, A. Y. (2016). *Freedom is a constant struggle: Ferguson, Palestine, and the foundations of a movement* (F. Barat, Ed.). Haymarket Books.

Dillard, C. (2021). *The spirit of our work: Black women teachers (re)member*. Beacon Press.

Duncan, K. E. (2020). "What better tool do I have?": A critical race approach to teaching civics. *The High School Journal, 103*(3), 176–189.

Freire, P. (1987). *Literacy: Reading the word and the world*. Praeger.

Henry, A. (2005). Black feminist pedagogy: Critiques and contributions. In W. Watkins (Ed.), *Black protest thought and education*. Peter Lang.

Howard, T. (2003). The dis(g)race of the social studies: The need for racial dialogue in the social studies. In G. Ladson-Billings (Ed.), *Critical race theory perspectives on social studies: The profession, policies, and curriculum* (pp. 27–44). Information Age Publishing.

Hunter, T. W. (1997). *To 'joy my freedom: Southern Black women's lives and labors after the Civil War*. Harvard University Press.

James, J. (1999). Radicalising feminism. *Race & Class: A Journal for Black and Third World Liberation, 40*, 15–32.

Johnson, K. A. (2009). Gender and race: Exploring Anna Julia Cooper's thoughts for socially just educational opportunities. *Philosophia Africana, 12*(1), 67–82.

Jones, M. S. (2020). *Vanguard: How Black women broke barriers, won the vote, and insisted on equality for all*. Basic Books.

Kelley, R.D.G. (2002). *Freedom dreams: The Black radical imagination*. Beacon Press.

Kelly, L. L. (2020). "I love us for real": Exploring homeplace as a site of healing and resistance for Black girls in schools. *Equity & Excellence in Education, 53*(4), 449–464. https://doi.org/10.1080/10665684.2020.1791283

King Encyclopedia. (n.d.). *Women's Political Council (WPC) of Montgomery*. The Martin Luther King Jr. Research and Education Institute. https://kinginstitute.stanford.edu/encyclopedia/womens-political-council-wpc-montgomery

Ladson-Billings, G. (Ed.). (2003). *Critical race theory perspectives on the social studies: The profession, policies, and curriculum*. Information Age Publishing.

Marshall, P. L. (2003). The persistent deracialization of the agenda for democratic citizenship education: Twenty years of rhetoric and unreality in social studies position statements. In G. Ladson-Billings (Ed.), *Critical race theory perspectives on social studies: The profession, policies, and curriculum* (pp. 71–98). Information Age Publishing.

Omolade, B. (1987). A Black feminist pedagogy. *Women's Studies Quarterly, 15*(3/4), 32–39. https://www.jstor.org/stable/40003434

Preston-Grimes, P. (2007). Teaching democracy before *Brown*: Civic education in Georgia's African American schools, 1930–1954. *Theory & Research in Social Education, 35*(1), 9–31. https://doi.org/10.1080/00933104.2007.10473324

Smith, B. (2000). *Home girls: A Black feminist anthology*. Rutgers University Press.

Stevens, M. (2020, November 8). *Kamala Harris's vice president-elect acceptance speech* [Speech Transcript]. *The New York Times*. https://www.nytimes.com/article/watch-kamala-harris-speech-video-transcript.html

Stewart, M. W., & Richardson, M. (1987). *Maria W. Stewart, America's first Black woman political writer: Essays and speeches*. Indiana University Press.

Taylor, K.-Y. (2020, July 20). Until Black women are free, none of us will be free: Barbara Smith and the Black feminist visionaries of the Combahee River

Collective. *The New Yorker.* https://www.newyorker.com/news/our-columnists/until-black-women-are-free-none-of-us-will-be-free

Taylor, U. (1998). The historical evolution of Black feminist theory and praxis. *Journal of Black Studies, 29*(2), 234–253. https://www.jstor.org/stable/2668091

Tyson, C. (2003). A Bridge over troubled water: Social studies, civic education, and critical race theory. In G. Ladson-Billings (Ed.), *Critical race theory perspectives on the social studies: The profession, policies, and curriculum* (pp. 15–26). Information Age Publishing.

Vickery, A. E. (2017). "You excluded us for so long and now you want us to be patriotic?": African American women teachers navigating the quandary of citizenship. *Theory & Research in Social Education, 45*(3), 318–348. https://doi.org/10.1080/00933104.2017.1282387

Wells-Barnett, I. B. (1895). *The red record: Tabulated statistics & alleged causes of lynching in the United States.* Read Books Ltd.

Yee, S. J. (1992). *Black women abolitionists: A study in activism, 1828–1860.* University of Tennessee Press.

CHAPTER 9

"Responsible, Capable, and Whole Human Beings"
The Value and Necessity of Indigenous Civics

Leilani Sabzalian and Michelle M. Jacob

> To me, educating a child means equipping him or her with the capability to succeed in the world he or she will live in. In our Inupiat communities, this means learning not only academics, but also to travel, camp, and harvest wildlife resources in the surrounding land and sea environments. Students must learn about responsibilities to the extended family and elders, as well as about our community and regional governments, institutions, and corporations, and significant issues in the economic and social system. (Okakok, 1989, pp. 411–412)

> At the core of Indigenous education are our ancestral teachings about how to be a good human and live a good life, and to fulfill our responsibilities to be good relatives. We think of these as our ethical or axiological commitments in what we very reluctantly might call, in English, Indigenous civics. (Bang & Brayboy, 2021, p. 165)

Indigenous peoples have a long history of critiquing whitestream schooling (Grande, 2015) and articulating our own visions of education. One poignant example occurred nearly three centuries ago. After a long round of negotiations with the Haudenosaunee Confederacy for the Treaty of Lancaster in Pennsylvania in 1744, the Commissioners from Virginia informed Haudenosaunee representatives that a college in Williamsburg could educate their youth. If they agreed to "send down half a dozen of their sons to that College, the Government would take Care that they should be well provided for, and instructed in all the Learning of the white People" (Franklin, 1784, para 3). After considering the offer, a Haudenosaunee representative responded, expressing gratitude for the offer and recognizing both the esteemed nature and expense of such an education, and then continued:

> We are convinced therefore that you mean to do us Good by your Proposal, and we thank you heartily. But you who are wise must know, that different Nations have different Conceptions of Things, and you will therefore not take it amiss if our Ideas of this Kind of Education happen not to be the same with yours. We have had some Experience of it: Several of our Young People were formerly brought up at the Colleges of the Northern Provinces; they were instructed in all your Sciences; but when they came back to us they were bad Runners, ignorant of every means of living in the Woods, unable to bear either Cold or Hunger, knew neither how to build a Cabin, take a Deer or kill an Enemy, spoke our Language imperfectly, were therefore neither fit for Hunters Warriors, or Counsellors; they were totally good for nothing. We are however not the less obliged by your kind Offer, tho' we decline accepting it; and to show our grateful Sense of it, if the Gentlemen of Virginia will send us a Dozen of their Sons, we will take great Care of their Education, instruct them in all we know, and make *Men* of them. (cited in Franklin, 1794, para 3)

This polite but piercing critique attests to a longstanding legacy of whitestream schooling being irrelevant, alienating, and damaging to Native children. Further, this vignette highlights a legacy of Indigenous peoples proposing solutions to education. Rather than transform whitestream schooling to better reflect the knowledges, skills, and needs of Indigenous youth, the speaker proposed an alternative: send us *your* children, and in doing so reminds us of the inherent brilliance in Indigenous education systems.

This chapter takes seriously the assertion that Indigenous leadership in education and in civics holds value not only for Indigenous children but for *all* children. Public schools have much to gain by learning from Indigenous values, philosophies, practices, and diplomacies—what we refer to here as Indigenous civics. Too often, however, Indigenous civics is discussed on the margins of civic education, if at all. Here, we move Indigenous civics from the margins to the center in two key ways: first, by unapologetically centering Indigenous theories as the basis from which we think about key civics concepts, including nationhood, sovereignty, and civic roles and responsibilities; and second, by framing Indigenous civics as the basis for *all* civic education, not just the education of Indigenous youth. As our discussion highlights, we believe Indigenous civics can support all students to "become responsible, capable, and whole human beings" (Alaska Native Knowledge Network [ANKN] 1998, p. 3).

A wealth of scholarship advocates for centering Indigenous knowledges within various disciplines, including science (Cajete, 2000; Kimmerer, 2013; Medin & Bang, 2014), environmental education and justice (Whyte, 2019; Wildcat, 2009), law (Borrows, 2000, 2019), philosophy (Burkhart, 2019; Cordova et al., 2007), and education (Battiste, 2013; Deloria & Wildcat, 2001; Jacob et al., 2018), among others. Though diverse in content and approach, each works to center Indigenous theories, while also recognizing the diversity of Indigenous realities and experiences. More recently, scholarship has addressed the need for civic education to take seriously structures and processes of colonialism as well as Indigenous nationhood and sovereignty (Bang & Brayboy, 2021; Haynes Writer, 2010; Sabzalian, 2019).

In "Indigenous Peoples and Civics in the 21st Century," Bang and Brayboy (2021) outline five key dimensions for civic education that support Indigenous sovereignty and our collective capacity to live in right relations with land and one another:

1. Understand and confront the ongoing dynamics of settler-coloniality in U.S. history and narratives of the United States that perpetuate violence, erasure, and invisibility of Indigenous peoples;
2. Develop the political and ethical commitments, meaning the civic responsibility, to uphold Indigenous sovereignty and engage in nation-to-nation relations;
3. Ethically hold and grapple with the heterogeneous conditions of migrations that differentially shape experiences and the racialization of "peoples of color, including Indigenous peoples from other places," and subsequently the complex work of relational solidarities across communities toward collective thriving;
4. Create forms of education that cultivate collective capacity to understand and generatively engage Indigenous peoples, our histories, sovereignties, knowledge systems, and distinct experiences with racialization and its impacts on Indigenous communities; and
5. Support the development of civic education for thriving Tribal nations and engaging the broader possibilities they open toward liberatory futures for all peoples. (pp. 185–186)

This chapter complements these recommendations by advocating for Indigenous civics to become central to theories and practices of civic education. In particular, we advocate that core questions and practices in Indigenous civics can help engender more just, humanizing, and ethical relations among peoples who live on Indigenous homelands, and the vast relational network of life those lands sustain.

ESSENTIAL QUESTIONS FOR INDIGENOUS CIVICS

Indigenous peoples have a long history of reflecting on questions at the heart of civic education: questions about what it means to be human and to live responsibly with one another and the world. These questions permeate Indigenous knowledge systems and stories and, more recently, have been published by Indigenous scholars. They have also informed Indigenous educational efforts designed to help students understand their roles and responsibilities and contribute meaningfully to the communities in which they live.

The following section outlines several essential questions for Indigenous civics that emerge from academic literature, Indigenous stories, and Indigenous-led efforts to make schooling more responsive to Indigenous students and homelands.

Academic Literature

In her book *How It Is: The Native American Philosophy of V.F. Cordova*, the late Apache philosopher Viola Cordova and colleagues (2007) proposed three questions that lie at the heart of philosophy:

1. What is the world?
2. What is it to be human in that world?
3. What is the *role* of a human in that world? (p. 83).

Through these questions, Cordova navigates the complex task of recognizing the distinctiveness of Native communities and worldviews, while also articulating commonalities among Native philosophies. Of particular importance here is Cordova's advocacy for the importance of Native philosophies: The time has come for Native peoples to give our explanations of reality and the ethics of being human; "that is the relevance of the study of philosophy for Native Americans: not to see ourselves as others see us, but *to look at ourselves through our own eyes*" (p. 53, emphasis added). Our rationale for Indigenous civics is similar: *Indigenous children deserve to learn about their civic roles and responsibilities through their own eyes.*

For Cordova, ethical questions (or what humans "*should* do") stem from how we define reality and the world we live in (p. 56). Civic education has been limited by Eurocentric definitions of reality—a world characterized and communicated to children in schools as material, mechanistic, and secular (Cordova et al., 2007; Grande, 2015). These definitions enable violent hierarchies, extraction, and exploitation, practices that harm Indigenous lands and lives—indeed all life on the planet. In contrast, Indigenous philosophies are often premised on the animate and sacred nature of the universe.

Importantly, Indigenous philosophies are deeper and more expansive than concepts like "balance" or "harmony," though these may be vital concepts to a community. Concepts are "starting points" and make sense within one's understanding of reality. Harmony and balance, for example, make sense in a world viewed as continually in motion or in flux. Inviting civics to take seriously Indigenous philosophies requires looking critically at how we define the reality, and asking, "What would it be like to live in a world that we considered a living being?" (Cordova et al., 2007, p. 56).

We believe that Indigenous realities can offer a basis for a more just and humanizing civics. In a living and sacred world in which all life is connected and valued, children must learn how to live in community with others. In this world, "'community' includes not only the family but the surrounding environment," and children must learn "to be aware not only of one's actions and their consequences toward other people, but toward the 'ground' one inhabits" (Cordova et al., 2007, p. 81).

Cordova also notes that while Indigenous philosophies may share similarities—the sacredness of the universe, the belief that humans are "a natural *part of* the Earth" rather than *"apart from* the Earth and the rest of its creations"* (Cordova et al., 2007, p. 151), the value of collectivity, or the belief that all beings have intelligence, among others—*ethics are developed in relation to place*. As such, Indigenous civics is locally responsive, as learning about one's roles and responsibilities should be developed in relation to the lands and communities in which one lives.

Like Cordova, Cherokee scholar Daniel Heath Justice (2018) also anchors his book *Why Indigenous Literatures Matter* around four guiding questions: How do we learn to be human? How do we behave as good relatives? How do we become good ancestors? How do we learn to live together? For Justice, these questions have everything to do with kinship, as our understanding of kinship shapes "how we abide in the world" (p. 90).

Justice contrasts the "horizontal model of relationship" found within many Indigenous communities to vertical and hierarchical forms relationality in settler society, and the consequences of each:

> If we have many relations to whom we owe more than superficial respect, a roughly if not entirely horizontal model of relationship, then monolithic settler colonial authority is difficult if not impossible to maintain or justify, and widespread exploitation of land, plants, and animals, as well as humans, is difficult to fully realize, because we recognize our implication in these relationships and their health. If, however, our familial obligations are vertical, with a clear hierarchy of authority that is mirrored by church, state, and industry, then a significant defensive network is eliminated. From there, other-than-human relations are more easily conceived as Others, and then as exploitable Others, and then simply as resources there for the taking, without reciprocity or consent. Violence begets violence; empathy and relationships diminish, human possibility grows narrower, more utilitarian, more narcissistic and selfish. And all life suffers. (p. 90)

Kinship, Justice offers, isn't romantic and "relationality isn't always positive and affirming" (p. 90); in fact, many Indigenous stories and traditions about kinship "aren't as much about making people like each other as about helping ensure our differences don't tear us apart" (p. 90). But Justice, like Cordova, argues that Indigenous philosophies have a long tradition of helping communities learn to live responsibly with land and with one another.

Being "human" is a learned process rather than a natural state. How children learn to be human, relate to other humans (including land and more than human relations), and understand their responsibilities to this kinship network lies at the heart of education in general, and civic education in particular. Unfortunately, the ways schools typically teach young children, Indigenous and otherwise, how to be in relation with land and others has been damaging. Western schooling often socializes students into the "deep structures of the colonialist consciousness," promoting individualism, competition, and a sense of separation from and superiority over Land and other communities (Grande, 2015, p. 99). This colonialist consciousness fuels logics and practices of domination, extraction, and oppression, harming Land and the various communities Land sustains. But just as children can learn forms of humanity that are rooted in separation, hierarchy, supremacy, and domination, they can also learn other ways to live and act in this world (Cordova et al., 2007; Deloria & Wildcat, 2001; Grande, 2015). Indigenous stories, which often foreground relationality and our responsibilities to the vast network of life that includes land and our more than human relations, offer a meaningful way to deepen children's understanding about what it means to live responsibly in place and with one another.

Indigenous Stories

In our work as Indigenous educators, we envision a world structured by the deep love and care that has sustained our communities despite legacies of oppression. We use a generative Indigenous feminist approach and name settler colonialism as the root cause of systemic oppressions that divide us from the land, each other, and even ourselves. Settler colonialism creates oppressive hierarchies in our lives and organizations that degrade our human and more than human relations. Indigenous ways of knowing and being help all of us living and working on Indigenous lands to counter settler colonialism and promote healing and transformation.

From an Indigenous perspective, all education takes place on Indigenous lands. Centering this idea creates space for centering Indigenous ways of knowing and being as we dream an equitable and inclusive collective future. In Indigenous education, stories are the backbone of our teaching, learning, and development. The benefits of engaging stories are many, including a stronger understanding and commitment to relationality and responsibility, which are the foundation of equity and inclusion. To demonstrate some of this importance, we engage some of Yakama peoples' treasured Coyote Stories, including Spilyáy (Legendary Coyote) Breaks the Dam[1] in which Spilyáy, one of our most revered teachers, demonstrates courage and generosity to set Salmon free so that people would not suffer with hunger. Spilyáy is a heroic leader who is not representative of toxic masculinity in settler colonialism. Rather, Spilyáy continually turns to his Sisters for advice and guidance, affirming Yakama teachings of the importance of women. Also, Spilyáy, while a wise and powerful leader, is also someone who makes mistakes and blunders. Spilyáy reminds us never to be held back by worry that we (or our efforts) are not "perfect." Instead, we can focus on a willingness to be accountable, transparent, and humbly ready to learn.

In Yakama teachings, humans are not the First People; plants, fish, water—all our more than human relations[2] are the First People. The time before humans is legendary time, and Yakama peoples have a rich storytelling tradition that has served as the backbone of our education and leadership training for generations. For example, we will share (briefly) lessons from a Yakama Creation Story. Tamanwiłá (Creator) was considering bringing humans into being and knew that doing so would have a deep impact on all People who were living and thriving on Mother Earth. Being a responsible and respectful leader, rather than hierarchically wielding power in any fashion desired, Creator called a Grand Council of all People, shared the idea of bringing humans into being, and asked what the People thought. After deeply considering this, Salmon and Water stepped forward, offering themselves as gifts to humans so we could survive.

Key lessons from this story:

True power is always in community.
Transparency and accountability are foundational.
Anyone who wishes to contribute is respectfully invited to do so.

We offer these two examples as beginning points for readers to learn more about the importance of Indigenous storytelling and storywork, as articulated by Q'um Q'um Xiiem, Jo-ann Archibald (https://indigenousstorywork.com). Indigenous educators have long advocated for the value of Indigenous stories in education, as they can teach children about living responsibly with others and with place (Archibald, 2008; Cajete, 1994; Jacob, 2020; Simpson, 2014). Importantly, stories recognize and respect the knowledge, dignity, and capacity of children (and all learners and listeners), a pedagogy that doesn't tell "children what to think or feel, but . . . *giv[es] them the space to think and feel*" (cited in Archibald, 2008, p. 134). As Lorna Mathias has offered, "a good story can reach into your heart, mind and soul, and really make you think hard about your relationship to the world" (cited in Archibald, 2008, p. 140). Civic education is often characterized by rote and rigid curriculum, but we see immense possibilities in stories as the basis for civic curriculum and a way to help students "think hard" about their roles, responsibilities, and relationship to the world.

An Example of Indigenous Civics

Indigenous communities have outlined frameworks that situate the knowledges within Indigenous stories as an essential part of preparing students to "become responsible, capable and whole human beings" (ANKN, 1998, p. 3). One meaningful example is the "Alaska Standards for Culturally-Responsive Schools" (ANKN, 1998).

After a series of meetings and listening sessions with Alaska Native Elders, educators, and community members hosted by the Alaska Rural Systemic Initiative, Alaska Native educators developed cultural standards for students, as well as educators, curriculum, schools, and communities serving Alaska Native students throughout the state. Importantly, the standards are designed to support *all* students living on Alaska Native homelands, recognizing "the unique contribution that indigenous people can make" in helping all students better understand the physical and cultural environment in which they live (ANKN, 1998, pp. 2–3).

The cultural standards outlined in the framework "are predicated on the belief that a firm grounding in the heritage language and culture indigenous to a particular place is a fundamental prerequisite for the development of culturally-healthy students and communities associated with that place" (ANKN, 1998, p. 2). Further, "teaching/learning *through* the local culture" is an important "foundation for all education" (p. 3). Though characterized as "cultural standards," we see the values, knowledges, and skills outlined in this document as an important example of Indigenous civics.

Civic knowledge, skills, dispositions, roles, and responsibilities permeate the framework. Students are encouraged to develop a deep knowledge of the land and community in which they live, and learn how to contribute meaningfully to the well-being of both. They are invited to reflect on the long-term consequences of their actions and develop solutions to problems in their community. Students are to appreciate the role of Elders and engage in meaningful interactions with them to learn about the community and its history and traditions. Local knowledge and culture, including oral histories and traditions, are framed as important foundations for student well-being and success. Students are encouraged to appreciate the vast kinship network in their community, including the spiritual dimension of the world and the role of traditional knowledge in maintaining a healthy physical environment. Cultural humility is another important outcome, as students are invited to recognize the situated nature of their knowledge, the place of their community in the broader world, and learn to "acquire insights from other cultures without diminishing the integrity of their own" (ANKN, 1998, p. 6). Cultural adaptation and change are also valued, and students are encouraged to think critically about the potential contributions and consequences of technology. These are just several examples of the way civics is framed generatively in relation to Indigenous lands and community.

The framework offers one model of Indigenous civics that can be "reviewed and adapted to fit local needs" (ANKN, 1998, p. 3). Designed through a process of community engagement, it exemplifies how Indigenous leadership in education can contribute to models and practices of civic education that account for the experiences and realities of Indigenous children, as well as *all* children living and learning on Indigenous lands. These standards written by Alaska Native Elders and educators were developed "in the spirit of sharing the indigenous perspective with all who live in this place called Alaska" (Alaska Department of Education & Early Development, 2012, p. v), a spirit of generosity that echoes the the promise of the Haudenosaunee earlier in this chapter—if we are responsible for your children, "we will take great Care of their Education."

Unfortunately, the rich insights embedded within Indigenous philosophies, stories, and frameworks are often ignored by civic education scholars and practitioners, who rarely engage the literature on Indigenous education or Indigenous studies. Although the field of civic education has been a "perfect stranger" (Dion, 2008) to Indigenous education, we see generative potential in Indigenous civics and what it can teach all children about being a good relative.

Indigenous philosophies situate humans within a sacred universe and kinship network in which humans have relational accountability to the rest of creation, a definition of the world that we believe can catalyze more just relational, ethical, and political commitments. Indigenous stories, as we shared above, remind us that humans have always learned about our civic roles and responsibilities from our more than human relations who have much to teach us about respect, community, humility, relationality, and diplomacy, among other values. Indigenous educators and communities have also offered generous and inclusive visions of education that can support all students to be in right relation with the communities and lands in which they learn.

THE VALUE, NECESSITY, AND LIBERATORY POTENTIAL OF INDIGENOUS CIVICS

Careful not to offer *the* Indigenous civics framework, we maintain that Indigenous civics is essential to the broader field of civic education, and a meaningful catalyst for various nation-based iterations, such as Alutiiq civics, Yakama civics, or Klamath civics. Indeed, this work is *already* taking place in Native nations "who continue to develop forms of their own civics education toward their own thriving" (Bang & Brayboy, 2021, p. 166).[3]

Here, we reiterate how Indigenous civics could support the thriving of Indigenous children, and potentially engender a more just and "liberatory future for all peoples" (Bang & Brayboy, 2021, p. 186). We draw this key insight from Anishinaabe legal scholar John Borrows (2000), whose theory "landed citizenship" connects civics to the land and Indigenous leadership. Recalling his grandfather's upbringing, and generations before him born and raised on the same lands, Borrows shared how his community's intergenerational experiences with place brought them "into citizenship with the land":

> We participate in its renewal, have responsibility for its continuation, and grieve for its losses. As citizens with this land, we also feel the presence of our ancestors, and strive with them to have the relationships of our polity respected. Our loyalties, allegiance, and affection is related to the land. The water, wind, sun, and stars are part of this federation. The fish, birds, plants, and animals also share this union. Our teachings and stories form the constitution of this relationship, and direct and nourish the obligations this citizenship requires. (p. 326)

Given the challenges that settler encroachment and the disregard of Indigenous laws have posed to sustaining his community's citizenship with the land, Borrows asks: "What is required to reinscribe these laws, and once again invoke a citizenship with the land?" (p. 326).

In response to his own question in the context of Canada, Borrows first paid homage to the necessary and "revolutionary message" that characterized political discourse and activism before him: "Indian control of Indian affairs" or "Aboriginal control of Aboriginal affairs" (p. 327). He then urged Indigenous peoples to move *beyond* that framework, arguing that in order to "preserve and extend our participation with the land, it's time to talk also of *Aboriginal control of Canadian affairs*" (p. 328, emphasis added).

Borrows (2000) argues that Indigenous leadership in Canadian affairs is necessary as many Indigenous peoples live outside of reservations, boundaries that include only a portion of Indigenous peoples' traditional homelands. As such, Indigenous leadership is an important way for Indigenous peoples "to influence and participate in our lands," including participating in "decision-making structures that have the potential to destroy our lands" (p. 330). More importantly, Indigenous leadership in Canadian affairs may influence *all people living on Indigenous lands* to be more attentive to land and Indigenous cultural practices and consider "the adverse impact of their activities on land itself" (p. 332). Indigenous leadership could also "expand to recognize land as a party to Confederation in its own right" (p. 332), a practice well established within Indigenous communities. Infusing Indigenous values and traditions into Canada's "governing ideas and institutions" could be transformative, and help "reconfigure Canada in an important way" (p. 332).[4]

Indigenous leadership within civics, and more broadly within society (McCoy et al., 2020), has the potential to transform dominant society in an important way, including how we all relate to one another and the land. Indigenous civics is also essential to fostering a society that respects Indigenous lands, rights, and sovereignty, all of which have been found to protect the lives, lands, and well-being of all beings living on Earth. It is not an accident that Indigenous peoples, who comprise 5% of the population, are responsible for maintaining 80% of the world's biodiversity within their territories (United Nations [UN], 2021, p. 137). As the recent report *Territories of Life* (ICCA Consortium, 2021) found:

> Indigenous peoples and local communities play an outsized role in the governance, conservation and sustainable use of the world's biodiversity and nature. They actively protect and conserve an astounding diversity of globally relevant species, habitats and ecosystems, providing the basis for clean water and air, healthy food and livelihoods for people far beyond their boundaries. (p. 10)

Movements to legally recognize the rights of nature, first in Ecuador and Bolivia, and later in the Ho-Chunk and Ponca Nations, emerged from within Indigenous communities (Borrows, 2000; LaDuke, 2019). Advocacy for the rights of lakes and rivers by Māori people in Aotearoa or the Yurok Tribe in California (Leonard, 2019), or for the rights of Manoomin (wild rice) by the White Earth Nation (LaDuke, 2019), make sense in a world that recognizes the value, dignity, and equality of creation. It is also no accident that Indigenous women have been "champions of climate change adaptation and mitigation" and "have always played a central role in safeguarding more than half of the world's land, including much of its forests" (UN, 2021, p. 137). Indigenous civics is feminist, committed to cultivating land-based solidarities that envision and work toward "a way of life free of exploitation and replete with spirit" (Grande, 2015, p. 243).

PLACING CIVIC EDUCATION WITHIN INDIGENOUS SOVEREIGNTY

> This isn't about pipelines, or jobs, or the best way to get our message out. This is about land and life for generations to come. This is about the kinds of worlds we collectively want to live in. Indigenous Worlds. Black Worlds. Beaver Worlds. Anti-Colonial Worlds. (Simpson, 2021, p. 57)

We believe the questions and stories that drive Indigenous civics are instructive for all children learning to be human in this world. Within Indigenous civics, and its nation-based iterations, we see generative and necessary shifts away from colonial ways of knowing and being in the world, and toward more responsible ways of carrying ourselves and relating to land and others. Indigenous civics shifts us away from viewing land as a resource, toward viewing land as a network of relationships of which we are a part; away from focusing on our rights as humans, and instead toward our responsibilities to land and to others (Aikau et al., 2015; Corntassel, 2012); away from viewing nationhood and diplomacy through a human-centered lens and toward more "complex ways of relating to the plant nations, animal nations, and the spiritual realm" (Simpson, 2021, p. 56); and away from viewing sovereignty through patriarchal white possessive logics of nation-states (Moreton-Robinson, 2015), to focusing instead on sovereignty as our "responsibility to carry ourselves; collectively as nations, as clans, as families as well as individually, as individual Mohawk [or Indigenous] citizens, in a good way" (Monture-Angus, 1999, p. 36). Indigenous civic education foregrounds "thinking intergenerationally" (Jacob, 2013), whether learning from Tamanwiɬá and the Grand Council of All People, valuing Elders and the guidance they can offer youth, considering future generations when we envision and enact social change, or nurturing in our young people the Elders they will become (Simpson, 2014).

We are aware that we left several important questions unaddressed, including how educators might utilize stories responsibly and teach *through*, rather than *about* culture (ANKN, 1998); how they might partner respectfully with Indigenous peoples to develop localized frameworks for Indigenous civics; or how to navigate the complex dynamics and tensions that surface when Indigenous peoples reproduce colonial logics and practices. We view these important questions as necessary problems of practice that require deep and critical engagement *after* civic education scholars and practitioners take seriously what it means to place civic education "*within* Indigenous sovereignty" (Nicoll, 2004)—that is, within the "awareness we are on Indigenous Lands containing their own stories, relationships, laws, Protocols, obligations, and opportunities, which have been understood and practiced by Indigenous peoples since time immemorial" (Carlson-Manathara & Rowe, 2021, p. 25). Indigenous sovereignty is not a "perspective" that civics education must accommodate but a reality that "we already exist within" (Nicoll, 2004, p. 29). Indigenous scholars and educators have offered beautiful models of Indigenous civics that live within Indigenous sovereignty. We hope that civic scholars and educators pay attention.

We thank you for engaging with our ideas in this chapter. You are now part of a long tradition of thinking with and through Indigenous storytelling. Our sharing in this chapter is itself a contemporary form of storytelling, as we seek to write into being a stronger understanding of the gift of Indigenous civics. You, as the reader/listener of our story, are now part of a powerful network of relationships; this way of respectful connecting has always served our communities. We invite you to share what you learned in this chapter with your students, colleagues, communities, and relatives. In doing so you take on an important storytelling role.

ACKNOWLEDGMENT

We would like to thank Shianne Walker (Klamath Tribes) for her contributions and feedback on this manuscript.

REFERENCES

Aikau, H. K., Arvin, M., Goeman, M., & Morgensen, S. (2015). Indigenous feminisms roundtable. *Frontiers: A Journal of Women Studies, 36*(3), 84–106.

Alaska Department of Education & Early Development. (2012). Guide to implementing the Alaska cultural standards for educators. https://www.asdn.org/wp-content/uploads/Implementing-AK-cultural-standards-1.pdf

Alaska Native Knowledge Network. (1998). Alaska standards for culturally responsive schools. www.ankn.uaf.edu/publications/ standards.html

Archibald, J. A. (2008). *Indigenous storywork: Educating the heart, mind, body, and spirit.* UBC Press.

Bang, M., & Brayboy, B.M.J. (2021). Indigenous peoples and civic education in the 21st century. In C. D. Lee, G. White, & D. Dong (Eds.), *Educating for civic reasoning & discourse* (pp. 165–189). National Academy of Education. https://naeducation.org/educating-for-civic-reasoning-and-discourse/

Battiste, M. (2013). *Decolonizing education: Nourishing the learning spirit.* Purich Publishing Limited.

Beavert, V. R., Jacob, M. M., & Jansen, J. W. (2021). *Anakú Iwachá: Yakama legends and stories.* University of Washington Press.

Borrows, J. (2000). "Landed" citizenship: Narratives of Aboriginal political participation. In W. Kymlicka & W. J. Norman (Eds.), *Citizenship in diverse societies* (pp. 326–342). Oxford University Press.

Borrows, J. (2019). *Law's indigenous ethics.* University of Toronto Press.

Burkhart, B. (2019). *Indigenizing philosophy through the land.* Michigan State University Press.

Cajete, G. (1994). *Look to the mountain: An ecology of Indigenous education.* Kiyaki Press.

Cajete, G. (2000). *Native science: Natural laws of interdependence.* Clear Light Publishers.

Carlson-Manathara, E., & Rowe, G. (2021). *Living in Indigenous sovereignty.* Columbia University Press.

Cordova, V., Moore, K. D., Peters, K., Jojola, T. S., Lacy, A., & Hogan, L. (2007). *How it is: The Native American philosophy of V.F. Cordova.* University of Arizona Press.

Corntassel, J. (2012). Re-envisioning resurgence: Indigenous pathways to decolonization and sustainable self-determination. *Decolonization: Indigeneity, Education & Society, 1*(1), 86–101.

Deloria, V., & Wildcat, D. R. (2001). *Power and place: Indian education in America.* Golden: Fulcrum.

Dion, S. D. (2008). *Braiding histories: Learning from Aboriginal peoples' experiences and perspectives.* UBC Press.

Franklin, B. (1784). "Remarks concerning the Savages of North America, [before 7 January 1784]," Founders Online. National Archives. https://founders.archives.gov/documents/Franklin/01-41-02-0280

Grande, S. (2015). *Red pedagogy: Native American social and political thought* (2nd ed.). Rowman & Littlefield.

Haynes Writer, J. (2010). Broadening the meaning of citizenship education: Native Americans and tribal nationhood. *Action in Teacher Education*, 32(2), 70–81.

ICCA Consortium. (2021). *Territories of life: 2021 report*. ICCA Consortium: worldwide. https://report.territoriesoflife.org

Jacob, M. M. (2013). *Yakama rising: Indigenous cultural revitalization, activism, and healing*. University of Arizona Press.

Jacob, M. M. (2020). *Huckleberries and coyotes: Lessons from our more than human relations*. Anahuy Mentoring, LLC.

Jacob, M. M., Sabzalian, L., Jansen, J., Tobin, T. J., Vincent, C. G., & LaChance, K. M. (2018). The gift of education: How Indigenous knowledges can transform the future of public education. *International Journal of Multicultural Education*, 20(1), 157–185.

Justice, D. (2018). *Why Indigenous literatures matter*. Indigenous Studies Series. Wilfrid Laurier University Press.

Kimmerer, R. (2013). *Braiding sweetgrass: Indigenous wisdom, scientific knowledge, and the teachings of plants*. Milkweed Editions.

LaDuke, W. (2019, February). The White Earth Band of Ojibwe legally recognized the rights of wild rice. *Yes! Magazine*. https://www.yesmagazine.org/environment/2019/02/01/the-white-earth-band-of-ojibwe-legally-recognized-the-rights-of-wild-rice-heres-why

Leonard, K. (2019, December). *Why lakes and rivers should have the same rights as humans* [Video]. TEDWomen. https://www.ted.com/talks/kelsey_leonard_why_lakes_and_rivers_should_have_the_same_rights_as_humans?language=en

McCoy, M., Elliott-Groves, E., Sabzalian, L., & Bang, M. (2020). Educating for right relations and land return. [Invited Testimony]. Center for Humans and Nature. https://www.humansandnature.org/restoring-indigenous-systems-of-relationality

Medin, D. L., & Bang, M. (2014). *Who's asking?: Native science, western science, and science education*. MIT Press.

Monture-Angus, P. (1999). *Journeying forward: Dreaming First Nations' independence*. Fernwood.

Moreton-Robinson, A. (2015). *The white possessive: Property, power, and Indigenous sovereignty*. University of Minnesota Press.

Nicoll, F. (2004). Reconciliation in and out of perspective: White knowing, seeing, curating and being at home in and against Indigenous sovereignty. In A. Moreton-Robinson (Ed.), *Whitening race: Essays in social and cultural criticism*. Aboriginal Studies Press.

Okakok, L. (1989). Serving the purpose of education. *Harvard Educational Review*, 59(4), 405–423.

Sabzalian, L. (2019). The tensions between Indigenous sovereignty and multicultural citizenship education: Toward an anticolonial approach to civic eduation. *Theory & Research in Social Education*, 47(3), 311–346. https://doi.org/10.1080/00933104.2019.1639572

Simpson, L. B. (2014). Land as pedagogy: Nishnaabeg intelligence and rebellious transformation. *Decolonization: Indigeneity, Education & Society, 3*(3), 1–25.

Simpson, L. (2021). *A short history of the blockade: Giant beavers, diplomacy, and regeneration in Nishnaabewin.* University of Alberta Press.

United Nations. (2021). State of the world's Indigenous peoples: Rights to lands, territories, and resources (Vol. 5.). United Nations. https://www.un.org/development/desa/indigenouspeoples/publications/state-of-the-worlds-indigenous-peoples.html

Whyte, K. P. (2019). Reflections on the purpose of Indigenous environmental education. In E. A. McKinley & L. T. Smith (Eds.) *Handbook of Indigenous education* (pp. 767–787). Springer.

Wildcat, D. R. (2009). *Red alert!: Saving the planet with Indigenous knowledge.* Fulcrum.

CHAPTER 10

"It Didn't Mean 'Me' When It Said 'We'"
Counterstories as Pedagogy When Citizenship Is Not Guaranteed

Brittany Jones

> I tell my students that they need to question any and everything that I give them. They should ask themselves if this is their reality and explain how it is and how it is not. I tell them all the time that the things I am supposed to teach them and what happens in real life can be different. I have to keep it real, when you Black in America the lessons from the textbooks don't always align with real life—our real life—the liberties, the rights, the freedoms that the textbooks say we supposed to have and how we are actually treated are different. The question almost everyday boils down to, who gets to be a citizen?
>
> —Randy, 9th-grade U.S. history teacher

The above quote originates from a study I conducted with Black social studies teachers examining their practices when teaching citizenship lessons to their Black students. This quote is striking for many reasons, as Randy (names used are pseudonyms) calls attention to the inconsistencies that exist within civic education. The question that Randy posed to his students at the end of this quote was critical for both himself and his Black students to grapple with as they engaged with learning the Reconstruction Amendments (13th, 14th, and 15th Amendments). In talking with Randy, he noted that almost every day he asked his students who gets to be a citizen? And if I were teaching this lesson, I might ask: Why are some people always afforded the rights of a U.S. citizen, while other people's access to citizenship is not as stable and fixed as the Constitution, social studies standards, and other curriculum materials suggest?

Black social studies teachers are expected to teach the Reconstruction Amendments as permanent laws that are fixed and afforded to all those who are born on U.S. soil. Although these words are codified, and perhaps solidified, by their place in the U.S. Constitution, lived experiences both historically and contemporarily, suggest that citizenship rights for Black people and people of Color are not always as definitive as the Constitution promises. Oftentimes, as noted by the teachers in this study, this instability of access to such citizenship is based on the color of one's skin and exacerbated by their other marginalized identities (e.g., Black woman; Crenshaw, 1991). For these Black teachers, and their Black students, what it means to be a citizen is much more nuanced than voting or participating on juries, as noted in the *C3 Framework for Social Studies Standards* (National Council for the Social Studies, 2013). To be a Black citizen in the United States is to understand how to navigate life when white supremacy denies those "inalienable" rights or when systems are created that impede one's right to vote.

With such incongruity between how Black teachers are expected to teach citizenship and their own lived experiences, this chapter explores how two Black social studies teachers navigated teaching a citizenship lesson, specifically the teaching of the Reconstruction Amendments, to their Black students. This chapter analyzes the pedagogies Black teachers employ to teach citizenship when their own lived experiences revealed how access to the rights of a U.S. citizen is often unstable and, in some instances, denied. Throughout their lessons, the teachers asked their students to challenge the term "we the people," questioning what a collective "we" means for communities of Color. By infusing their own stories within their civics lessons, the teachers contested dominant narratives of citizenship, pushing their students to reframe what it means to be Black and simultaneously a U.S. citizen.

This chapter begins by exploring a brief history of Black citizenship in the United States. Next, I provide an overview of the framework used to analyze the interviews with the teachers, and last, I examine how the teachers incorporated counterstories to make their citizenship lessons more accurate for their Black students.

BLACK CITIZENSHIP IN THE UNITED STATES

For Black people in the United States, full access to citizenship rights has always been in flux. It is impossible to discuss Black citizenship without considering the ways U.S. policies and systems have consistently questioned Black humanity by situating Black people as non-human (Mills, 1997). During the Colonial Era, white men passed laws intended not only to confine enslaved peoples' place in society but as a mechanism for control to limit Black advancement (DeLombard, 2019). For example, a Virginian law passed in 1662 stated that the status of the mother determined the enslavement status of Black children, which legally expanded the definitions of who was to be considered an enslaved person. In 1787, members of the Constitutional Convention signed Article 1, Section 2 of the Constitution, better known as the Three-Fifths Compromise, which limited Black humanity to only 60 percent of a human. In 1857, the Supreme Court ruled in the *Dred Scott v. Sandford* case that the Constitution was never intended to grant citizenship to people of African descent—free or enslaved.

Following the abrupt end of Reconstruction, white intimidation, poll taxes, and literacy tests constrained Black access to voting—a definitive action defining citizenship. In 1967, the National Advisory Commission on Civil Disorders published the *Kerner Commission Report* specifying how African Americans had been systemically and structurally excluded from U.S. citizenship. Despite this alarming report, Congress ignored almost all the recommendations made by the committee, which would have increased Black access to full citizenship rights (Rigeur & Beshlian, 2019). Contemporarily, policing and the criminal justice system have severely impacted Black access to full citizenship through mass incarceration (Alexander, 2010). While these are just a few examples historicizing the fragility of Black citizenship in the United States, it is very clear that there has always been a connection between race and who has access to full citizenship rights. Given this history, the question becomes: Why are race and citizenship rarely taught in tandem in K–12 social studies classrooms?

CIVIC EDUCATION

Scholars of social studies education have examined the dissociation between race and citizenship lessons in K–12 education. Brown et al. (2011) found that while citizenship education remains a central piece of social studies education, a strong link connecting race and citizenship is absent from social studies research. Similarly, in explaining the changing constructs about who has access to citizenship, Vickery (2016) maintained that citizenship "is a legal status that gives citizens certain rights and privileges, it also becomes a social construct and discursive practice that has changed over time to exclude certain bodies from belonging and participating" (p. 29). Busey and Dowie-Chin (2021) argued that global antiblackness perpetuates ideas that situate Blackness and the ability to be a citizen as distant entities that social studies education should reconcile.

Additionally, I contend that as much as citizenship education needs to include a discussion of race, there should also be an emphasis placed on the ways Black people have resisted (and continue to resist) racist policies aimed at constraining their access to citizenship. In its simplest form, a fight for citizenship is a fight for the recognition of one's full humanity. Enslaved peoples fought for their humanity by resisting slavery in a variety of ways including pretending illness, damaging tools, escaping, or planning and enacting rebellions (Stampp, 1956). Black soldiers enlisted to fight against the Confederacy as an act of resistance and attempt to gain full citizenship rights (Berry, 1995). During Jim Crow, despite fear tactics such as lynchings, Black people organized and marched for their right to enfranchisement (Berry, 1995). Today, Black people continue to organize and protest to ensure that policies reflect the idea that Black lives do indeed matter. Given this legacy of Black resistance, an accurate teaching of citizenship cannot omit the ways in which the United States has denied citizenship status based on race, and subsequently, the ways Black people have resisted their *sometimes* explicit second-class status.

THEORETICAL FRAMEWORK

Counterstories

Counterstories were useful to guide my analysis of the teachers' interviews in this study. Counterstories, a tenet of critical race theory (CRT) that analyzes how race and racism permeate society (Delgado & Stefancic, 2017), challenge racist discourses and beliefs in society by amplifying marginalized voices through "recognition of the experiential knowledge of People of Color" (Matsuda et al., 1993, p. 6), while simultaneously providing space for marginalized peoples to share their lived realities that oftentimes disrupts the status quo (Solórzano, 1997). While counterstories have many purposes, the ways they "value the knowledge of People of Color" (Dixson & Rousseau Anderson, 2018, p. 123) by critiquing and challenging dominant or normalized narratives (Decuir & Dixson, 2004) as a "first step on the road to justice" (Ladson-Billings & Tate, 1995, p. 58) was most pertinent to this study. The participants in this study used counterstories to contest the narratives presented in curricula that contended Black Americans gained *full and permanent* citizenship rights with the passing of the Reconstruction Amendments. Their counterstories not only added accuracy and complexity to their lessons on the Reconstruction Amendments but also created a more equitable learning space that, as Miller and colleagues (2020) noted, amplified the voices of "silenced and marginalized populations ... geared toward the ultimate goal of revealing the truth" (p. 273) that our society is embedded with and structured by racism.

Counterstories and Social Studies

Ladson-Billings and Tate (1995) introduced CRT into education as a way to assess how systemic racism impacted education. Ladson-Billings's (2003) use of CRT to critique the ways social studies, as a field, tends to evade acknowledgment of race and racism continues to spark more social studies scholars to incorporate CRT as a framing for their research. Social studies scholars have used counterstories as a tool to discuss race and racism in elementary social studies (An, 2017), as a strategy to create more inclusive pedagogies and curricula for social studies teachers (Rodríguez, 2020), and as a method of amplifying the experiences of teachers of Color (Duncan, 2020, 2022) and students of Color in social studies classrooms (Howard, 2004). Duncan's (2020) study illustrated how a Black civics teacher incorporated her own counterstories and her students' counterstories in her instruction. Duncan commented that the students' use of counterstories was important in the course because "a few of Ebony's (the teacher in the study) students believed racism to be a thing of the past that ended with the signing of the Voting Rights Act in 1965" (p. 185). By listening to the experiences of their peers, the more naïve students in Ebony's class were able to understand that racism is still very much present in the United States, as exampled through the experiences of their classmates.

MIA AND RANDY'S STORIES

The stories that I reflect on in this chapter come from a larger study in which I conducted interviews and think-alouds with five Black social teachers across the United States, inquiring how they approached teaching topics such as enslavement or Reconstruction. This chapter focuses on the interviews and think-alouds from Mia and Randy. Mia, a social studies teacher with 17 years of experience, teaches U.S. history at an urban public high school that serves predominately Black students. Randy, a social studies teacher with 10 years of experience, teaches financial literacy and African American history at an urban high school that serves predominately Black students. As a qualitative method, I used think-alouds (Patton, 2002) during the interviews where I asked teachers to walk me through how they create lessons on the Reconstruction Amendments.

The teachers' use of counterstories when teaching the Reconstruction Amendments illuminates what Tillet (2012) noted about "civic estrangement," where Black people operate as both citizens and noncitizens because their access to full citizenship is not always attainable. The teachers used their lived experiences to emphasize perspective taking and empathy, and to disrupt the notion that "the law is fair for all." Pedagogically, the stories served multiple purposes: they rendered civic lessons more relatable for their students, they disrupted societal stereotypes of Black people, and they made space for students to share their own stories with racism. In the following sections, I share how Mia and Randy used stories to provide a different perspective on their realities of citizenship.

"It Must Have Not Meant 'Me' When It Said 'We'"

Mia walked me through how she prepares to teach a lesson on the Reconstruction Amendments to her students. Mia noted that the essential or overarching question that she poses to her students before she begins teaching is, "Have these Amendments stood the test of time?" Mia's story is below.

> I tell them a story about how one day I was driving, in my Beamer, minding my business, jamming to Mary J. and next thing I know someone pulled me over. When I first saw the lights, I frantically looked down to see if I was speeding. I wasn't. I thought perhaps my taillight was out; in fact, I convinced myself the taillight was out because why else would I be pulled over? The officer comes to my window, and before I could apologize for the light being out, he harshly asked—is this your car? I responded in a calm yet taken-aback tone, of course—this is my car and why are you stopping me? The officer ignored my question and asked for my license and registration. I gathered the materials, but in my head, I thought ain't this sum ish. After checking my credentials, I asked the officer again why he pulled me over, to which he responded, "I wanted to make sure." He then told me to have a good day. Was I not allowed to have a Beamer? In what world are officers allowed to just pull people over just because they needed to check? This must be against the law? Ain't I a citizen? All of these questions flooded my head after that incident. I came to the conclusion that when the Constitution said "we," it must not have meant me. But it did not end there. I took down the officer's badge number and reported him. Whether anything happened to him, I'm not sure, but I knew I wasn't just gonna let him get away with it.

As Mia finished sharing her story, she commented that, in past years, by the time she got to the end of that story the students were so engaged they wanted her to keep sharing. She recalled that a student once yelled out, "F the police and you lucky you alive—they don't see us as citizens. This happened to me before." Mia noted that her story was a great segue into her lesson because it prompted students to ask whether the police pulling her over was legal, whether a citizen should be treated like she was treated, and what caused a police officer to randomly pull her over. Thinking about these questions in tandem to the teaching of the Reconstruction Amendments are important because it allows students to contend with other factors that may affect one's access to the rights of a citizen.

"I Ain't Gonna Lie—I Was Scared"

Randy, a high school U.S. history teacher, walked me through how he prepares to teach a lesson on the 14th Amendment to his students. Randy noted that each year he teaches this lesson, he ends with a personal story. When I asked him about the utility of the story, Randy explained: "It leaves them with another point of view, it leaves them with something to think about, and I think my story might help them [his Black students] in the future. Randy's story is below.

> I was at my friend's 14th birthday party and he's white and lived in a white neighborhood and there was a semi busy road near where he lived. His mom needed something for the party, so we walked to the store to get it. On the way to the store, we had silly string from the party, and I just remember running around the neighborhood, spraying it and messing with each other. But you know, you go out in the suburbs, people leave their garages open, so they see us. So, we get to the store, we buying the stuff for his mom and cop cars pull up. At that time, I was about 6'4, so they point me out and say, "Sir can you come with us? We got calls of somebody breaking into cars and vandalizing properties." I tell them I didn't do that, but they put me in the car first. My friend got to sit outside and wait for his mom to come. I tell my students, I ain't gonna to lie to you—I was scared. I also tell them I might not be here to speak to you if it happened during this present time because I either might have been shot by a neighborhood watch person like brother Trayvon; or an officer might have had their knee on my neck. I end my story asking my students—is this how a citizen is treated? If I wasn't a tall Black boy, would this have happened? At the end of the day it motivated me to learn my rights as a citizen.

As Randy finished his story, he commented that he always asked his students to reflect on this story and be prepared to discuss their reflections in the next class. He remarked that when his students came back to class, they thanked Randy for sharing his story because it resonated with them as they, too, have been profiled by the police. His students also appreciated the story because it made them feel seen. Randy concluded:

> We all have stories, especially our kids, when the textbooks and curriculum expect us to teach these amendments through one lens I need to add in my story because if not—I'd be doing a disservice to my students and to my own experiences.

LEVERAGING STORIES AS PEDAGOGY

Unfortunately, Black social studies teachers are an underrepresented group in the social studies literature (Duncan, 2022) but, as illustrated by Mia and Randy, there is much the field can learn from Black social studies teachers and their pedagogies. The teachers' utilities of their counterstories were significant components of how they chose to teach the Reconstruction

Amendments. Not only were their counterstories engaging, but these stories aligned with the rich histories of Black teachers employing emancipatory pedagogies for their Black students (Cooper, 1930; Woodson, 1933). In both lessons, the teachers employed counterstories to complicate their civics curriculum by illustrating how citizenship is not always stable—especially when you have Black skin.

Mia's Story as Pedagogy

Mia's story described a situation where the police wrongfully pulled her over. Using her story as a pedagogical tool when teaching her civics lesson on the 14th Amendment was effective because it illustrated the inconsistencies between what the students are expected to learn and the lived experiences of Black people. When civic education is taught without the inclusion of race and racism, students of Color who experience oppression and injustices are not able to connect the civic education they learn in their social studies classrooms with their lived experiences that strip them of their full rights of a citizen and their humanity. While Mia's civics curriculum claimed that the 14th amendment guaranteed all persons born or naturalized in the United States access to full rights of a citizen, her counterstory not only challenged this dominant narrative as she was unlawfully pulled over by a police officer, but as Dixson and Rousseau Anderson (2018) maintained, it added value and legitimacy to the knowledges held by people of Color.

Mia's counterstory served not only as an alternate narrative to the curriculum but also made space for her students to relate to the material. Similar to Duncan's (2020) study, by sharing her counterstory Mia created space for her students to communicate how they, too, have been wrongfully pulled over by a police officer for simply being Black. The inclusion of Mia's counterstory in the lesson allowed for students not to have to experience their oppression in isolation; rather, they were able to share how their rights as U.S. citizens had also been denied. Last, Mia's counterstories reflected the history of racism that Black people have had to endure since their forced arrival here over 400 years ago, while simultaneously illustrating how Black people have resisted white supremacy. This resistance, shown at the end of Mia's story, where she commented that "it did not end there" because she reported the police officer, is a nod to Ladson-Billings and Tate (1995), who asserted that counterstories are a "first step on the road to justice" (p. 58).

Randy's Story as Pedagogy

Randy's story described a time when he was 14 years old where he was racially profiled and forced to sit in a police car while his white friend had the privilege of sitting on the sidewalk. Randy's counterstory, as pedagogy, emphasized how Black experiences are often unaccounted for when teaching lessons about citizenship. At the end of his story, Randy stated, "when the textbooks and curriculum expect us to teach these amendments through one lens, I need to add in my story, because if not, I'd be doing a disservice to my students and to my own experiences." Similar to the Black teachers in Duncan's (2022) study, Randy felt a personal responsibility, a duty, to include his story in his lesson to prepare his students for future discrimination they may encounter.

Randy's centering of Black emotion within his counterstory speaks to the ways counterstories often disrupt the status quo and harmful stereotypes (Solórzano, 1997) that situate Black people as subhuman bodies merely existing, without emotions such as fear (Jones, 2022). Through his counterstory, Randy disrupted these stereotypes and challenged the status quo by acknowledging that he feared for his life when, as a 14-year-old, not only was he unlawfully placed into the back of a police car, but he was the only child placed in the car while his white friend watched. The notion that Black people fear because of their existence in an oppressive society is missing from social studies standards and curricula that too often portray Black people as one dimensional, sometimes messiah-like figures (Alridge, 2006) who are able to experience suffering but lack the ability to fear (Jones, 2022). Randy's counterstory not only nuances the relationship between citizenship education and race but dispels notions of toxic Black stereotypes and masculinity (Ferguson, 2020). As a 6'4" Black man, Randy's application of fear in his narrative demonstrated that Black men also have the ability and the right to feel afraid.

WHAT'S IN A STORY?

During an interview, Charlie Rose asked Toni Morrison why she writes about race and why she focuses solely on Black life in her writing. Morrison poignantly responded: "What I am interested in is writing without the gaze, without the white gaze" (Morrison, 1998). Like Morrison, Mia and Randy were also interested in teaching their civics lessons without the white gaze. For them, this white gaze was civics curricula that failed to include and critique race and racism and its influence on access to citizenship. To mitigate this harm, these teachers integrated their own experiences, their stories, into their civics lessons as both a counter and as an act of resistance to speak back to colorblind civics lessons. Using stories as part of their pedagogy provided a more complex and truthful teaching of citizenship in the United States.

We can learn many things by including counterstories as part of our pedagogies teaching civics. As Mia and Randy demonstrated, stories increase engagement among students, stories relate the past to the present, and perhaps most importantly, stories provide diverse accounts of the past that are erased from social studies and civics curricula. When Black teachers and other teachers of Color include their own stories or stories of their Elders and Ancestors, they are providing a different perspective from which students can learn. Though Mia and Randy's civics curricula did not include how race affects one's access to the rights afforded to citizens, their stories did. Though Mia and Randy's civics curricula did not associate the history of racism in the United States with the ongoing fragility of Black citizenship, their stories did. Their stories filled a crucial gap missing from civics curricula that not only made their lessons more accurate but also corroborated some of their students' experiences, and prepared others on how to respond to the racism they may experience in their own lives. As Randy so powerfully stated, "we all have stories, especially our kids . . . I need to add in my story because if not, I'd be doing a disservice to my students and to my own experiences."

REFERENCES

Alexander, M. (2010). *The new Jim Crow: Mass incarceration in the age of colorblindness*. Pantheon Books.

Alridge, D. P. (2006). The limits of master narratives in history textbooks: An analysis of representations of Martin Luther King, Jr. *Teachers College Record, 108*(4), 662–686.

An, S. (2017). Teaching race through AsianCrit-informed counterstories of school segregation. *Social Studies Research and Practice 12*(2), 210–231.

Berry, M. F. (1995). *Black resistance/white law: A history of constitutional racism in America*. Penguin.

Brown, A. L., Crowley, R. M., & King, L. J. (2011). Black Civitas: An examination of Carter Woodson's contributions to teaching about race, citizenship, and the Black soldier. *Theory & Research in Social Education, 39*(2), 278–299.

Busey, C., & Dowie-Chin, T. (2021). The making of global Black anti-citizen/citizenship: Situating BlackCrit in global citizenship research and theory. *Theory & Research in Social Education, 49*(2), 153–175.

Cooper, A. J. 1930. "On Education." In E. Bhan & C. Lemert (Eds.), *The voice of Anna Julia Cooper* (pp. 248–258). Rowman & Littlefield.

Crenshaw, Kimberlé (1991). Mapping the margins: Intersectionality, identity politics, and violence against women of color. *Stanford Law Review, 43*, 1241–1299.

DeCuir, J., & Dixson, A. (2004). So when it comes out, they aren't that surprised that it is there: Using critical race theory as a tool of analysis of race and racism in education. *Educational Researcher, 33*(5), 26–31.

Delgado, R., & Stefancic, J. (2017). *Critical race theory: An introduction* (Vol. 20). New York University Press.

DeLombard, J. M. (2019). Dehumanizing slave personhood. *American Literature, 91*(3), 491–521.

Dixson, A. D., & Rousseau Anderson, C. (2018). Where are we? Critical race theory in education 20 years later. *Peabody Journal of Education, 93*(1), 121–131.

Duncan, K. E. (2020). What better tool do I have? *The High School Journal, 103*(3), 176–189.

Duncan, K. E. (2022). "That's my job": Black teachers' perspectives on helping Black students navigate white supremacy. *Race Ethnicity and Education, 25*(7), 978–996.

Ferguson, A. A. (2020). *Bad boys: Public schools in the making of Black masculinity.* University of Michigan Press.

Howard, T. (2004). "Does race really matter?" Secondary students' constructions of racial dialogue in the social studies. *Theory & Research in Social Education, 32*(4), 484–502.

Jones, B. L. (2022). Feeling fear as power and oppression: An examination of Black and white fear in Virginia's US history standards and curriculum framework. *Theory & Research in Social Education, 50*(3) 431–463.

Ladson-Billings, G. (Ed.). (2003). *Critical race theory perspectives on the social studies: The profession, policies, and curriculum.* Information Age Publishing.

Ladson-Billings, G., & Tate, W. (1995). Toward a critical race theory of education. *Teachers College Record, 97*(1), 47–68.

Matsuda, M., Lawrence, C., Delgado, R., & Crenshaw, K. (Eds.). (1993). *Words that wound: Critical race theory, assaultive speech, and the First Amendment.* Westview Press.

Miller, R., Liu, K., & Ball, A. F. (2020). Critical counter-narrative as transformative methodology for educational equity. *Review of Research in Education, 44*(1), 269–300.

Mills, C. W. (1997). *The racial contract.* Cornell University Press.

Morrison, T. (1998). From an interview on Charlie Rose [Video]. Public Broadcasting Service. https://www.youtube.com/watch?v=F4vIGvKpT1c

National Advisory Commission on Civil Disorders. (1967). Kerner Commission Report on the Causes, Events, and Aftermaths of the Civil Disorders of 1967.

Patton, M. (2002). *Qualitative research and evaluation methods* (3rd ed.). Sage.

Rigeur, L., & Beshlian, A. (2019). The history and progress of Black citizenship. *Du Bois Review, 16*(1), 267–277. https://doi.org/10.1017/S1742058X19000158

Rodríguez, N. N. (2020). "This is why nobody knows who you are:"(Counter) Stories of Southeast Asian Americans in the Midwest. *Review of Education, Pedagogy, and Cultural Studies, 42*(2), 157–174.

Solórzano, D. (1997). Images and words that wound: Critical race theory, racial stereotyping, and teacher education. *Teacher Education Quarterly, 24*(3), 5–19.

Stampp, K. M. (1956). *Peculiar institution: Slavery in the ante-bellum south.* Vintage Books.

Tillet, S. (2012). *Sites of slavery: Citizenship and racial democracy in the post-civil rights imagination.* Duke University Press.

Vickery, A. E. (2016). "I worry about my community": African American women utilizing communal notions of citizenship in the social studies classroom. *International Journal of Multicultural Education, 18*(1), 28–44.

Woodson, C. G. (1933/1990). *The Mis-education of the Negro.* Africa World Press.

CHAPTER 11

The Black Lives Matter at School Guiding Principles
Fostering Black Cultural Citizenship Through Critical Civic Empathy

Denisha Jones and Sarah A. Mathews

The Black Lives Matter (BLM) movement was born when three Black women—Patrisse Cullors, Opal Tometi, and Alicia Garza—used the hashtag #BlackLivesMatter as a rallying cry to the state-sanctioned terror against Black lives. Inspired by this Black freedom struggle, the Black Lives Matter at School (BLMAS) movement began in Seattle in 2016 when teachers at John Muir Elementary School wore shirts explicitly stating, "Black Lives Matter/We Stand Together" (Hagopian, 2020, p. 2). Today, the BLMAS movement is guided by four national demands: (1) Mandate Black history and ethnic studies, (2) Hire more Black teachers, (3) End zero tolerance, and (4) Fund counselors, not cops.

Soon after the Seattle teach-ins, educators in Philadelphia used the Black Lives Matter Global Network's *What We Believe* statement to identify 13 guiding principles (13GPs) to incorporate into classrooms. These 13GPs include empathy, loving engagement, restorative justice, diversity, globalism, Black families, Black villages, intergenerational, trans affirming, queer affirming, collective value, Black women, and unapologetically Black. The national BLMAS movement uses these principles to develop a curriculum affirming Blackness, centering communal values, supporting individuals' authentic selves, and transforming notions of justice. Though not officially labeled as a civic education project, we examine how teaching the 13GPs contributes to cultural citizenship education for Black lives (Jones, 2022; Jones & Mathews, 2023; Mathews & Jones, In press).

This exploration has led us to problematize traditional notions of citizenship (Westheimer & Kahne, 2004), civic engagement (Gaby, 2017), and the civic empowerment gap (Levinson, 2010). Most scholarship related to the civic lives of young people includes implicit and explicit conceptualizations of civic life normed to white, middle- to upper-class, straight, cis, able-bodied, American, and Christian identities and ways of being. Constructing research on civic education through a lens of civics defined for and by those positioned as dominant effectively renders those positioned as nondominant, less civically engaged, lacking civic empowerment, and failing or unable to enact their civic identity (Woodson & Love, 2019).

In this chapter, we explore how teachers' utilization of the 13GPs supports the tradition of Black citizenship education and fosters cultural citizenship for Black lives. We begin by elucidating the problems located in the literature on civic engagement and civic empowerment. We then explore the literature on cultural citizenship in relation to critical race pedagogies (CRP) and critical citizenship education to explore how the 13GPs reinforce this framework. Finally, this chapter will feature examples of critical race pedagogies (CRP) from pre-K–12 grade teachers who incorporate the 13GPs into their classrooms to explore how three principles—empathy, loving engagement, and restorative justice—reinforce cultural citizenship and expand notions of civic engagement.

DE-CENTERING WHITENESS IN RESEARCH ON CIVICS

Civic education remains a widely theorized and researched endeavor in the never-ending quest to build a stronger democracy through public education. Social studies education helps students learn the civic knowledge, skills, and dispositions deemed necessary for democratic participation. A frequently used framework, Westheimer and Kahne (2004) outlined three archetypes of "good" citizenship: (1) the personally responsible citizen, (2) the participatory citizen, and (3) the justice-oriented citizen (p. 240).

Studies investigating civic engagement through civic participation led Levinson (2010) to assert the existence of "a profound civic empowerment gap in the United States that disproportionately muffles the voices of non-White, foreign-born, and especially low-income citizens and amplifies the voices of White, native-born, and especially wealthy citizens" (p. 331). Woodson and Love (2019), however, provide an essential lens for critiquing gap research, noting how deficit-oriented assumptions often guide these comparative studies. They remind us that "Black children are perpetually measured against a yardstick created for other histories, cultures, and relationships to school and society. In many instances, Black children's perceived potential is solely defined by middle-class White children's actualities" (p. 93). The authors argue that traditional notions of civic engagement are not "equally available, relevant, and ideal for Black children" (p. 93).

Missing from most analyses of Black youth civic engagement is a nuanced understanding of how Black children are routinely socialized and educated to believe only outsiders can solve the problems in their communities.

Black children constantly internalize messages that their communities are not worthy investments (Kozol, 1991) and that only outsiders, mainly white liberals, can solve their problems (Love, 2019). Further, when the curriculum frames Blackness as the community's problem, how do we expect youth to solve something they are educated to believe lies within their very existence (Brown & Brown, 2021; ross, 2021)? Woodson and Love (2019) note that "comparing Black children's (understandable critical) civic attitudes to the more positive civic orientations of many middle-class White children makes Black kids appear disengaged, hopeless, nihilistic, and apathetic" (p. 94).

Levinson and scholars concerned about the "civic empowerment gap" acknowledge some contextual factors contributing to these findings, such as attending segregated schools and experiences with racism (Littenberg-Tobias & Cohen, 2016). However, the studies they rely on fail to examine contextual differences in the lives of Black, Latino, and white children. The "civic empowerment gap" positions BIPOC and poor children on the losing end of a perceived gap constructed solely on the expectations and experiences of white children and beliefs about good citizenship as defined by white scholars. Thus, comparative research on civic engagement must decenter whiteness and explore how racially marginalized children, and their communities, define and construct their civic worlds.

BEYOND DEFICIT VIEWS OF YOUTH CIVIC ENGAGEMENT: CRITICAL CIVIC PRAXIS

Instead of accepting deficit narratives about Black youth civic engagement, some scholars examine the diverse ways youth engage in civic life that are not typically measured or studied. Building on the work of youth participatory action research scholars, Mirra and Garcia (2017) offer a model of critical civic learning and development that includes "developing critical consciousness, identifying multiple identities/perspectives, connecting to pursue social action, resisting injustice creatively, and embodying critical civic praxis" (p. 150). By analyzing the disconnect between civic ideals and civic inequalities, Mirra and Garcia make a case for developing new theories and frameworks for civic education.

We find critical civic praxis an important model for understanding how racially marginalized children engage as civic actors and how teachers can facilitate civic engagement. Critical civic praxis provides a framework to problematize traditional notions of citizenship and decenter white normative civic ideals. When we apply critical civic praxis to Westheimer and Kahne's three types of citizens, we can recognize how core assumptions of the personally responsible citizen, participatory citizen, and justice-oriented citizen fail to include space for racially marginalized youths. We go beyond looking for examples of good character, willingness to participate in established systems, and questioning injustices as markers of civic engagement through critical civic praxis. Instead, we make space to witness the many civic beliefs, ways of being, and actions that BIPOC utilize to make sense of their world. We now explore how cultural citizenship and critical race pedagogies provide a theoretical framework to center Black lives in civic research.

CULTURAL CITIZENSHIP AND CRITICAL RACE PEDAGOGIES

Cultural citizenship offers another framework for decentering whiteness in civic research. Latino scholars coined "cultural citizenship" while defining how marginalized groups engaged in cultural actions assert their rights as citizens (Flores & Benmayor, 1997; Rosaldo, 1997). Cultural citizenship is defined "as a broad range of activities of everyday life through which Latinos and other groups claim space in society and eventually claim rights" (Flores & Benmayor, 1997, p. 15). These activities foster empowerment and agency while problematizing historical constructions of citizenship that sought to marginalize BIPOC as subordinates (Rosaldo, 1997). In our previous studies on how the BLMAS 13GPs foster cultural citizenship education for Black lives, we identified similar themes of agentic teaching to support young children as civic actors in the present capable of grappling with big ideas (Jones & Mathews, 2023).

Critical race pedagogy (CRP) grew out of the critical pedagogy's limitations, situating racism as endemic to education and calling for the need to explore power dynamics, incorporate reflectivity, and center liberatory pedagogies (Jennings & Lynn, 2005; Lynn et al., 2013). CRP has four broad categories. Education must (1) help students understand that institutionalized racism exists, (2) include strategies that help individuals understand how power functions in creating and limiting access to education, (3) provide time for self-reflection, and (4) promote liberatory frameworks to seek justice and equity in educational experiences. Together, these frameworks provide a theoretical foundation for exploring cultural citizenship education for Black lives. Through the testimonials of how teachers use the 13GPs in the classroom, we provide an approach for analyzing civics centered on Black lives.

METHODOLOGY

This chapter includes counterstories (Bell, 2020) from pre-K–12 teachers gathered through a narrative qualitative research study (Kim, 2016; Riesman, 2008). Narrative inquiry provides a space to center marginalized voices and challenge the master narrative (Duncan 2019, 2021). Narrative research also captures "the histories and perspectives that are brought to the table, and the conversation and the lives of those that interact and connect with us as scholars, as teachers, and as colleagues" (Berry & Bowers Cook, 2019, p. 87). By accessing teachers' narratives, we examined the nuanced ways teachers implemented the 13GPs to expand civics. This chapter explores:

> How do teachers implement principles that center and affirm Blackness to facilitate relational, critical, and cultural civic education?

Participants

We used purposive sampling (Patton, 2014) to solicit seven teachers active in the BLMAS movement to participate in this study (Table 11.1). Author One (Denisha) recruited teachers at every level—two preschool, one kindergarten,

Table 11.1. Participant Demographics

Participant Name	Self-Identified Demographic Information	Ages/Grades Taught	Type of School	Years of Teaching Experience	# of BLMAS WoA
Leah	Black Puerto Rican, Female	Kindergarten	Private School	21	4
Makayla	Multiracial, Female	3s and 4s	Preschool/ECC	10	4
Rachel	White, Female	Pre-K 4s	Public School	9	3
Alicia	African American, Female	1st Grade	Public School	4	4
Mateo	Latino White Man	9th- to 12th-grade Music Teacher/Restorative Justice	Public School	16	4
Liliana	Multiethnic, Female	9th- to 12th-grade Spanish	Public School	11	4
Kendall	White, Female	Middle School Art	Public School	5	4

one 1st grade, one middle school, and two high school teachers—to explore similarities and differences between how teachers incorporate the 13GPs across grade level. Every teacher had participated in at least three BLMAS Weeks of Action (WoA). Although we tried to recruit a variety of participants, only one self-identified as male. Participants taught in New York, the Washington DC area, or the Midwest.

Data Collection

Each teacher participated in two hour-long, semi-structured interviews through Zoom. Author One conducted all interviews because she is actively involved in the BLMAS movement and had already established rapport with the participants. The first interview gathered background information, the teachers' history with BLMAS, and their rationale for and processes of implementing the curriculum in their classrooms. We asked teachers to provide the activity or lesson plans they used as an elicitation tool during that first interview. This stage allowed participants to describe how they incorporated the 13GPs in their classrooms. The second interview was conducted after the 2021 BLMAS WoA, allowing participants to share how they adapted their teaching due to COVID-19 and answer researchers' follow-up questions. While watching the recordings, Author Two (Sarah) transcribed the data verbatim.

Data Analysis

We utilized a reiterative data analysis process to analyze the narratives produced by study participants. During each transcription read, we used a variation of Charmaz's (2006) incident-by-incident approach, where each incident in the narrative was selected and explored for story structure, political and social context, and similar and contrasting story elements (Grbich, 2007). The lesson plans added context and details to support the teachers' narratives. After the initial reading, we independently looked across the critical incidents, searching for similar themes (Auerbach & Silverstein, 2003), which often meant returning to previous transcripts to apply newly generated themes. We also drew on Auerbach and Silverstein's (2003) notion of elaborative coding, which allowed us to apply our cultural citizenship and critical civic practices frameworks to the data. After each researcher exhausted their analysis, we compared our themes until we reached a consensus.

FINDINGS

The teachers incorporated the 13GPs in a variety of ways. Some teachers aligned their instruction with the outline provided through the BLMAS

Table 11.2. Empathy, Loving Engagement, and Restorative Justice

Principle	BLMAS Website
Empathy	We are committed to practicing empathy; we engage comrades with the intent to learn about and connect with their contexts (para 2).
Loving Engagement	We are committed to embodying and practicing justice, liberation, and peace in our engagements with one another (para 3.)
Restorative Justice	We are committed to collectively, lovingly, and courageously working vigorously for freedom and justice for Black people and, by extension, all people. As we forge our path, we intentionally build and nurture a beloved community that is bonded together through a beautiful struggle that is restorative, not depleting (para 1).

curriculum for the WoA or Year of Purpose, focusing on principles during recommended days or months. Others interspersed the GPs throughout the year. Some participants explicitly taught about one principle, while others asked students to determine which GP they thought applied to a particular lesson or activity. Teachers used children's literature, role-playing, issues-oriented instruction, community engagement activities, project-based learning, art, and music to help students explore the 13GPs. These efforts help students recognize white supremacy, unlearn and relearn Black history, and build or affirm their own cultural identity. In this chapter, we focus on three GPs—empathy, loving engagement, and restorative justice—to decenter whiteness in civic education and advocate for frameworks supporting cultural citizenship education for Black lives.

Table 11.2 provides the language for these three GPs as stated on the BLMAS website. These GPs describe relational commitments for engaging in collaborative action for Black lives. As we describe how the teachers rationalize and incorporate the principles into their classrooms, we argue for their inclusion in frameworks for exploring civic attitudes and beliefs that center Black experiences.

Empathy

At the early childhood level, many teachers focused on empathy as the first step to introducing the big ideas of the 13GPs. For example, when Makayla and her early childhood colleagues worried about how to introduce these ideas at the youngest level, she was encouraged by a consultant, who said, "Just do empathy. Like just focus on empathy. Like low key, keep it simple." (Unless indicated otherwise, all data comes from individual interviews.)

Makayla also acknowledged that "empathy is the foundation for the rest of the guiding principles. Because you can't be trans-affirming and not empathetic."

Makayla also has students practice displaying empathy by incorporating children's literature and role-playing with puppets. The class read the picture book *Strictly No Elephants* (Mantchev & Yoo, 2015) about a pet club that excluded certain animals. A boy who owned an elephant started a new club with other children whose pets were also excluded. Makayla reflected on the class discussion, saying,

> Granted, no one has a pet elephant, a pet skunk, or a giraffe. But the kids really like it, and they really get it. Because then you'll get, "Well, then they can't come to mine." And others were like, "Okay, so now you're perpetuating that." We break down those kinds of thought processes.

This example demonstrates how young children were wrestling with notions of fairness and could empathize with those excluded. When it comes to empathy, Makayla says, "I just kept reminding them like, 'We do this all the time! We're just naming it.'"

Alicia also used a children's book, *Desmond and the Very Mean Word* (Tutu & Ford, 2012), to teach empathy. This text tells the story of the late activist Desmond Tutu as a young boy riding a new bicycle through his segregated South African neighborhood when a group of white boys shouted a very mean word at him. In her lesson plan, Alicia shares a synopsis of the book:

> He first responds by shouting an insult, but soon discovers that fighting back with mean words doesn't make him feel any better. With the help of kindly Father Trevor, Desmond comes to understand his conflicted feelings and sees that all people deserve compassion, whether or not they say they are sorry (Tutu & Ford, 2012).

When describing this lesson, Alicia said, "I really wanted to get them to think about what it means to not have forgiveness from others, but forgiveness for yourself."

At the secondary level, teachers also felt *empathy* was a principle that students often gravitated toward. High school Spanish teacher Liliana begins each year by saying

> "Look, I have light-skinned privilege. This work, I feel is my duty. But I don't have the right as a non-Black woman, no matter how I identify as Brown, or whatever that is . . . my experiences will never compare to what Black students go through in this country every single day, and my Black brothers and sisters and colleagues." I'm very upfront with them and say that no matter what I go through, no matter what my perspective is, it will never compare.

Liliana insists that her students understand her desire to learn about their lives and connect with their situations; however, this does not mean she can necessarily relate to their experiences. Her recognition of the privileges she receives from having light skin provides an important context for practicing the type of empathy that does not assume one can fully understand another's experience. As a relational practice, empathy highlights the need to listen and learn from others and provides a missing component from traditional measures of civic beliefs, attitudes, and dispositions.

Loving Engagement

The fairness component of *loving engagement* is easy for early childhood teachers to incorporate into their classrooms because young children frequently articulate when they think things are unfair. Alicia described how important it was for teachers to model loving engagement at this level. She said, "I'm going to show you what it looks like. I'm going to show you what it feels like." Early childhood teacher Leah shared, "I think that it is definitely important that we teach them those interruptions, where like, 'Yeah, does that seem fair? No.' But we also have to give kids the actual narrative that we want them to have." In addition to addressing fairness, loving engagement asks us to consider the unfair advantages we receive. Leah shared the following questions as prompts to support young children in practicing loving engagement:

> Practicing love and justice can be hard. Can you think of a time when something was unfair in your favor, such as when you accidentally got more than someone else? How did that make you feel? What did you do? Would you make the same choice now? Why or why not? If it's hard to give things up, even if you know it's not fair for you to have them, what makes it easier for us to do it? How can we help people decide to think about the good of the community? Are there times when individual people are more important than the community? How can we help communities make those kinds of decisions?

To make our communities centers of justice, peace, and liberation, we must reflect on fairness from multiple sides of a situation.

For many of these teachers, the loving engagement began with creating a safe space for their students to reflect on their own beliefs while engaging with their peers' perspectives. Secondary Spanish teacher Liliana described this process, saying

> You have to be intentional about creating a safe space first. I make sure that my students understand that we, in a consensus manner, come together to create our values and our guidelines of our classroom—what it's going to look like, how we're going to interact with one another—so that we create the foundation

to be able to have these discussions. Because they are hard discussions. They're gut-wrenching discussions. They're uplifting discussions. They're affirmative discussions. But they're difficult, especially for white students.

Liliana also shared that she tells her students

> I don't have the right to determine for you as Black students what your idea of liberation is, what your idea of justice is, the methods of action that you feel necessary to take. It's just my place to create the space so that you can have the opportunity to speak your mind and that your voice will be valued, respected, loved, and cared for in this room. And that you can see yourselves in the curriculum that I teach.

As a relational practice, teachers model loving engagement by creating an environment that models for students how to engage in collective liberation work.

Mateo incorporates restorative circles in his advising course. Yet, reflecting on how he plans for these experiences, Mateo shared:

> Using the 13 guiding principles, we can't guarantee that trouble won't happen. Because we can't do that, a safe space is not possible. But I try to mitigate . . . I'm thinking in advance of where issues like pain and violence would happen.

During one discussion, a student asked him, "How is it that we can use the word 'queer' now but not the N-word?" He shared how he helped the students think through the complexity of this response:

> I was like, "A dope question, which in a way, I didn't know how to answer. I'm taking my cues from y'all but also from my queer community and my Black community. Right?" And then we began talking about . . . people are not a monolith. I identify as queer. A bunch of my friends who identify as queer love the word queer. I have friends who are gay and lesbian who tell me, "Don't you ever refer to me as a queer because back in the '80s, I lost a lot of friends to that." And, in my own school, you know, we have Black teachers who use the N-word. And we have older Black teachers who are like, "Don't you ever use that word to refer to me."

He finalized this example, saying, "All we can do is stay in relationship, right our wrongs, apologize . . . some folks are going to be harmed by the same things, but some folks are going to be lifted because people have different experiences." Loving engagement in Mateo's classroom is established by an instructor that is vulnerable about his experiences and demonstrates that he is trying to hear and consider all perspectives on issues. Moreover, Mateo models the complexity of striving for justice for diverse groups that often approach actions and concepts differently. Instead of issuing a blanket rule that offensive words will not be allowed in their space, Mateo models how practicing loving engagement for each other means grappling with different beliefs and opinions and finding ways to honor and value them.

Restorative Justice

The restorative justice guiding principle merges empathy and loving engagement to help fight against collective injustice. Restorative justice rejects punitive discipline that disposes of those who commit harm and puts forth a practice to build collective liberation by engaging with all people to restore relationships. Young children learn that apologizing for harm is not enough. To practice restorative justice, we must repair the harm with the intent that we will make better choices in the future. Allowing for second chances and restorative accountability centers nurturing relationships over punishments.

Rachel used Lana Button's book *Willow Finds a Way* (2013) in her preschool class. This book describes how the protagonist stood up to another student who was forcing the other children to do as she wanted, or she would not invite them to her birthday party. Rachel shared:

> I think it was the first year that I taught it. I hadn't introduced it with a specific principle in mind (there's a few that kind of fit into that specific book). At the end, basically, there's a bully who is being hurtful to a lot of people, and Willow, the main character, is trying to think of a way to like say "no" [and] to stand up to this bully. And she does find a way. Then the bully ends up feeling really sad and lonely and gets kind of isolated from the rest of the class because they all stand up against her. Willow comes back and invites her back into the fold and kind of says, "Hey, I still am willing to be your friend."

This story provides a way for young children to recognize that practicing restorative justice means supporting those who engage in harmful behaviors so they can learn and make a different choice.

Alicia shared how she modeled restorative justice through her interactions with her students. She shared that she told them:

> "You might do something that upsets Miss. You know, does Miss ever put you out or make you feel bad? You know, what does Miss say?" They talked a lot about how I give them opportunities to apologize and I treat them the same all the time.

Teachers model restorative justice by providing children with opportunities to change their behavior and remain valued and loved community members. By reminding children they have space to make mistakes and better choices, Alicia encourages them to practice restorative justice with each other.

Art educator Kendall introduces students to the restorative justice principle with the following quote: "Something that's restorative makes things better, healthier, or stronger, especially after it has been damaged." She incorporates muralist Kah Yangni's graphic art piece "Free Them All" to illustrate how art can be a political act. Working with Survived and Punished NYC, Kah Yangni created art to pressure the governor of New York to release incarcerated people during the pandemic (Kah Yangni, 2020). Kendall's students are then encouraged to create artistic expressions that depict their understandings of, and experiences with, restorative justice. Given the complexity of exploring restorative justice as both healing those who were harmed and restoring those who caused harm, this project allowed her students to create their own depictions of this principle.

As mentioned above, Mateo explicitly incorporates restorative circles in his teaching, especially during his advisement period. Each student is responsible for creating a lesson for their assigned class session, "unpoliced" by their instructor. To articulate how he uses restorative justice practices, he shares an example of a student's presentation about Sigmund Freud that featured a potentially misogynistic video about Freud's concept of penis envy. He shared how he followed up with a restorative circle and reflected:

> We had a restorative circle that lasted like 7 minutes, just making sure that everybody was cool. And then we name it, right? Like, say, "Hey, what we're doing right now, is we're engaging in the restorative justice principle. I felt like this video could be disrespectful or violent to some folks. Let's talk about it." And then students were really empathetic. And then I said, "Hey, that is you being empathetic toward others. Like, you were listening. You're trying to learn a different point of view."

The restorative circle practice provided the space for those harmed by the video to share their perspective so that others could practice empathy. As a practice, restorative circles embody loving engagement, model empathy, and center therapeutic relationships, reinforcing the intersectionality of these principles.

DISCUSSION

In this chapter, we demonstrate that the principles of empathy, loving engagement, and restorative justice are relational civic practices missing from Westheimer and Kahne's (2004) and noncritical civic frameworks, measures of youth civic engagement, and civic education practices. We argue that the 13GPs are criteria for cycles of critical civic praxis (Mirra & Garcia, 2017) and foster cultural citizenship education for Black lives. Empathy allows for identifying multiple identities and perspectives, loving engagement can lead to creative ways to resist injustice that center liberation and peace, and restorative justice ensures that our pursuance of social action is built on developing relationships and nurturing the community.

Our findings highlight how empathy combined with loving engagement and restorative justice closely resemble critical civic empathy. When Makayla's students use puppets to role-play how their peers may feel in a particular setting, they learn to listen to others' stories and connect with them, no matter their experience. It is not enough to say the bully was wrong. Instead, these young children are tasked with understanding a bully's motivation and imagining actions they can take to stop bullying while practicing loving engagement. *Desmond and the Very Mean Word* helps Alicia's students understand complex emotions in a situation, even what it means to have compassion for those who may not show you compassion in return. These young children learn the importance of choosing to respond to harmful actions with actions that heal. Mateo facilitates a restorative justice circle to help students identify why things might be problematic for others and how they can redress situations. By modeling loving engagement and restorative justice in their classrooms, these teachers are helping students shape narratives, practice processes in the "safest" ways possible, and determine their own liberation, supporting their use of critical race pedagogies.

Empathy as part of the BLMAS 13GPs relates to Mirra's (2018) notion of critical civic empathy. Her typology of empathy denotes four zones: false empathy, imaginative refusal, individual empathy, and critical civic empathy. False empathy and imaginative refusal are not motivated by a belief in collective liberation through collective struggle (mutual humanization). Instead, these typologies differ in orientation toward action. False empathy can lead to social action only for selected groups, while imaginative refusal seeks to prevent collaborative action. The third typology, individual empathy, "refers to the most popular understanding of empathy as the ability to walk a mile in someone's shoes while avoiding consideration of what it means to support them as fellow citizens" (Mirra, 2018, p. 11). Mirra argues that though there is some interest in mutual humanization, individual empathy does not require social action.

Critical civic empathy combines a motivation for mutual humanization and social action to push beyond narrow conceptions of empathy and requires moving beyond oneself. Critical civic empathy is not about self-reflection but a "recognition of the ways that individual experiences shape (and are shaped by) participation in civic life," (Barnes, 2019, p. 3). As we reexamine Westheimer and Kahne's (2004) three types of citizens, we note the absence of these guiding principles. Personally responsible citizens are examples of false empathy. The participatory citizen framework does not foster loving engagement as necessary for social action. Restorative justice can expand notions of the justice-oriented citizen beyond critiquing societal injustice to creating spaces and practices where mutual humanization is the goal.

The BLMAS curriculum, and particularly the 13GPs, decenter white stories, experiences, and perspectives in ways that challenge traditional notions of civic knowledge, skills, and attitudes. All 13GPs offer contemporary cultural knowledge that center and affirm Black lives rather than focusing on deficit-oriented "civic empowerment gap" models. By centering notions of empathy, loving engagement, and restorative justice, these teachers are helping students reimagine what it means to "civically engage" and maintain their authentic selves with the agency to participate as citizens in their community in the quest for individual and communal liberation.

REFERENCES

Auerbach, C., & Silverstein, L. B. (2003). *Qualitative data: An introduction to coding and analysis* (Vol. 21). New York University Press.

Barnes, M. E. (2019). Review: Education for empathy: Literacy learning and civic engagement. [Review of the book *Education for Empathy: Literacy learning and civic engagement* by Nicole Mirra]. *Journal of Language & Literacy Education. 15*(1), 1–10.

Bell, L. A. (2020). *Storytelling for social justice: Connecting narrative and arts in antiracist teaching*. Routledge.

Berry, T. R., & Bowers Cook, E. J. (2019). Critical race perspectives on narrative research in education: Centering intersectionality. In J. T. DeCuir-Gunby, T. K. Chapman, & P. A. Schultz (Eds.) *Understanding critical race research methods and methodologies: Lessons from the field* (pp. 86–96). Taylor and Francis.

Brown, K. D., & Brown, A. L. (2021). Anti-Blackness and the school curriculum. In C. A. Grant, A. N. Woodson, & M. J. Dumas (Eds.), *The future is Black: Afropessimism, fugitivity, and radical hope in education* (pp. 7–15). Routledge.

Button, L, & Howells, T. (2013). *Willow finds a way*. Kids Can Press.

Charmaz, K. (2006). *Constructing grounded theory: A practical guide through qualitative analysis*. Sage.

Duncan, K. E. (2019). "That hate on me!" Black teachers interrupting their white colleagues' racism. *Educational Studies, 55*(2), 197–213. https://doi.org/10.1080/00131946.2018.1500463

Duncan, K. E. (2021). "They act like they went to hell!": Black teachers, racial justice, and teacher education. *Journal for Multicultural Education, 15*(2), 201–212. https://doi.org/10.1108/JME-10-2020-0104

Flores, W. V., & Benmayor, R. (1997). Constructing cultural citizenship. In W. V. Flores & R. Benmayor (Eds.), *Latino cultural citizenship: Claiming identity, space, and rights* (pp. 1–23). Beacon Press.

Gaby, S. (2017). The civic engagement gap(s): Youth participation and inequality from 1976–2009. *Youth & Society, 49*(7), 923–946. https://doi.org/10.1177/0044118X16678155

Grbich, C. (2007). *Qualitative data analysis: An introduction*. Sage.

Hagopian, J. (2020). Making Black lives matter at school. In D. Jones & J. Hagopian (Eds.), *Black lives matter at school: An uprising for educational justice* (pp. 1–24). Haymarket Books.

Jennings, M. E., & Lynn, M. (2005). The house that race built: Critical pedagogy, African-American education and the re-conceptualization of a critical race pedagogy. *Educational Foundations, 19*(3–4), 15–32.

Jones D. (2022). Enacting cultural citizenship education for Black liberation: A dream for social studies education. In A. E. Vickery & N. N. Rodríguez (Eds.), *Critical race theory and social studies futures: From the nightmare of racial realism to dreaming out loud* (pp. 120–129). Teachers College Press.

Jones, D., & Mathews, S. (2023). Teaching Black Lives Matter at school: 13 guiding principles as cultural citizenship education for young children. In S. DeZutter (Ed.), *International perspectives on educating for democracy in early childhood: Recognizing young children as citizens* (pp. 240–259). Routledge.

Kah Yangni I [@kayangni]. (2020, April 18). Free them all [Image and post]. Instagram. https://www.instagram.com/p/B_IMzv2nghp/

Kim, J. (2016). *Understanding narrative inquiry: The crafting and analysis of stories and research.* Sage.

Kozol, J. (1991). *Savage inequalities.* HarperCollins.

Levinson, M. (2010). The civic empowerment gap: Defining the problem and locating solutions. In L. Sherrod, J. Torney-Purta, & C. Flanagan (Eds.). *Handbook of research on civic education* (pp. 331–361). John Wiley & Sons.

Littenberg-Tobias, J., & Cohen, A. K. (2016). Diverging paths: Understanding racial differences in civic engagement among white, African American, and Latina/o adolescents using structural equation modeling. *American Journal of Community Psychology, 57*, 102–117. https://doi.org/10.1002/ajcp.12027

Love, B. L. (2019). *We want to do more than survive: Abolitionist teaching and the pursuit of educational freedom.* Beacon Press.

Lynn, M., Jennings, M. E., & Hughes, S. (2013). Critical race pedagogy 2.0: Lessons from Derrick Bell. *Race Ethnicity and Education, 16*(4), 603–628.

Mantchev, L., & Yoo, T. (2015*). Strictly no elephants.* Simon & Schuster.

Mathews, S. A., & Jones, D. (In press). Black Lives Matter in school: Using the 13 Guiding Principles as critical race pedagogies for Black citizenship education. *Journal of Social Studies Research.* https://doi.org/10.1016/j.jssr.2022.03.001

Mirra, N. (2018). *Educating for empathy: Literacy learning and civic engagement.* Teachers College Press.

Mirra, N., & Garcia, A. (2017). Civic participation reimagined: Youth interrogation and innovation in the multimodal public sphere. *Review of Research in Education, 41*(1), 136–158. https://doi.org/10.3102/0091732X17690121

Patton, M. Q. (2014). *Qualitative evaluation and research methods* (4th ed.). Sage.

Riesman, C. (2008). *Narrative methods for the human sciences.* Sage.

Rosaldo, R. (1997). Cultural citizenship, inequality, and multiculturalism. In W. V. Flores & R. Benmayor (Eds.), *Latino cultural citizenship: Claiming identity, space, and rights* (pp. 27–38). Beacon Press.

ross, k. m. (2021). On Black education: Anti-blackness, refusal, and resistance. In C. A. Grant, A. N. Woodson, & M. J. Dumas (Eds.), *The future is Black: Afropessimism, fugitivity, and radical hope in education* (pp. 7–15). Routledge.

Tutu, D., & Ford, A. (2012). *Desmond and the very mean word*. Candlewick.
Westheimer, J., & Kahne, J. (2004). What kind of citizen? The politics of educating for democracy. *American Educational Research Journal, 41*(2), 237–269.
Woodson, A. N., & Love, B. (2019). Outstanding: Centering Black kids' enoughness in civic education research. *Multicultural Perspectives, 21*(2), 91–96. https://doi.org/10.1080/15210960.2019.1606631

Endnotes

Chapter 3

1. This chapter was born out of a conversation, thus, this first part will follow the format of an introduction.
2. See Monreal & Tirado (2021) for more information.
3. See Fernandez (2021) and Rodriguez & Gonzàlez Ybarra (2020) for further discussion.
4. See Ender (2021) for more on counter-narratives.
5. See Busey (2019, 2021) for more information.

Chapter 4

1. We refer to the Arab-Palestinians who remained in the territory that today designates the State of Israel after the 1948 war. In contrast to Palestinians who live in the Palestinian authority, Gaza or East Jerusalem, these Arab-Palestinian possess Israeli citizenship. Arab-Palestinians have a complex identity repertoire and the significance of different identities has varied over time; for example, while their Israeli identity has been more dominant after Israel gained statehood, their Palestinian identity became increasingly emphasized in the aftermath of the 1967 war together with an Arab national identity (Amara & Schnell, 2004). Scholars usually differentiate between Arab-Palestinian citizens' legal Israeli identity and their emotional attachment to Palestinian and Arab national identities (Rouhana, 1997; Smooha, 1992).

Chapter 5

1. To undermine the social power conferred by the racial descriptor white, we lowercase it and uppercase peoples of Color, particularly those racialized as Black.
2. Pseudonym.
3. While Mario was not a formal historian, we use historian here to recognize and honor his knowledge as one.

Chapter 9

1. A complete version of this story can be found in *Anakú Iwachá: Yakama Legends and Stories* (Beavert, Jacob, & Jansen, 2021).
2. This framing of "more than human relations" (as opposed to "non-humans") is a simple but important way Indigenous teachings can help us think about and use language as a tool to articulate a collective vision for inclusion (Jacob, 2020).

3. Some nations have outlined their goals in formal frameworks. The Navajo Nation, for example, developed Diné content standards for language, culture, history, character, and civics (https://oscad.navajo-nsn.gov/Resources/Dine-Content-Standards), a prime example of nation-based civics.

4. Borrows (2000) anticipated that his message of Indigenous control of Canadian affairs might be read as violating key principles within treaties, like Gus Wen Tah, the two-row wampum belt that some interpret (given the two parallel, purple rows) as meaning "a separate nation-to-nation relationship between First Nations and the Crown," which prohibits interference (p. 334). For Borrows, however, the white rows "represent a counter-balancing message that signifies the importance of sharing and interdependence" (p. 336).

Index

The letters *n* and *t* after a page number refer to note and table, respectively.

13 GPs (guiding principles), 153, 159–165
14th Amendment, 141, 146–147, 148. *See also* Reconstruction
1619 Project, The (Hannah-Jones), 20

Abolition of slavery, 116, 118
Abu-saad, I., 42, 43
Accountability movement, 7
Adekile, A., xiii
African American youth civic engagement. *See* Black student activism; Youth spoken word (YSW)
Agency, 87–88, 156
Aikau, H. K., 136
Alaska Department of Education & Early Development, 133
Alaska Native Knowledge Network, 126, 132, 136
Alaska Standards for Culturally Responsive Schools, 132
Alayan, S., 43
Alexander, M., 143
Al-Haj, M., 43
Alridge, D. P., 149
Amara, M., 41n1, 43
An, S., 145
Anakú Iwachá (Beavert et al.), 130n1
Anderson, M., 9
Anti-Black racism, 62–63, 109–110
Aparicio, A., 33
Aponte-Martinez, G., 95
Appiah, K. A., 51

Arab-Palestinian civics
background and context, 41–43, 50
congruence and disjuncture, 43–44, 49
identity, 48–50
research framework, 43–44
research methodology, 44–45
research themes, 45–49
Archibald, J. A., 131
Archibald, Jo-ann (Q'um Q'um Xiiem), 131
Artistic expression and activism, 166. *See also* Youth spoken word (YSW)
Arvin, M., 136
Asian American Resource Workshop, 75
Asian Prisoner Support Committee, 78t
Au, W., 72
Auerbach, C., 158
Authoritarian patriotism, 8, 21, 25
Ayers, W., 58, 59, 60, 63, 64, 66, 67

Baldwin, M., 63
Baldwin, Marshall, 63
Ball, A. F., 144
Bañales, J., 59
Bang, M., 125, 126, 127, 133, 134
Banks, J., xi, xii, xiii
Banks, J. A., 57, 58, 59, 111
Barnes, M. E., 165
Barriers to high-quality civic education, 6–10
Barton, K. C., 44
Battiste, M., 126

Baum, N., 42
Beavert, V. R., 130n1
Bell, D., 4
Bell, L.A., 156
Belonging, 8–9, 21
Beltrán, C., 34
Benavot, A., 43
Benmayor, R., 156
Bernal, D. D., 32
Berry, D. R., 110
Berry, M. F., 144
Berry, T. R., 157
Beshlian, A., 144
Black educators' personal perspectives on civic education
civics education backgrounds, 20–22
civics for current students, 24–26
collective sense-making, 26
democratic patriotism, 25–26
the ideal, 23
multiple perspectives, 24–25
reasons for hope, 27–28
Black feminist pedagogy
and anti-racism, 119–120
and Black feminist thought, 112–113
guiding questions, 120
RESPECT framework, 113–119, 120
Black humanity, 142–143, 148
Black Lives Matter at School (BLMAS)
about, 153
guiding principles, 156, 159–166
research methods, 156–158
research results, 158–164
Black Lives Matter Global Network, 153
Black Lives Matter (BLM) movement, 17, 153
Black masculinity stereotypes, 149
Black student activism, 61–66. *See also* Youth spoken word (YSW)
Black student–led walkout, 61–63, 66
Black women activism, 109, 110–112, 114–115, 119, 120–122
Blain, K. N., 116
Blaming, 20
Blanco, M. Y., 32
Blass, N., 44

BLMAS (Black Lives Matter at School). *See* Black Lives Matter at School (BLMAS)
Bolivar, A., 33
Borrows, J., 126, 134, 134n4, 135
Bowers Cook, E. J., 1597
Boxerman, A., 42
Boydston, J. A., 57
Boylorn, R. M., 21
Braun, V., 45, 97
Brayboy, B.M.J., 125, 127, 133
Brenes, T., 34
Brewton-Johnson, M., 110
#BringHieuHome, 80, 82f. *See also* Southeast Asian civic action
Brown, A. L., 7, 10, 57, 58, 143, 155
Brown, C.-A., 18–19, 20–21
Brown, K. D., 7, 10, 155
Brown, Willie, 62
Buenavista, T. L., 72, 73
Bui, T., 74
Burkhart, B., 126
Burroughs, Nannie Helen, 112
Burroughs, N. H., 112
Busey, C., xi, 3, 5, 6, 7, 8, 12, 143
Busey, C. L., 32n5, 37, 57, 58
Button, L., 163

C3 Framework for Social Studies Standards, 142
Cajete, G., 126, 131
Calderón, D., 4
Cammarota, J., 95
Canada and Indigenous leadership, 134
Carcerality, 71, 73–74
Carillo, R., 44
Carlson-Manathara, E., 136
Carrizales, A., 9
Carrillo, R., 51
Carruthers, C., 116
Castro, A., xiii
Castro, A. J., 72
Chang, J., 86
Character education, 25
Charmaz, K., 158
Chávez, A., 33
Checkoway, B., 95

Index

Chevrier, B., 9
Chow, G. K., 71
Ciechanowski, K. M., 44, 51
Citizenship
  barriers to, 28
  communities of Color, xii–xiii
  cultural frameworks, xii
  ideal of, 28, 58, 109, 153–154, 155–156
  and migration, 72
  and race, 3, 6, 13, 35
  rights of, 41–42, 109, 142, 146, 156
Civic disjunction, 9
"Civic empowerment gap," 154, 155
Civic estrangement, 8–9, 145
Civic identity, 10–11, 44, 49–50
Civic internal dissonance, 45–49
Clarke, V., 45, 97
Clay, K., xii, xiii, 5, 6, 9, 12, 13
Clay, K. L., 34, 41
Cohen, A., 43, 44
Cohen, A. K., 6, 9, 155
Cohen, C., 94
Cohen, C. J., 94
Cohn, D., 73
Coles, S. C., 110
Collazo, T., 44, 51
Collective action, 117–118, 127
Collectivism tenet, 117–118
Collins, P. H., 112–113, 115
Colonialism, 127, 130
Colonialist consciousness, 130
Colorblind racism, 6
Combahee River Collective, 117–118
Communism threat, 74
Community, xii, 64–66, 81–84, 97, 127–128
Community cultural wealth, 59–60, 63, 65, 66, 86
Community tour project, 63–66
Congruent civic experiences, 44, 46, 49
Context relevance and identity, 50
Contreras, F., 34
Cooper, A. J., 148
Cooper, Anna Julia, 112
Cordova, V., 126, 128–129, 130
Corntassel, J., 138

Counter-narratives, 4, 11–12, 18, 23, 59, 77. *See also* Counterstories as pedagogy
Counterstories as pedagogy
  background, 141–142
  Black humanity, 142–143
  race and dissonance, 143–144
  rationale, 149–150
  and research, 156–157
  teachers' counterstories, 145–149
  theoretical framework, 144–145
Courageous conversations, 11
Coyote stories, 130–131
Cranfill, Henry, 62–63
Crenshaw, K., 59, 60, 142, 144
Critical awareness, 27
Critical civic empathy, 165
Critical civic praxis, 155–156
Critical consciousness, 21
Critical liberationist theory, 103
Critically relevant civics, 12
Critical patriotism, 12–13, 25
Critical perspective, 23, 24
Critical race pedagogy, 156. *See also* Critical race theory (CRT)
Critical race praxis, 5–6, 10–11
Critical race theory (CRT), 4–6, 13, 19–20, 59, 110, 112, 144
Crowley, R. M., 57, 59, 143
Cullors, Patrisse, 153
Cultural capital, 59–60
Cultural citizenship, xii, 73, 154, 156
Cultural complexity, 45–49
Cultural diversity, 24
Cultural humility, 132
Cultural identity, 59, 99
Culturally relevant pedagogy, 6, 10
Culturally responsive pedagogy, 6, 10
Cummings, R., 7, 9, 10, 11
Curriculum dissonance, 45–46, 148–149
Curriculum flaws, 3, 5, 6, 43

Dabach, D., xiii
Dabach, D. B., 35–36
Davis, A. Y., 114, 118
Davis, C., 96, 97
Decentering Whiteness, xi–xii, 154–155, 166

Decuir, J., 144
#*DefendBoun*, 77, 80, 82f, 84
Deficit perspective, 60, 154, 155
Delgado, R., 4, 5, 77, 144
DeLombard, J. M., 142
Deloria, V., 126, 130
Democratic values, xi
Demographic shifts, 24
Denney, S. M., 50
Denzin, N., 76
Deportation, 71, 74
Desegregation/segregation, 43, 61–63
Desmond and the Very Mean Word (Tutu & Ford), 160, 165
Dewey, J., 96
Dialogue, 11, 77, 80
Diera, C., 34
Dillard, C., 121
Dilworth, P., xii
Dilworth, P. P., 57, 58
Dion, S. D., 133
Disconnectedness from civic life, 9–10
Discrimination. *See* Structural racism
Disjunctive civic experiences, 44, 46, 49
Displacement, 74
Dissent. *See* Resistance
Diverse approach to civic activism, 98–99, 102–103
Dixson, A., 144
Dixson, A. D., 144, 148
Dominant narrative, xi, 11–12, 18, 25, 32, 36, 57, 142, 153–154
Double consciousness, 8, 9
Dowie-Chin, T., xi, 57, 58, 143
Dred Scott v. Stanford, 143
Drop the Charges, 77, 83–85f
Du Bois, W.E.B., 8
Duncan, K., xii, 3, 4, 5, 7, 9, 10, 11, 12
Duncan, K. E., 25, 59, 112, 145, 147, 148, 149, 156

East Chicago, Indiana, 64–65
Educational outcomes, 13
Educational policies, 41
Education as democracy insurance, 111–112
Education as key to liberation, 119
Elliott-Groves, E., 134
Ellis, L., 44, 51
Emancipatory education, 5, 10–13, 117, 148–149
Emancipatory tenet of anti-racist civics, 117
Emotion, 149
Empathy as guiding principle, 159–161, 165
Empowerment, 22, 23, 46, 47, 156
Ender, T., 5, 10, 11, 12, 32n4
English proficiency, 7
"Enoughness," 21, 50, 103
Enslavement, 7, 116, 118, 142–143
Epistemology tenet of anti-racist civics, 114–115
Epstein, T., 6, 10, 11
Escobar, M., 73
Estreicher, S., 42
Exclusion, 22, 24, 72, 149, 154–155, 160. *See also* Inclusion

Failed citizenship, 58–59
Fairness, 160, 161
Falkner, A., 72, 77, 81
False empathy, 165
Fear, 149
Feliciano-Santos, S., 33
Ferguson, A. A., 149
Fernandez, J. S., 32n3
Fierros, C. O., 32
Fiore, M., 94, 95
First People, 131
Fisher, M. T., 94
Flgov.com, 20
Flores, T., 33
Flores, W. V., 72, 81, 156
Florida Board of Education, 19–20
Fones, A., xiii
Fones, A. K., 35–36
Ford, A., 160
Franke, M., 34
Franklin, B., 125–126
#*FreeSaelee*, 84
"Free Them All" (Kah Yangni), 164
Freire, P., 64, 66, 72, 96, 112
Funds of knowledge, 44

Gaby, S., 154
Gadsden, V. L., 34
Gándara, P. C., 34
Garcia, A., 34, 155, 164
Garza, Alicia, 153
Geller, R. C., 34
George Washington Carver high school, 61
Gillborn, D., 41
Ginwright, S., 95
Gist, C., 6, 10
Goeman, M., 136
Gonzales, R. G., 36
Gonzalez, L., 95, 103
González, N., 43, 46
González Ybarra, M., 32n3, 34, 41
Gordon, B. M., 57, 59
Gotanda, N., 59, 60
Gotkine, E., 42
Gramlich, J., 74
Grande, S., 125, 128, 130, 135
Grbich, C., 158
Greenberg, J. B., 44
Greenhouse Fellowship, 64–66
Gross, K. N., 110
Guerra, S. I., 33
Gus Wen Tah, 134n4
Gutiérrez, K. D., 41, 44, 51

Hagopian, J., 153
Halagao, P. E., xii
Hall, H. R., 96
Hannah-Jones, Nicole, 20
Harnish, J., 72
Hart, D., 44
Haudenosaunee Confederacy, 125–126
Hawkman, A. M., 25
Hayes, B., 41, 44, 50
Hayes, C., 6
Haynes Writer, J., 127
Heilig, J., 7, 10
Henry, A., 110
Heroification, 7, 8
Herrera, M., 32
Hidden curriculum, 5
Hill, M. L., 94
Hogan, L., 126, 128–129
hooks, b., 66, 72, 77, 115

Hope, E. C., 95
Horizontal model of relationship, 129
Howard, T., 18, 109, 145
Howard, T. C., xii
Howells, T., 163
Hughes, S., 156
Humanity and Indigenous worldview, 130
Hunter, T. W., 118

ICCA Consortium, 135
Identity, 36, 37, 48–50, 77, 80–81
Images and accessibility, 82–83
Incarceration. *See* Carcerality
Inclusion, 28, 36, 43, 50. *See also* Exclusion
Indigenous civics
  background, 126–128
  Canadian affairs, 134
  example, 132–133
  and formal schooling, 125–126
  kinship network, 129–130, 132, 133
  philosophies and worldview, 128–130, 133, 134, 134n4
  questions from academic literature, 128–130
  and sovereignty, 127, 135–136
  and stories, 130–131, 131n2, 136
  as universal civics, 133–136, 133n3
  value of, 133–135
Indigenous Peoples and Civics in the 21st Century (Bang & Brayboy), 127
Individual racism, 62–63
Ingalls, R., 95
Ishimoto, M., 34
Ishizuka, K. L., 86
Israel, 41–42
Israeli citizenship and Arab Palestinians, 41, 41n1

Jabareen, Y. T., 42, 43
Jacob, M. M., 126, 130n1, 131, 131n2, 136
Jagers, R. J., 95
Jamal, A., 42
James, J., 114
James-Gallaway, A. D., 61, 62

Jansen, J., 126, 130n1
Jennings, M. E., 156
Jocson, K., 96
Johnson, K. A., 112
Johnson, M., xi
Johnson, M. W., 59
Johnson, W. F., 34
Jojola, T. S., 126, 128–129
Jones, B. L., 149
Jones, D., 153, 156
Jones, M. S., 110
Jones, T. J., 57
Journell, W., xi, 3, 9
Juarez, B., 6
Justice, D., 129
Justice, Daniel Heath, 129
Justice-centered education, 59–60, 66–67

Kahne, J., xi, 18, 20, 34, 94, 153, 154, 164, 165
Kah Yangni I, 164
Kang, H.-K. S., 77
Kawano, Y., 77
Kelley, R. D., 67
Kelley, R.D.G., 114
Kelly, L. L., 113
Keren, M., 42
Kerner Commission report (Rigeur & Beshlian), 143
Kim, J., 95, 156
Kim, R., 96, 105
Kimmerer, R., 126
Kinchloe, J., 45
King Encyclopedia, 118
King, L., 7
King, L. J., 57, 58, 143
Kinship network, 129–130, 132, 133
Kirshner, B., 34, 95
Kissling, M. T., 25
Knesset, 42
Knight Abowitz, K., 72
Knowles, R. T., 72
Kozol, J., 155
Kramer, K., 44, 51
Krogstad, J. M., 33
Kumashiro, K., 58, 59, 60, 63, 64, 66, 67

Kuoch, J., 72, 73–74
Kuttner, P. J., 94

LaChance, K. M., 126
Lacy, A., 126, 128–129
Ladson-Billings, G., xi, xii, 3, 4, 6, 10, 21, 44, 51, 57, 58, 59, 80–81, 109, 110, 112, 112, 144, 148
LaDuke, W., 135
"Landed citizenship," 134
Land stewardship, 132, 134, 135
Lannegrand-Willems, L., 9
Latinx community and civics
    conclusions, 37–38
    connections from research, 37
    introduction and goals, 31–33
    Monreal letter, 35–36
    Rodriguez letter, 33–34
    Tirado letter, 36–37
LaVega high school, 61–62
Lawrence, C., 144
Lawston, J. M., 74
Ledesma, M. C., 4, 11
LeMee, G. L., 19
Leonard, K., 135
Letters to teachers of Latinx students. *See under* Latinx community and civics
Levinson, B. A., 72–73
Levinson, M., 36, 153, 154
Liberationism, 96, 103
Literary activism, 95–96
Littenberg-Tobias, J., 6, 9, 155
Liu, K., 144
Lo, J., 103
Local history. *See* Local stories
Local stories, 25, 57–58, 63–66
Lopez, M. H., 94
Love, B., xiii, 23, 94, 97, 103, 154, 155
Love, B. L., 21, 51, 155
Loving engagement as teacher's guiding principle, 161–163, 165
Low, B., 94
Ludden, J., 73
Lynn, M., 156

Mahamid, H., 43
Mantchev, L., 160

Marshall, P. L., 109, 111, 112
Mathews, S., 153, 156
Mathews, S. A., 153
Mathias, L., 131
Matsuda, M., 144
Mayorga, E., 6, 10, 11
McBride, C. E., 9
McCoy, M., 134
McCully, A. W., 44
McLaren, P., 45
McLellan, J. A., 44
McTier, S. A., 96
Medin, D. L., 126
Meiners, E., 58, 59, 60, 63, 64, 66, 67
Mentoring, 103
Merchant, N., xiii
Merchant, N. H., 35–36
Mexican American/Mexican community, 33
Miami-Dade Grand Jury Report, 21
Miles, J., 34
Miller, R., 144
Miller-Lane, J., xii
Mills, C. W., 142
Milner, H. R., 6, 10
Mirra, N., 34, 155, 164, 165
Modeling, 163, 165
Moje, E. B., 44, 51
Moll, L. C., 41, 44
Monreal, T., 31n2, 32
Monture-Angus, P., 136
Monzó, L., 45
Moore, K. D., 126, 128–129
More-than-human relations, 133n2. *See also* Horizontal model of relationship
Moreton-Robinson, A., 136
Morgensen, S., 136
Morrison, T., 149
Muhammad, G., 95, 103
Multicultural citizenship, xii
Mutual humanization, 165–166
Myers, J. P., 9

National Advisory Commission on Civil Disorders, 143
Nationalism, 41, 42

Native American Philosophy of V. F. Cordova (Cordova et al.), 128
Nature rights, 135
Navajo Nation, 133n3
Navarro, O., 18
Nelson, J., 6, 10, 11
Neoliberal policies, 41
Ngai, M., 73
Nicoll, F., 136
Noe-Bustamante, L., 33
Noguera, P., 95
Nontraditional actions, 98–99
Northeast Region Pardons Project, 74, 78t
NPR, 20

Ochoa, G., 34
Okakok, L., 125
Omolade, B., 110, 113
Organization of this work, xiii–xvi

Paris, D., 21, 48, 51
Parker, A. W., 72
Parker, W., xi
Parkhouse, H., 11
Pasek, J., 110
Passel, J. S., 33
Patiño-Longoria, F., 32
Patler, C., 36
Patton, M., 145
Patton, M. Q., 157
Payne, K. A., 72, 77, 81
Peled, Y., 42
Peller, G., 59, 60
Pelligrino, A. M., 95
Perchec, C., 9
Pérez, G. M., 33
Personal context of action, 97–98, 100–101t
"Personally responsible citizen," xi
Petchauer, E., 94
Peters, K., 126, 128–129
Pew Research, 33
Philadelphia, PA, 153
Pinkney, A., 3, 5, 6, 7, 10, 12
Pinson, H., 43, 44
Plurality, xi–xii
Poetry. *See* Youth spoken word (YSW)

Police abuse, 19, 146, 147, 153
Political-social activism tenet, 116–117
Pollock, M., 34
Power misuse, 25. *See also* Police abuse
Power structure, 27, 97, 113, 131, 156
Pozzoboni, K. M., 96
Preston-Grimes, P., 58, 111–112

Quinn, T., 58, 59, 60, 63, 64, 66, 67
Q'um Q'um Xiiem (Archibald, Jo-ann), 131

Rabinowitz, D., 41
Race-citizenship dissociation, 143
Racism. *See* Structural racism; individual racism
Rahman, S., 34
Rationale for civic activism, 100–101t, 101–103
Reach of civic action, 85–86, 87
Reconstruction period, 141–142, 145, 146
Reflection, 26–27, 96, 99, 156
Reflexive teaching, 26–27
Relational accountability, 133, 135–136
Relationship with the land, 132, 134, 135, 136
Representation of marginalized groups, 7, 43. *See also* Decentering Whiteness
Resh, N., 43
Resistance
    contemporary, 47, 58, 62–63, 65, 66, 75
    and counter-narratives, 12
    historical, 143–144, 148, 149, 163
Resource pedagogies, 43–44
Respect for Elders, 132
RESPECT framework. *See under* Black feminist pedagogy
Restorative justice as guiding principle, 163–164, 165
Revolutionary movement, 114
Richardson, C., 44
Riesman, C., 156
Rigeur, L., 143
Rights of nature, 135

Rios, V. M., 34
Risk evaluation and civic action, 99–100
Rodriguez, G., 32n3, 34
Rodriguez, N., 7, 10, 11
Rodríguez, N., xiii
Rodríguez, N. N., 72, 73, 145
Roediger, D. R., 62
Rogers, J., 34
Role-play, 165
Rombalski, A., 34
Rosa, J., 33
Rosaldo, R., xii, 72, 156
Rosas, G., 33
Ross, k. m., 155
Rouhana, N., Xn1
Rousseau Anderson, C., 144, 148
Rowe, G., 136
Rubin, B., xii, xiii, 5, 6, 9, 12, 13
Rubin, B. C., 34, 41, 44, 50

Sabzalian, L., xi, xii, 126, 127, 134
Safe space, 161–163
Salam, S., 21
Saldaña, J., 76
Salinas, C., xiii
Sánchez-Jankowski, M., 94
Sánchez Loza, D., 34
Schaeffer, K., 24
Schnell, I., 42, Xn1
School closure, 61
School walkout, 61–63
SEAFN, 75
Seattle, WA, 153
Segregation/desegregation, 43, 61–63
Self-care, 98–99
Self-determination tenet, 115
Self-love, 98–99
Sen, A., 37
Shafir, G., 42
Shavit, Y., 44
Shear, S., xi
Sherman, R. F., 95
Silencing, 154–155
Silva, C., 33, 37
Silverstein, L. B., 158
Simanski, J. F., 74
Simpson, L., 135, 136
Simpson, L. B., 131

"Sleeping giant" narrative, 31, 34
Smith, B., 115, 118
Smooha, S., Xn1
Snyder, J., xi
Social injustice, 24, 26, 33–34
Social media. *See* Southeast Asian civic action: toolkits
Solórzano, D. G., 72, 97, 144, 149
Southeast Asian civic action
  background, 74
  citizenship notions, 72–74
  community action, 75–86
  role of researcher, 75
  stories, 77, 80, 88
  sustaining resistance, 81–86
  theory and practice, 86–88
  toolkits, 75–81
Southeast Asia Resource Action Center, 71, 74
Spencer Foundation report (Bang & Brayboy), 127
"Spilyáy Breaks the Dam," 130–131
Spoken word. *See* Youth spoken word (YSW)
Stampp, K. M., 144
Status quo acceptance, 47–48
Stefancic, J., 4, 5, 77, 144
Steinberg, R., 45
Stereotypes, 36, 37, 149
Stevens, M., 110
"Stop Anti Asian Violence," 86–87f
Stories, 25, 57–58, 63–66, 77, 80, 88, 130–131, 131n2, 136. *See also* Counter-narratives; Counterstories as pedagogy
Stout, C., 19
Stovall, D., 5, 10, 58, 59, 96
Strictly No Elephants (Matchev & Yoo), 160
Structural racism
  Arab Palestinians, 46–47
  and counterstories, 143, 144–145, 150
  and emancipatory education, 3, 4, 5, 6, 13
  and resistance, 58, 66, 109, 110
Stumpf, J., 74
Su, C., 6

Takaki, R., 37
Tal, A., 42
Tate, W., 144, 148
Tate, W. F., 4, 10
Taylor, U., 110
Teach-ins, 153
Territories of Life (ICCA Consortium), 135
Textbooks, 43
Thomas, D., xiii
Thomas, K., 59, 60
Three-Fifths Compromise, 143
Tiers of action, 84–85
Tillet, S., xiv, 3, 4, 5, 6, 7, 8, 11, 12, 145
Tirado, J., 32n2
Tobin, T. J., 126
Tometi, Opal, 153
Traditional activism, 98
Traditional civic education, xi, 3, 17, 27–28, 57, 111
Training for civic action, 102
Truong, T., 74
Truth-telling, 118–119
Tuhiwai Smith, L., 77
Turner, F. F., 61
Tutu, D., 160
Tyson, C., 109, 110, 111, 112
Tyson, C. A., 59

Um, K., 72
United Nations, 135
U.S. Census Bureau, 64
U.S. Constitution, 4, 141, 142, 146–147, 148
U.S. Department of Homeland Security, 74
U.S. Department of State, 73
U.S. policies and Black citizenship, 142–143

Vang, C. Y., 73, 74
Van Horn, S. E., 25
Vélez-Ibáñez, C. G., 44
Vickery, A., xii, xiii, 4, 6, 8, 10, 11, 21
Vickery, A. E., 57, 59, 109, 111, 112, 113, 143
Villarreal, A., 33

Vincent, C. G., 126
Voice, 21, 97

Waco, Texas, school walkout, 60–63
Walker, I., 3, 5, 6, 7, 8, 12
Wampum belt, 134n4
"War on Drugs," 74
Washing Society, 118
Watkins, W. H., 57
Watson, V. M., 95, 103
Weinstein, S., 94
Wells-Barnett, I. B., 118
West, A., 94
West, R., 18–19, 21–22
Westheimer, J., xi, 18, 20, 34, 153, 154, 164, 165
"What We Believe" statement, 153
Wheeler-Bell, Q., 72
White allies, 26
"White gaze," 149
Whiteness centering, xi
White supremacy, 5, 57, 59, 62, 63, 111
Why Indigenous Literatures Matter (Justice), 129
Whyte, K. P., 126
Wildcat, D. R., 126, 130
Wilkenfeld, B., 44
Willow Finds a Way (Button), 163
Wilson, A., 63, 66
Winn, M. T., 94, 95
Women's Political Council, 118
Women's suffrage movement, 115
Wong, T. K., 74
Woodson, A., xiii, 5, 6, 7, 8, 12, 94, 97, 103

Woodson, A. N., 21, 51, 154, 155
Woodson, C. G., 148
Wynter, S., 61

Yakama Creation Story, 130n1, 131
Yakama people, 130–131, 130n1
Yancy, G., 57
Yates, M., 44
Yeager Washington, E., 19
Yee, S. J., 117
Yoder, P., xiii
Yoo, T., 160
Yoshisato, M., 34
Yosso, T. J., 58, 59, 60, 62, 63, 64, 66, 72, 97
Youniss, J., 44
"Youth control complex," 34
Youth poets. *See* Youth spoken word (YSW)
Youth spoken word (YSW)
  action expectation, 101–103
  background, 93–94
  cultural identities, 100–101
  engagement in diverse activism, 98–100, 103–104
  power of words, 95–96
  rationale for action, 100–101
  research methodology, 96–97
  spoken word concept and function, 94
  theoretical framework of research, 96
Yun, F.E.E., 34
Yurich, G., 36

Zavella, P., 33
Zenkov, K., 95

About the Editor and Authors

Carla-Ann Brown is a university school assistant professor in the College of Education at the University of Florida P.K. Yonge Developmental Research School as well as a Fulbright Distinguished Teacher. Her primary research areas focus on personalized and universally designed student experiences through standards and project-based culturally sustaining learning and instruction.

Aviv Cohen is an associate professor at the Seymour Fox School of Education of The Hebrew University of Jerusalem, Israel. He serves as the co-head of the Undergraduate Program in Educational and Social Leadership. His interests include democratic civic education, multicultural education, teacher education, and the use of qualitative methods in educational research.

Camea Davis is a poet, educator, and educational researcher with a heart for urban youth and communities. Her research focuses on youth activism, racial justice in teacher education, critical collaborative ethnography, and critical poetic inquiry.

Kristen E. Duncan is an assistant professor of social studies education at Clemson University. Her research focuses on the ways Black teachers discuss race and racism with their students and the ways race is presented in text and media. She is a former middle school social studies teacher and instructional coach.

Tommy Ender is an associate professor of educational studies in the Feinstein School of Education and Human Development at Rhode Island College. Dr. Ender also holds a joint appointment in the Department of History. He is currently researching how music can be used a lens into the past in secondary and post-secondary settings.

Sabryna Groves is currently pursuing a PhD in Technology and Teacher Education at Texas A&M University. Their research interests pertain to examining whiteness as it emerges in social studies curriculum and pedagogy.

Michelle M. Jacob (Yakama) loves imagining and working toward a future in which kindness, fierceness, and creativity saturate our lives and institutions in delicious and inviting ways. Dr. Jacob does this in her popular The Auntie Way Writing Retreats and Anahuy Mentoring professional development workshops, in which she draws from her Yakama cultural teachings to encourage and support attendees in developing clear visions that bring about radical and sustainable social justice. Dr. Jacob is an enrolled member of the Yakama Nation and is Professor of Indigenous Studies and Co-Director of the Sapsikʷałá Program in the Department of Education Studies at the University of Oregon where she's also affiliated faculty in Indigenous, Race, and Ethnic Studies and in Environmental Studies.

ArCasia D. James-Gallaway is a proud first-generation college graduate, native Texan, and former social studies teacher. She draws on these dispositions as an interdisciplinary historian of education and teacher educator in the Teaching, Learning, and Culture Department at Texas A&M University, where she is an assistant professor and a faculty affiliate in the Gender and Women's Studies Program. Dr. James-Gallaway's work aims to bridge past and present perspectives on African American struggles for educational justice.

Brittany Jones is an assistant professor of social studies education at the University at Buffalo. Her research examines the teaching of critical Black histories, with a specific focus on Black emotionality, and explores the intersections of discourse, power, and oppression within social studies curricula.

Denisha Jones is the executive director of Defending the Early Years. She is a part-time faculty member in the Art of Teaching program at Sarah Lawrence College and the School of Education at Howard University. Since 2017, she served on the steering committee for the national Black Lives Matter at School Week of Action. Her first co-edited book, *Black Lives Matter at School: An Uprising for Educational Justice*, was published in December 2020 by Haymarket Books.

Erica Kelley is a residency coach in Chattanooga, Tennessee, where she works with preservice teachers, program graduates, and mentor teachers on incorporating anti-racist and culturally responsive practices in their daily work with students. Her doctoral research, completed at the University of South Carolina, centered on the intersection of transformational coaching, critical race praxis, and reimagined civics instruction with Black students in mind. She has served as a civics curriculum developer for the Tennessee Department of Education, sat on the state social studies standard-setting committee, and received the 2022 NAACP Educator of the Year award by her local chapter.

About the Editor and Authors

Sarah A. Mathews is an associate professor of curriculum and instruction and social studies education within the Department of Teaching and Learning at Florida International University. Dr. Mathews's research focuses on multicultural and global citizenship education as well as the impact of youth participatory research as transformative civic engagement. Her research and teaching efforts focus on the current state of civic education in K–16 educational institutions and the potential to prepare future citizens in the United States and abroad.

Timothy Monreal is assistant professor of learning and instruction at the University at Buffalo. His academic research lies at the intersection of Latinx studies, social studies education, and cultural studies.

Aline Muff is a postdoctoral fellow at the Seymour Fox School of Education, The Hebrew University of Jerusalem. She completed her doctoral research at Queen's University Belfast and was a postdoctoral researcher at the University of Haifa. Her research interests include citizenship education in diverse societies, the role of education in conflict settings, and the teaching of difficult histories.

Natasha C. Murray-Everett is the director of social justice at the Tower Hill School, a K–12 independent school in Delaware. She is a former elementary school teacher and teacher educator/professor. Her research explores how teachers (and students) engage in race dialogue. She examines how dialogue can serve to explore one's racial and ethnic identities and the racial and ethnic identities of others. She looks at how these understandings can shape one's ideologies of race and racism and influence teaching practices and relationships with students, particularly with students of Color. The heart of her work is to engage students and educators in racial and social justice education.

Tiffany Mitchell Patterson is a manager of social studies at District of Columbia Public Schools, with over a decade of experience as a social studies educator and teacher educator. Her research interests include racial and social justice in education, education activism, critical civic education, Black feminism, and teaching Black and underrepresented histories in social studies education. Education is her revolution.

Gabriel Rodriguez is an assistant professor in the Department of Education Policy, Organization & Leadership at the University of Illinois Urbana-Champaign. His research centers on learning from Latinx youth and youth of Color in the context of demographically changing schools and communities.

Leilani Sabzalian (Alutiiq) is an associate professor of Indigenous studies in education and co-director of the Sapsikʷałá program at the University of Oregon. Dr. Sabzalian's heartwork is supporting the next generation of Indigenous educators to become teachers within their communities and creating more just and humanizing spaces for Indigenous students in public schools. Her research also prepares all educators to challenge colonialism in curriculum, policy, and practice.

Crystal Simmons is an associate professor of social studies education at SUNY Geneseo. Her research interests are K–12 Black history education, teacher education, and anti-racist pedagogy.

Jesús Tirado is an assistant professor at Auburn University. His work (both research and as a teacher educator) seeks to interrogate into the ways that we understand the world around us and our place in that world.

Van Anh Tran is the assistant director of field experience at the Lurie College of Education at San José State University. A former history teacher in East San Jose, she is excited to be supporting the field experiences of teacher candidates in a community that she loves. Van Anh is passionate about supporting humanizing and sustaining pedagogies, curriculum, and instruction.

Elizabeth Yeager Washington is professor and coordinator of Secondary Education and Social Studies Education at the University of Florida, as well as a Fulbright Distinguished Scholar. Her research and teaching interests include civic education and the teaching of controversial issues, difficult history, and social issues.

Rasheeda West is a facilitator with the University of Florida Literacy Institute and an instructor in the School of Teaching and Learning. She earned her doctorate degree from the University of Florida in curriculum and instruction, with a focus on the relationship between teaching, schools, and society. Her aim is to support students and teachers in leveraging literacy for social justice.

Asif Wilson is an assistant professor of curriculum and instruction at the University of Illinois Urbana–Champaign. His research broadly focuses on justice-centered pedagogies in P–20 educational contexts.

Ashley N. Woodson is the associate vice president of academic outreach at Albion College, and founding director of Virtual Freedom Schools for the Abolitionist Teaching Network. Her research and activism supports Black children's civic identity and positive racial identity development. She is a mom of two and other mother to many.